D1499634

Parallel MIMD Computation

MIT Press Series in Scientific Computation
Dennis B. Gannon, editor

The Massively Parallel Processor, edited by J. L. Potter, 1985
Parallel MIMD Computation: The HEP Supercomputer and Its Applications,
    edited by J. S. Kowalik, 1985
Synchronization of Parallel Programs, by F. André, D. Herman, and
    J.-P. Verjus, 1985

PARALLEL MIMD COMPUTATION:

THE HEP SUPERCOMPUTER AND ITS APPLICATIONS

edited by J. S. Kowalik

The MIT Press
Cambridge, Massachusetts
London, England

Library of Congress Cataloging in Publication Data

Main entry under title:

Parallel MIMD computation.

(The MIT Press series in scientific computation)
Includes bibliographical references and index.
1. Denelcor HEP (Computer) 2. Parallel processing (Electronic computers) I. Kowalik, Janusz S. II. Title: Parallel MIMD computation. III. Series.
QA76.8.D436P37   1985   001.64   85-39
ISBN 0-262-11101-2

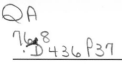
Contents

SERIES FOREWORD

It is often the case that the periods of rapid evolution in the physical sciences occur when there is a timely confluence of technological advances and improved experimental technique. Many physicists, computer scientists, and mathematicians have said that such a period of rapid change is now under way. We are currently undergoing a radical transformation in the way we view the boundaries of experimental science. It has become increasingly clear that the use of large-scale computation and mathematical modeling is now one of the most important tools in the scientific and engineering laboratory. We have passed the point of viewing the computer as a device for tabulating and correlating experimental data; we now regard it as a primary vehicle for testing theories for which no practical experimental apparatus can be built. NASA scientists speak of "numerical" wind tunnels, and physicists experiment with the large-scale structure of the universe.

The major technological change accompanying this new view of experimental science is a blossoming of new approaches to computer architecture and algorithm design. By exploiting the natural parallelism in scientific applications, new computer designs show the promise of major advances in processing power. When coupled with the current biennial doubling of memory capacity, supercomputers are on their way to becoming the laboratories of much of modern science.

In this series we hope to focus on the effect these changes are having on the design of mathematical and scientific software. In particular, we plan to highlight many major new trends in the design of numerical algorithms and the associated programming and software tools that are being driven by the new advances in computer architecture. Of course, the relation between algorithm design and computer architecture is symbiotic. New views on the structure of physical processes demand new computational models, which then drive the design of new machines. We can expect progress in this area for many years, as our understanding of the emerging science of concurrent computation deepens.

In *Parallel MIMD Computation*, Janusz Kowalik has brought together a wide-ranging group of computer scientists and physicists whose recent research shares an important common thread. Each has been involved in the development or the pioneering use of the HEP supercomputer and has participated in the design of the software tools and programming techniques that have become part of the foundation of parallel computation. Based on a radical new model of parallel execution, the HEP has stimulated a substantial amount of new research in parallel algorithm and software design. In particular, this machine has provided researchers with their first large-scale MIMD computer. This architectural feature opened a new dimension for experimental algorithm design. Although this book is a collection of original contributions, it succeeds in presenting a remarkably coherent view of the potential of the HEP model of computation.

Dennis B. Gannon

PREFACE

The demand for more powerful computers is rapidly growing and can only be met by a radical change in computer architecture. The demand for massive amounts of computing power arises from two broad classes of problems:

a. problems requiring numerical computation, such as aerodynamics, computer graphics, weather forecasting, oil reservoir simulation, and
b. problems requiring symbolic processing or a combination of symbolic and numeric computation, such as expert systems, computer vision, robotics, natural language understanding and other applications of artificial intelligence.

The first class of problems is historically earlier and has attracted much more attention from the computer designers and vendors. Almost all of the supercomputers representing the state-of-the-art in computing machinery have been designed primarily for numerical computing. The main architectural feature of the most successful commercial high-performance machines is arithmetic pipelining that allows concurrent processing of overlapped operations. These super computers are very effective for applications that have a high percentage of vectorisable operations. They are not suitable for problems dominated by scalar or non-numerical computation. The pipelined supercomputers such as CRAY-1 and CYBER 205 can be considered as relatively modest extensions of the conventional single-processor mainframes. To increase computer performance by the factors of a hundred or a thousand we must look to machines with multiple processors, capable of truly parallel execution.

Current design efforts in parallel architecture indicate three potential directions:

1. array processors working in lock-step,
2. multiprocessors which typically share resources and work asynchronously,
3. massively parallel aggregates of processors that have either a flexible configuration or a specialized configuration to solve limited classes of problems.

In the second category we can identify a very general class of machines capable of processing multiple streams of instruction on multiple streams of data (MIMD). So far only a few MIMD computers have been built and used. In the United States the best known MIMD computers are: CRAY X-MP, CRAY-2, S-1, and DENELCOR Heterogeneous Element Processor (HEP).

The MIMD computer architecture employs tightly coupled high-performance processors whose number typically can vary from 2 to 16. The question of extending these systems to a much higher number of processors is still open. Using many processors to solve one partitionable problem would require small granularity of the computationally independent subtasks and this implies extensive communication between processors and memory banks. This need for communication may significally reduce systems high-performance. In this regard the HEP multiprocessor offers remarkable originality in design. The computational synchronization is implemented in hardware with a low overhead allowing efficient usage of small granularity. Also, the memory latency which can slow-down any multiprocesor system is overcome by the use of pipelining. A computational process waiting for data is queued up until its memory access is satisfied, thus permitting other processes to execute. These two important features of HEP suggest that the HEP architecture may be extendable and also be a basis for highly efficient and powerful future MIMD machines.

The purpose of this book is to introduce MIMD computing to a wider audience of researchers and potential users. This volume is a collection of several research papers on the MIMD computation and the HEP machine which have been contributed by the HEP designer and by scientists who have experimented with this system. Most of these computational experiments are related to numerical analysis type problems. Can HEP also be used efficiently for nonnumeric problems, for example, logic programming and symbolic processing? This is certainly a challenging question whose answer (particularily if the answer is: yes) would be of interest to the fast growing community of developers and users of the Artificial Intelligence technology.

We have found the HEP multiprocessor to be an excellent tool for experimenting with the MIMD computation and programming. Being an innovative general purpose machine and the first commercial MIMD machine in the world, the HEP system has provided us with a timely opportunity to get seriously acquainted with parallel computing and have a glimpse of the future computation.

The book contains fourteen original contributions divided into four sections: Architecture, Performance, Programming and Languages, and Applications. The Appendix describes the use of monitors in FORTRAN, providing tutorial on the barrier, self-scheduling DO-loop, and Askfor monitors.

Thanks are due to Bruce Wilson and George Roberts of Boeing Computer Services for supporting the project.

Janusz S. Kowalik

BOEING COMPUTER SERVICES,
Artificial Intelligence Center,
Bellevue, November 1984.

Contributors

Stephen J. Allan, Colorado State University

Steve Allan holds the B.S. degree in Mathematics (Utah State) and M.S. and Ph.D. degrees in Computer Science (Iowa State). His research interests include compilers and languages for parallel machines. He is a member of ACM and the IEEE Computer Society.

Robert G. Babb II, Oregon Graduate Center

Robert Babb is an Assistant Professor of Computer Science and Engineering with the Oregon Graduate Center. He received the B.S. degree in astrophysics and mathematics from the University of New Mexico in 1969. In 1974 he received the M.Math. degree in computer science from the University of Waterloo, Ontario, Canada, and the Ph.D. degree in electrical engineering and computer science from the University of New Mexico.

From 1974 to 1976 he was an Assistant Professor in the Computer Science and Statistics Department at California Polytechnic State University, San Luis Obispo. From 1976 to 1978, he was a Visiting Assistant Professor of Computer Science at New Mexico State University. From 1978 to 1982, he was a Software Research Engineer with Boeing Computer Services Company, Seattle, developing methods and tools for large-scale software engineering.

His current research interests center on the application of Large-Grain Data Flow methods to software engineering, data-driven parallel processing, and super computer system architecture.

J. J. Dongarra, Argonne National Laboratory

Jack Dongarra received his Ph.D. in 1980 from the Department of Mathematics at the University of New Mexico. His research interests are in numerical analysis and mathematical software. His specialties include numerical linear algebra and algorithm and software development for high performance computers. He is a computer scientist at Argonne National Laboratory, Chairman of the SIAM Special Activities Group on Supercomputing and an editor of the SIAM series on Frontiers.

Paul O. Frederickson, Los Alamos National Laboratory

Paul Frederickson is a Staff Member in Computer Research and Applications Group. He received his B.S. and M.A. degrees in Mathematics from the University of Maryland and his Ph.D. in Mathematics from Nebraska University. His research interests include numerical analysis, large-scale scientific computation, parallel processing, applied mathematics, multigrid techniques for elliptic boundary-value problems, numerical solution of fluid mechanics problems, and parallel algorithm development.

John Gabriel, Argonne National Laboratory

John Gabriel works as a Computer Scientist at Argonne National Laboratory. His current work is on inference about physical systems, particularly problems in Automated Diagnosis of Faults in Plant. He is a Fellow of the Institute of Physics of London, has undergraduate degrees in Mathematics, Physics and Electrical Engineering together with a M.Sc. (1st class Hons) in Physics from the University of Otago, New Zealand. His interests include Logic Programming, Group Representations in Quantum Mechanics, Design of Digital Logic Systems, and Control Theory. Prior to joining Argonne as a Solid State Scientist in 1962, he was an Assistant Lecturer in the Dept. of Physics U. of Otago (1952-5), a Theoretical Physicist in the N.Z. DSIR Nuclear Sciences Division (1955-8), and a Senior Special Research Fellow in Theoretical Physics Division UKAEA Harwell (1958-62).

Robert E. Hiromoto, Los Alamos National Laboratory

Robert Hiromoto is a Staff Member in Computer Research and Application Group. He received his B.S. in Physics from California State University, and Ph.D. in Physics from the University of Texas at Dallas. His expertise is in general relativity and parallel processing, and his current research interests and involvements are in parallel implementation of existing sequential algorithms, data flow technique for processing large structured computational kernels in parallel, and new parallel algorithms for numerical simulation.

Darrell L. Hicks, Michigan Technological University

Darrell Hicks is a Professor in the Department of Mathematical and Computer Sciences. He is a consultant to KMS FUSION, Inc., and Idaho National Engineering Laboratories, and a member of the summer faculty at Sandia National Laboratories, Albuquerque. He was a Research Mathematician at Air Force Weapons Laboratory

Kirtland between 1962 and 1969, a member of the technical staff at Sandia National Laboratories between 1969 and 1981, and a Professor of Mathematics at the University of Colorado, Denver, from 1981 to 1983.

He holds the degrees of B.S. and Ph.D. in Mathematics from the University of New Mexico, Albuquerque. His research has been supported by several agencies: Department of Education, NSF, AFOSR and Los Alamos National Laboratory.

He has published over fifty articles and research reports, in proceedings and various journals (Mathematics of Computation, Acta Metalurgica, Journal of Applied Physics, Computer Methods in Applied Mechanics and Engineering, Journal of Computational Physics, etc.).

His current research interests and activities include application of supercomputers to problems in computational continuum dynamics, parallel processing and applications of Artificial Intelligence.

Roger W. Hockney, Reading University, U.K.

Roger Hockney received the B.A. and M.A. degrees in the natural science tripos (physics) from Cambridge University, Cambridge, England, and the Ph.D. degree in numerical analysis and plasma physics from Stanford University, Stanford, California.

At Stanford, as a student of Professor O. Buneman, Professor G. Forsythe, and Professor G. Golub, he developed the rapid FACR algorithm for the solution of Poisson's equation, and the particle-mesh method for the simulation of plasmas and galaxies. He has also worked in experimental physics on the Cyclotron at the University of Michigan, Ann Arbor, as an English-Speaking Union Teaching Fellow, and in the British nuclear power industry with the English Electric Company, Ltd. Before returning to England in 1970 to take up the new Chair of Computer Science at Reading University, he held a Senior Postdoctoral Research Fellowship at the NASA Langley Research Center, Langley AFB, VA. and was a member of the Research Staff at the IBM Research Laboratories, Yorktown Heights, NY. He specializes in developing simulations methods using particles and implementing them on the new generation of parallel computers. He has coauthored two books on these topics: "Computer Simulation Using Particles" (New York: McGraw Hill, 1981) and "Parallel Computers" (Philadelphia, PA: Heyden, 1981).

Harry F. Jordan, University of Colorado

Dr. Jordan received the B. A. degree from Rice University, Houston, Texas, and the M.S. and the Ph. D. degrees from the University of Illinois, Urbana, Illinois. He has been with the University of Colorado, Boulder, Colorado, since 1966 and is now a Professor in the Department of Electrical and Computer Engineering, and of Computer Science. His interests in computer systems center on the interface between hardware and software. His involvement with MIMD parallel processing began with the design of The Finite Element Machine in association with ICASE and NASA Langley Research Center, Hampton, Virginia. He became associated with the HEP computer and a consultant to Denelcor, Inc., in the summer of 1980.

Janusz S. Kowalik, Boeing Computer Services

Janusz Kowalik received a Ph. D. degree from the Polish Academy of Sciences, Warsaw. He held research and teaching positions at the Norwegian University of Technology, Trondheim, Norway, Australian National University, Canberra, Australia, and Sir George Williams University, Montreal, Canada. Most recently he was a Professor of Computer Science and Mathematics at Washington State University, Pullman, Washington. Currently he is Manager of Technology Transfer in Artificial Intelligence Center, Boeing Computer Services Company, Bellevue, Washington. His research interest include high-speed computation, applied artificial intelligence, and coupling symbolic and numerical computation in expert systems.

Swarn P. Kumar, Colorado State University

Swarn Kumar is presently an assistant professor in the Department of Computer Science at the Colorado State University. She received her M.Sc. (Applied Mathematics and Operations Research) from the Panjabi University, India, an M.A. (Math) from the University of Idaho, followed by a M.S. and Ph.D. in computer science from the Washington State University. Her research interests include super computers and high speed computing, computational complexity, and distributed networks. She has an extensive experience in the numerical applications of HEP machine, dating back to her doctoral research, and the results of her work have been published in leading journals and proceedings.

Tim G. Lindholm, Artificial Intelligence Applications Institute, Edinburgh

Tim Lindholm received a B.A. from Carleton College, Northfield, Minnesota in Mathematics (1983). After receiving his B.A., Tim worked as a research assistant at Argonne National Laboratory for a year. He is currently working in Prolog implementation and optimization at the Artificial Intelligence Applications

Institute, Edinburgh. His interests include logic programming languages, abstract machine design, and applications of multiprocessing.

Robert E. Lord, Washington State University

Robert Lord is presently Director of the Computing Center and Associate Professor of Computer Science and holds the degrees of B.S., M.A., and Ph.D. in Physics, Mathematics and Computer Science, respectively. He served as a consultant to Denelcor during the design and development phases of HEP and was involved in both software and hardware. Following a five-year period of utilizing analog computers for simulation of continuous systems, he became involved in digital computing in 1960. During the past years he has worked in the areas of computer architecture and system software but has kept his interest in continuous system simulation.

Olaf M. Lubeck, Los Alamos National Laboratory

Olaf Lubeck is a Staff Member in Computer Research and Applications Group. He received his B.A. in Physics from the University of Colorado and M.S. in Meteorology from Naval Postgraduate School. His expertise and current research interests include parallel processing and applying computational models and algorithms to parallel architectures.

Ewing L. Lusk, Argonne National Laboratory

Ewing Lusk is a computer scientist at Argonne National Laboratory. He received a B.A. at the University of Norte Dame and a Ph.D. in mathematics from the University of Maryland in 1970. He was at Northern Illinois University until he joined Argonne in 1982. His research interests include automated theorem proving, logic programming, and multiprocessing, with particular emphasis on the development of high-performance software for automated reasoning.

James W. Moore, Los Alamos National Laboratory

James Moore is a Section Leader in Computer Research and Application Group. He received his B.S. and M.S. degrees in Mathematics from New Mexico State University. His expertise is in parallel computer languages and architectures, operating systems and graphics. His current research interests include mapping applications programs onto parallel architectures.

Rod R. Oldehoeft, Colorado State university

Rod Oldehoeft holds the B.A. degree in Mathematics (Southern Illinois) and M.S. and Ph.D. degrees in Computer Science (Purdue). His research interests include operating systems, performance evaluation, software engineering, and parallel processing. He is a member of the IEEE Computer Society and ACM.

Karl J. Ottenstein, Michigan Technological University

Karl Ottenstein received the B.S., M.S. and the Ph.D. in computer science from Purdue University, W. Lafayette, IN, in 1974, 1975, and 1978, respectively. He joined the Department of Mathematical and Computer Sciences at Michigan Technological University, Houghton, MI, in 1978 where he is currently an Assistant Professor. His research interests include program optimization, parallel processing, programming methodologies and environments, and software metrics. Dr. Ottenstein has been a visiting scientist at Los Alamos National Laboratory and the IBM T. J. Watson Research Center. He has been a member of the ACM since 1973 and has been a referee or reviewer for numerous journals, publishers and granting agencies.

Ross Overbeek, Argonne National Laboratory

Ross Overbeek works as a computer scientist at Argonne National Lab. He received his M.S. degree from Penn State University in 1970, and his Ph.D. in 1971. After receiving his doctorate, he accepted a position at Northern Illinois University, where he remained until joining Argonne in 1983. Most of his research has related to automated reasoning, logic programming, database systems, and multiprocessing. He has authored a number of textbooks in computing, as well as papers in each of the indicated research areas.

Melvin R. Scott, Sandia National Laboratories

Melvin Scott received his Ph.D. in Applied Mathematics from the University of Vermont. He is currently the Supervisor for Applied Mathematics at Sandia National Laboratories in Albuquerque, New Mexico. He is coeditor-in-chief of the journal Applied Mathematics and Computation and associate editor for the Journal of Nonlinear Analysis and UMAP Journal. He is primarily interested in the development of software for super computers and is the author of a book and numerous papers on the subjects of applied mathematics and numerical analysis.

Burton J. Smith, Denelcor, Inc.

Burton J. Smith is Vice President, Research and Development, of Denelcor, Inc., and is the principle architect of the HEP computer system, the first commercial MIMD computer. Dr. Smith has been with Denelcor full time since June 1979, and was a consultant to the company from March 1973 to June 1979. He was an assistant professor of electrical engineering with the University of Colorado's Denver campus from September 1972 to September 1978, and an associate professor from September 1978 to June 1979.

Dr. Smith received the BSEE degree (summa cum laude) from the University of New Mexico in 1967 and the SM, EE, and ScD Degrees from MIT in 1968, 1969, and 1972, respectively. He was an NSS Graduate Fellow in 1978 - 79, and is a member of Eta Kappa Nu and Sigma Xi. His research has been in the areas of hardware description languages, optical computing, parallel computer architecture and software, and the relationships among parallel architectures, programming languages, and applications.

D. C. Sorensen, Argonne National Laboratory

Dr. Sorensen received his Ph.D. in 1977 from the Department of Mathematics at University of California San Diego. His research interests are in numerical analysis. His specialties include numerical linear algebra, numerical methods for nonlinear optimization, and algorithm and software development for parallel computers. He is an associate editor of the SIAM Journal on Scientific and Statistical Computing. He was assistant professor of mathematics at University of Kentucky from 1977-1980, visiting associate professor at Department of Operations Research, Stanford University in 1980 and at the Department of Mathematics, University of California San Diego 1982 and is now a computer scientist at Argonne National Laboratory.

PART 1

ARCHITECTURE

1.1   HEP Architecture, Programming and Performance

Harry F. Jordan†
University of Colorado
Boulder, Colorado

Introduction

The Denelcor HEP computer seems to represent a fairly natural next step in the evolution of computer architecture. It can be characterized as a shared memory, pipelined multiprocessor. The overall speed of a computer is influenced first by the electronic circuitry used to implement it and second by the amount of parallel activity which the architecture allows to be accomplished simultaneously. Over the history of computer development, advances in circuit technology have accounted for most of the improvement in overall speed. The HEP is implemented with rather conservative circuit technology for its historical date and owes its significance to a distinct departure from previous machines with respect to architecture. The key is to allow more activity to occur in parallel and, as in the vector computers, the HEP does this in a way that appears explicitly in program structure.

The increase in speed due to enhanced parallelism has been the province of computer architecture beginning with the move from serial by bit to parallel by word operation, moving through processor and I/O overlap and now focusing on the area of concurrent data operations. Flynn [1] characterized the concurrency of data operations with respect to instruction streams by dividing architectures into four categories based on the number of instruction streams and the number of data streams. Single (SI) or multiple (MI) instruction streams may be combined with single (SD) or multiple (MD) data streams to form an architectural category. The scheme does not seem suitable for "Data Flow" machines [2] which are outside the scope of this paper.

In this paper, the categories SISD, SIMD and MIMD will be used from the instruction set point of view without regard to whether multiple operations are carried out on separate complete processors or whether the "parallel" operations are processed by a pipeline. A machine in which a single instruction specifies operations on several data items is a SIMD machine. The advantage of this point of view is that pipelining then becomes an independent architectural variable which may be combined with Flynn's categories in an orthogonal manner. Data operations in the SISD case do not become parallel until pipelining is applied; the simple technique of fetch-execute overlap is one application of pipelining to SISD computers. The Illiac IV computer [3] is a non-pipelined SIMD computer for vector and matrix processing. A machine with a very similar instruction set architecture but which uses pipelined arithmetic units to support vector operations is the Cray I [4], which we will call a pipelined SIMD computer.

Non-pipelined or "true" SIMD machines have the architecture shown in Fig. 1 (a). This structure has been used in numerous machines of a more special purpose nature [5], [6], [7]. SIMD computers which have seen widespread commercial use have tended

---

† Some of this work was done while the author was a consultant to Denelcor Inc.

1

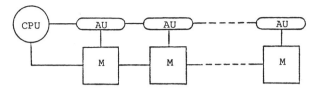

a)   True SIMD or Vector Computer

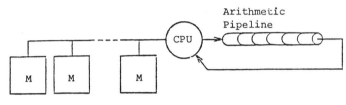

b)   Pipelined SIMD

```
AU  - Arithmetic Unit
CPU - Central Processing Unit
M   - Memory Module
```

Figure 1: SIMD Architectures.

to be of the pipelined variety [4], [8]. These correspond to the general architectural configuration shown in Fig. 1 (b). Of course no commercial machine uses a single form of parallelism. Multiple pipelines are used to enhance speed and scalar arithmetic units are overlapped. The move from "true" to pipelined SIMD machines is dictated by an improved cost/performance ratio along with added flexibility in vector length. The numerous arithmetic units of the "true" SIMD computer are only partially used at any instant so that pipelining can keep the amount of parallel activity constant while significantly reducing the hardware requirement. Pipelining also avoids the disadvantage of having vectors whose lengths are not even multiples of the number of arithmetic units in the "true" SIMD case.

Two prototypical forms of MIMD computers or multiprocessors [9] are shown in Fig. 2 (a). Although not widely available commercially, successful systems of both the shared memory form [10] and the distributed memory form [11] have been built. Fig. 2 (b) shows the configuration of an MIMD machine in which multiple instruction streams are supported by pipelining rather than by separate complete processors. The application of pipelining to multiple instruction stream execution can have the advantages of reduced hardware and increased flexibility in the number of instruction streams: the same advantages as were seen in the SIMD case. Since multiple, independent memory

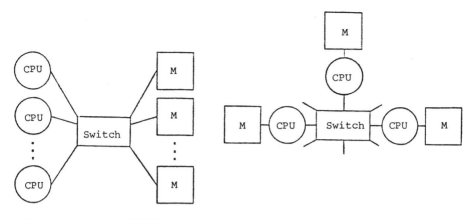

a)   True MIMD or Multiprocessor

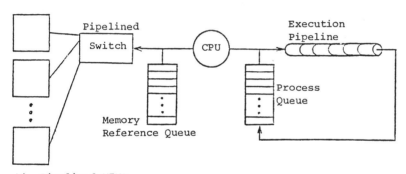

b)   Pipelined MIMD

CPU - Central Processing Unit
M   - Memory Module

Figure 2: MIMD Architectures.

requests are generated by the parallel instruction streams, pipelining can also be applied effectively to the memory access path. The Denelcor HEP is a commercially available pipelined MIMD computer [12], [13], [14], [15] of the type described above, and this chapter reports experience in applying this machine to a selection of scientific applications programs and measuring its performance.

Applications programs for machines falling into different architectural categories require different structuring of solution algorithms for efficient operation. Put differently, given a program with a particular structure, the ways in which architectural parallelism can be applied are different. For example, programs written in a sequential programming language for a sequential machine will take full advantage of a pipelined SISD machine. To apply an SIMD machine to an already written, sequential program requires an automatic vectorizing compiler [16], [17] with a degree of success depending on program structure. MIMD machines can execute multiple sequential programs in parallel for increased throughput, but work on automatic parallelizing compilers to speed up the execution of a single, sequential program using an MIMD architecture has just begun [18].

All forms of architectural parallelism are applicable to the many large problems arising out of numerical linear algebra [19], but SIMD machines are tailored to them and can achieve extremely high performance in operations on long enough vectors. It is easy to partition the components of a vector over different instruction streams, but the flexibility afforded by multiple streams is not needed, and synchronization overhead may be excessive if parallelism is restricted to the level of single vector operations. Vector processing may be performed quite efficiently with respect to other work on an SISD computer as a result of predictable lookahead characteristics, but again the architecture is not specialized to it. The number of linear algebraic applications, the often large size of these problems and the considerable algorithm research which has taken place in this field make this type of application an important standard against which to measure performance of any parallel architecture.

In numerous applications, the opportunity for parallel data operations is evident, but the operations differ from datum to datum, or there is enough irregularity in the structure of the data to make SIMD processing difficult or impossible. In these applications, one must either be content with pipelined SISD processing or move into the MIMD environment. Where multiple data items have irregular or conditional access patterns, MIMD processing may be preferred even when vectors are involved, as in the case of sparse matrix operations. At a higher level of algorithm structure is functional parallelism, in which large modules of the program operate in parallel and share data only in specific, easily synchronized ways.

The implementations of several algorithms in the above categories on the HEP pipelined MIMD computer are described below. The programs are of small to medium size, but all represent central parts of large scientific codes. The size of the codes allows an analysis of the efficiency of the architecture which is applicable to large code performance but simple enough to extract information about utilization of specific parts of the architecture. Few direct comparisons with other machines of a detailed nature have been carried out, and interpretation is complicated by circuit technology differences. The major thrust of this paper is to determine the extent to which the type of parallelism inherent in pipelined MIMD machines can be effectively utilized in different types of computations underlying large scale applications.

The HEP Architecture

The HEP computer is an MIMD computer consisting of one or more pipelined MIMD Process Execution Modules (PEMs) which share memory. Even within a single PEM the HEP is an MIMD computer. There is no qualitative difference in the way processes are created and managed or in the way in which they communicate in a one PEM system versus a multi-PEM one. Only the number of instructions actually executing simultaneously, about 12 per PEM, changes when more PEMs are added to a system. The results of measurements on a single PEM system are thus characteristic of the pipelined MIMD architecture of Fig. 2 (b). A multi-PEM HEP system consists of several units having the architecture of Fig. 2 (b) and sharing a single data memory consisting of one or more memory modules. The PEMs and memory modules are connected together by means of a pipelined, message switched interconnection network. Thus, it is a mixture of the architecture of Fig. 2 (b) with that of the left hand configuration in Fig. 2 (a).

There are several separate pipelines in a PEM, but the major flavor of the architecture can be given by considering only one, the main execution pipeline. In pipelined SIMD machines, the operating units are broken into small stages with data storage in each stage. Complete processing of a pair of operands involves the data passing sequentially through all stages of the pipeline. Parallelism is achieved by having different pairs of operands occupy different stages of the pipeline simultaneously. The different operand pairs represent different components of vectors being operated upon. In HEP, independent instructions (including operands) flow through the pipeline, with an instruction being completely executed in eight steps. Independence of activity in successive stages of the pipeline is achieved not by processing independent components of vectors but by alternating instructions from independent instruction streams in the pipeline. An instruction from a given stream must be completed before the next instruction from the same stream may be started, but instructions from other streams are started through the pipeline in the meanwhile. Multiple copies of process state, including program counter, are kept for a variable number of processes - up to 128 per PEM. The hardware implements what can be viewed as extremely fine grained multiprogramming by issuing instructions from different processes successively into the pipeline. Fig. 3 contrasts pipelined SIMD processing, in which pairs of operands occupy pipeline stages, with pipelined MIMD, in which instructions accompany their operands in the pipeline. Divide instructions do not progress according to the above descriptions since floating point divide makes use of a parallel rather than a pipelined implementation.

The previous paragraph describes the register to register instructions of the HEP. Those dealing with main memory (data memory) behave differently. There are four types of memory in a HEP system: program memory, register memory, constant memory and data memory. Program memory is normally read-only and is local to a PEM. Register and constant memories are also local to a PEM and are similar in use, except that constant memory may not be altered by a user process. There are 2048 registers and 4096 constants so that, even if many processes run in parallel, each has access to some private working storage. Data memory is shared between PEMs, and words are moved between register and data memories by means of Scheduler Function Unit (SFU) instructions.

A process is characterized by a Process Status Word (PSW) containing a program counter and index offsets into both register memory and constant memory to support the writing of reentrant code. Under the assumption that multiple processes will cooperate on a given job or task, and thus share memory, memory is allocated and protected on the basis of a structure called a task. Each of up to 16 tasks is described by a Task Status Word (TSW) containing base and limit values for each memory type. The 128 possible processes are divided into a maximum of 64 user and 64 supervisor

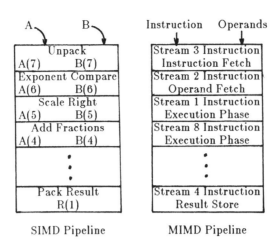

Figure 3: SIMD Versus MIMD Pipelining.

processes, which must belong to tasks of corresponding types. Aside from this restriction, a task may have any number of processes from zero to 64. Within this limit, a user process can create another process within the same task to share its computation. A single instruction serves to produce a running process from a word representing a PSW. A trap condition creates a trap handling process in the supervisor task associated with the user task causing the trap condition. Placing processes in different tasks serves to limit the memory which they may share. Thus, independent jobs would normally be assigned to different tasks. Instruction issuing maintains a fair allocation of resources between tasks first and processes within a task second. An active process is represented by a Process Tag (PT) which points to one of the 128 possible PSWs. The main scheduler issues the next instruction corresponding to a queued PT into the execution pipeline every 100 ns. The flow of PTs is outlined in Fig. 4, which also shows the structures involved in accessing data memory.

The completion time for an SFU instruction (data memory access) is larger than for other instructions, even though the pipeline step time is still 100 ns. When an SFU instruction is issued, the PT leaves the main scheduler queue and enters a queue in the SFU. When a PT comes to the head of the SFU queue, a memory transaction is built and sent into the attached node of a pipelined, message-switched routing network. The transaction propagates through the switch to the appropriate memory bank and returns to the SFU with status and perhaps data. The PT is then relinked into the queue of the main scheduler. The pipelining of messages through the switch and data memory modules makes SFU instructions behave as if issued into a pipeline longer than the eight step execution pipeline, but with the same step rate. The number, quoted above, of about 12 processes executing simultaneously per PEM represents an average of the main execution and memory pipeline lengths. The SFU instruction scheduler and the switch routing strategy make the length of this pipeline somewhat indeterminate. It is between 20 and 30 steps in a small, moderately loaded system.

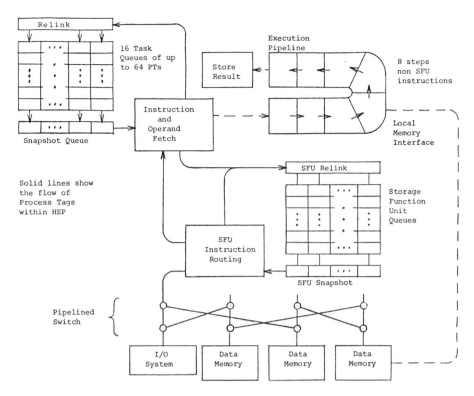

Figure 4: The Principal Pipelines in HEP.

Potentially, an instruction may be completed every 100 ns. Thus, 10 Million Instructions Per Second (MIPS) is an execution rate representing a maximum utilization of the hardware of one PEM. The fact that one instruction may require the result of another which is still in the pipeline is handled by a synchronization mechanism associated with operands and results of instructions. Each cell in register and data memories has a full/empty state, and synchronization is performed by having an instruction wait for its operands to be full and its result empty before proceeding. The synchronizing conditions are optionally checked by the instruction issuing mechanism, and, if not fulfilled, cause the PT to be immediately requeued with the program counter of the PSW unaltered. Only registers have a third state, reserved, which is set for the result register of an instruction currently in the execution pipeline. The most useful functions on the state are wait for full, read and set empty and wait for empty, write and set full. A test and change of the state is performed in an indivisible manner, as required by the synchronization for which it is used.

One other hardware mechanism illustrated in Fig. 4 is a separate, synchronous interface to a section of data memory. This "local memory" interface is pipelined with eight steps, as are most other execution units. Accesses may only use the local interface if they do not involve the full/empty state of a memory location. The pipeline step time is 100 ns for both local and switch access to data memory. The number of steps, however, is 8 for the local interface and 20-30 for access through the switch. The existence of two memory access paths will be used below to study the influence of pipeline length on program execution time in the pipelined MIMD environment.

Another mechanism which has a significant effect on performance measurements on the HEP is instruction lookahead. This represents a departure from the scheme of only allowing instructions from different streams to occupy slots in the pipeline simultaneously. The lookahead mechanism only comes into play when no PT is waiting in the task queues to issue an instruction at this pipeline step time. In this case, some simple checks are made to see if the next instruction for the PT obtained on the last cycle is independent of the instruction just issued into the pipeline. This is simple single stream lookahead and is blocked by branch instructions, operand-result dependencies and other factors. The major performance effect of this feature is on the execution time of a single process. Measurements show about a 25% faster execution on FOR-TRAN produced code. This means that an algorithm which might potentially show a speedup of 12 as a result of parallelization will only speed up by a factor of 9, merely because the one process program is already using some of the available parallelism.

All of the PEMs in the HEP are connected to all of the data memory modules by a pipelined switch. The switch consists of a network of interconnected nodes, each of which has three bi-directional ports. Memory references are formed into read or write request messages and sent into the switch by the SFU associated with some PEM. Messages are passed from node to node until they reach the correct memory module, which does the memory access and sends back a reply indicating the completion status. The full/empty synchronization on memory cells may result in a failed transaction with a failure reply being sent back to the requesting PEM by the memory. The SFU in a PEM is responsible for re-issuing synchronized requests until the full/empty state of the addressed location is correct. The switch nodes are pipelined and move messages on to the next node at the 100 ns step rate used in the rest of the machine, but they have no internal queues. Thus, a message arriving on an input port must be sent to some output port during the cycle. The nodes perform a "hot potato" routing by trying to send each message to the output port which brings it closest to its destination. The topology of the node network is somewhat flexible, being limited by the wire length and port restrictions, but the idea is to have multiple paths from any source to any destination. If two messages arrive simultaneously at a node and request the same output port, one of them will be misrouted and follow a different path to its destination. The entire switching network thus forms a dynamic message queue, which may have as many as three messages per switch node in the process of being routed.

In order to make such a pipelined switch function effectively, provision must be made for:

1) limiting the average number of misroutings;
2) handling switch overflow;
3) limiting worst case routing time.

The number of misroutings is kept small by associating an integer, called age, with each message, and incrementing it each time the message is misrouted. The age is then used as a priority in the conflicts which arise when two messages at a node request the same output port. The age is a four bit number and invokes the mechanism for limiting worst case routing time when it reaches its maximum of 15. The topology of the switch viewed as a graph guarantees the existence of an Eulerian path which traverses each edge, and thus reaches each output port, in a cycle. Such an Eulerian path is recorded in the switch nodes along with the optimal routing table, and, when a message attains an age of 15, it is sent on the Eulerian circuit of the switch. The Eulerian path makes the switch a ring so that age 15 messages follow each other in line and do not conflict with each other. Since an age 15 message naturally wins a conflict with a lower age message, it is guaranteed to reach its destination in a number of steps less than three times the number of switch nodes. Switch overflow comes into play when a message is misrouted to an output port which is connected to a PEM or memory module rather than another switch node. Such "leaking" messages are handled by requiring all devices connected to the switch to re-transmit a leaked message into the switch in preference to a new message which it might generate. This rule makes switch overflow self-limiting.

Each PEM connected to the switch can generate request messages at a rate of 10 million messages per second (MMPS), and each memory module can service requests to generate replies at 10 MMPS. It is thus possible for the switch to become filled in a case where several PEMs are running many processes, all of which reference the same memory module. In many programs, interleaving memory by having sequentially numbered locations in different memory modules would reduce the frequency of this kind of congestion. Interleaving memory on the HEP has the drawback, however, that the utility of the local memory interface is reduced. Local memory associates a specific memory module with a specific PEM for unsynchronized accesses only. It is most important for single stream programs which reference memory without using the full/empty state. Even with interleaving, however, the use of a single memory location to synchronize a large number of processes spread over more than one PEM can cause the switch to fill as a result of messages entering the switch faster than a single memory can handle them.

The Programming Model

Programming of the applications reported was done in HEP Fortran and is thus close to the machine language level. Minimal modifications were made to Fortran to give a user access to the MIMD environment of the HEP. To allow for the fact that an independent process usually requires some local variables, the process concept is tied to the Fortran subroutine. The Fortran extension is merely a second version of the CALL statement, CREATE. Control returns immediately from a CREATE statement, but the created subroutine, with a unique copy of its local variables, is also executing simultaneously. The RETURN in a created subroutine has the effect of terminating the process executing the subroutine. Parameters are passed by address in both CALL and CREATE, though some care must be taken in the linkage to see that changing addresses, such as array elements, are frozen at the value associated with executing the CREATE and remain static during the created subroutine's execution.

The only other major conceptual modification to Fortran allows access to the synchronizing properties of the full/empty state of memory cells. Any Fortran variable may be declared to be an "asynchronous" variable. Asynchronous variables are distinguished by names beginning with a $ symbol and may have any Fortran type. They may appear in Fortran declarative statements and adhere to implicit typing rules based on the initial letter. If such a variable appears on the right side of an assignment, wait for full, read and set empty semantics apply. When one appears on the left of an assignment, the semantics are wait for empty, write and set full. To initialize the state (not the value) of asynchronous variables, a new statement:

$$\text{PURGE } a_1, a_2, ..., a_n$$

sets the states of $a_1, a_2, ..., a_n$ to empty regardless of their previous states.

A pedagogical HEP Fortran example is shown in Fig. 5. The main program and two instances of the subroutine run in parallel to compute an array of cosines of sums of pairs of angles. Note that correct operation of the program depends on the order of evaluation of the expression in statement 10. It is assumed the memory access for the leftmost occurrence of $A ($B) in the expression is executed before that for the rightmost occurrence of $A ($B). Since optimizing compilers do not guarantee this, the accesses should appear in two successive Fortran statements.

The HEP Fortran extensions of CREATE and asynchronous variables are the simplest way to incorporate the parallel features of the hardware into the Fortran language. Since process creation is directly supported by the HEP instruction set and any memory reference may test and set the full/empty state that is associated with each memory cell, the Fortran extensions are direct representations of hardware mechanisms. Other types of interprocess synchronization must be implemented using these extensions. For example, the critical section, a section of code which must be

```
          PROGRAM MAIN
          REAL $ANGLE1(100), $ANGLE2(100)
          REAL COSSUM(100)
                .
                .
          Read in the $ANGLE arrays.
                .
          PURGE $A, $B
          CREATE TRIG($A, $ANGLE1)
          CREATE TRIG($B, $ANGLE2)
          DO 10 J = 1, 100
10        COSSUM(J) = $A*$B - $A*$B
C         COS(A1 + A2) = COS(A1)*COS(A2) - SIN(A1)*SIN(A2)
                .
                .
          END

          SUBROUTINE TRIG($X, $ANGLE)
          REAL $ANGLE(100)
          DO 20 I = 1, 100
          Y = $ANGLE(I)
          $X = COS(Y)
20        $X = SIN(Y)
          RETURN
          END
```

Figure 5: A HEP Fortran Example

executed by only one process at a time, has been used in numerous discussions of parallel programs [20]. It can be implemented with an asynchronous variable initialized to full. At the beginning of the critical section, a process reads and empties this variable, and, at the end of the section, writes it and sets it full. No other process attempting to enter its critical section will be able to complete the asynchronous read of this same variable until the first process has refilled it.

The FORK and JOIN statements [21], [22] are a standard way of passing from single stream to multiple stream execution and back again. FORK is trivially implemented in HEP Fortran by multiple creates, but JOIN requires each process to report completion before executing the Fortran RETURN so that the main program can wait on them before proceeding. Another way of controlling single versus multiple stream execution is the Barrier [23]. A set of parallel processes executing a Barrier statement must all complete the code preceeding the barrier before any process executes a statement following it. This allows the introduction of precedence constraints on program segments without the creation and destruction of process state and local variables, which is inherent in FORK and JOIN. The barrier mechanism is a simple and powerful aid to producing correct parallel programs and has been used in many of the applications discussed below. It can be costly in terms of performance in some cases, and some of the measurements reported shed light on this subject.

Effective Parallelization of Application Code

As mentioned, one way to use pipelined MIMD machines is to execute independent sequential programs simultaneously for increased throughput. If enough jobs can be held in memory at once, the independence of instructions in separate streams implies maximally efficient use of the parallel hardware, with no "holes" in the pipelines resulting from synchronization delays between streams. The interesting problem, however, is to apply this type of machine to large scientific applications where turnaround time is to be minimized. We thus limit the discussion to the problem of executing one job which is partitioned over multiple instruction streams so that total execution time is minimized.

In MIMD processing, there are two main ways of partitioning work across multiple instruction streams: partitioning on function and partitioning on data. Functional partitioning involves assigning different functional sections of a program to different instruction streams. These may communicate or share data in well defined ways but are independent enough to use the parallel hardware without significant synchronization overhead. When one functional section produces results which are consumed by the next, this organization is sometimes called macro-pipelining. On an SISD computer, it would be characterized by coroutines. Data partitioning involves using different instruction streams to process different items of a multi-item data structure. Functional partitioning tends to introduce a limited amount of parallelism, both because the number of distinct large functions is usually limited and because a single function often dominates execution time. If many smaller functions are identified, the amount of data shared is usually large enough that synchronization overhead becomes prohibitive. Hence some data partitioning must usually be applied to yield more than a few parallel processes computing simultaneously.

An extremely simplified characterization of parallel programs is useful in indicating how to proceed in parallelizing an application. It also yields a useful empirical probe into the degree of success achieved. Let the number of parallel hardware units be P This corresponds to P arithmetic units in an SIMD machine, a ratio of vector speed to scalar speed of P in a pipelined SIMD machine, P processors in MIMD and P pipeline stages in a pipelined MIMD machine. Consider P as variable and let the execution time on a machine with hardware parallelism P be $T(P)$. $P = 1$ and $T(1)$ correspond to the SISD case.

The simplest model of a parallel program is that it consists of a fraction f of operations which must be performed sequentially and a fraction $(1-f)$ of operations which can be spread across P hardware units with a speedup of P, i.e. unit efficiency. The execution time for such a program on a machine with hardware parallelism P would be:

$$T(P) = f \times T(1) + (1-f) \times \frac{T(1)}{P} \ . \tag{1}$$

The corresponding speedup and efficiency are:

$$S(P) = \frac{T(1)}{T(P)} = \frac{P}{f \times P + (1-f)} \ \text{ and } \ E(P) = \frac{S(P)}{P} = \frac{1}{1 + f \times (P-1)} \ . \tag{2}$$

The qualitative demands on successful parallelization come from observing that, if one wants at least 50% efficiency of hardware utilization, the fraction f of sequential code must be no larger than $1/(P-1)$. This may be quite small if P is large, so even a small amount of unparallelized code may have a significant effect on efficiency. One consequence is the importance of a good scalar processor in an SIMD machine, since this serves to keep P small. Another consequence is that an environment which allows parallelizing even a small amount more code can have a significant effect on efficiency. In an MIMD machine, sequential operation arises both from single stream execution and from synchronizations, such as critical sections, which cause all instruction streams but one to wait.

An empirical probe into the degree of parallelism in a parallel program can be obtained by assuming an execution time of the form $T(P)$, executing the program for several values of P and determining the fraction $(1-f)$ of parallel code by the method of least squares. This model fits a situation in which the parallel fraction of the code is done by P processes which do not change, except in the amount of work each performs, as P is varied. The model also requires hardware in which the P processes can be executed by non-interfering hardware units. This is the case in a true multiprocessor with P or more processors and is closely approximated in the pipelined MIMD hardware of a single HEP execution module, provided P is no more than about five. Above $P = 5$ single instruction stream lookahead begins to limit parallelism in HEP.

Many applications programs discussed fit the required program format very well. They are composed of an arbitrary number of "self-scheduling," identical processes which result from a FORK near the beginning of the program and JOIN together near its end. The self-scheduling characterization comes from the total work being divided into a number of chores which is large relative to P. Each process obtains a chore, and, when finished, determines and performs the next unassigned chore. This technique can give uneven execution time if the number of chores per process is small but is a powerful technique when the execution time of a chore is data dependent. We will thus use the probe to determine how well an application has been parallelized. It must be kept in mind that all limits to parallel execution, including such things as critical section lockout, producer-consumer delays and multiple readers and writers synchronization delay, will all be lumped into an increase in the fraction f of sequential code in the model of Eq. 1.

Many of the process synchronizations which limit speedup on the HEP can be looked at as critical sections in the code. In fact, the basic hardware synchronization mechanism of shared full/empty memory cells essentially imposes critical section properties on multiple processes accessing the same variable. We can modify Eq. 1 by assuming that the cost of parallelizing the fraction $(1-f)$ of the code is a critical section of length t_c in each process. The amount of work done by each process in the parallel section is:

$$\frac{(1-f) \times T(1)}{P} + t_c$$

It may be possible for all other processes to complete their critical sections while a given process is doing its fraction of useful work. This can only occur when

$$\frac{(1-f) \times T(1)}{P} \geq (P-1) \times t_c .$$

Conflict for critical section access can occur in this case, but a justification for using the best case analysis of perfect overlap is that, if the critical section is made up of short segments executed in a loop, the delays occuring on the first pass cause the processes to fall into synchronism. Thus, no delays occur on subsequent passes through the loop, and the best case timing is well approximated. In this case, the total execution time can be written:

$$T(P) = f \times T(1) + (1-f) \times \frac{T(1)}{P} + t_c , \quad (1-f) \times T(1) \geq P \times (P-1) \times t_c .$$

When the amount of time a process spends doing useful work is shorter that the total time spent by other processes sequentially passing through their critical sections, the useful work is masked by critical section delay, and the best case time becomes:

$$T(P) = f \times T(1) + P \times t_c , \quad (1-f) \times T(1) < P \times (P-1) \times t_c .$$

Combining the cases, the best case analysis gives:

$$T(P) = f \times T(1) + t_c + \max\left[(1-f) \times \frac{T(1)}{P}, (P-1) \times t_c\right] . \tag{3}$$

This expression has a minimum at

$$P_m \approx \frac{1}{2} + \left(\frac{(1-f) \times T(1)}{t_c}\right)^{\frac{1}{2}} , \quad \frac{t_c}{(1-f) \times T(1)} \ll 1 ,$$

and rises linearly with P for $P > P_m$. The rise in execution time is observed in most of the measurements when the number of processes becomes large.

The above analysis assumes no limit on the number P of processes which may execute in parallel. In the HEP, the degree of simultaneous execution is limited by the lengths of the various pipelines and can be characterized by an average pipeline length, U. One can then consider U to be the maximum number of processes which can run in parallel on the hardware without slowing execution. The addition of further processes does not speed the completion of the $(1-f) \times T(1)$ workload which can be parallelized but does increase the number of processes executing critical sections. Taking this limit into account, the execution time model becomes:

13

$$T(P) = f \times T(1) + t_c + \max\left(\frac{(1-f)\times T(1)}{min(P,U)}, (P-1)\times t_c\right). \qquad (4)$$

This execution time model fits many of the measured results very well, except that the sharp corners predicted by the max and min functions are smoothed by statistical effects on the hardware process scheduling.

Applications Programs on a Single PEM

Results of timing and analysis of several different applications codes, ranging from a one page subroutine through an 1800 line Fortran package for sparse linear system solution [24], will be presented. The programs are categorized into three types. The first is the "dusty deck" Fortran program, written for a sequential processor and obscure enough in its origin or short enough in execution time that a redesign of the program is not practical. Mechanical parallelization of the program, preferably with an automatic, parallelizing compiler, is the correct approach to this type. The second type is the "vector program" which comes from the realm of numerical linear algebra and is well suited to SIMD computers. Some interesting comparisons of SIMD and MIMD performance can come from this type. The third type of program is the "non-vectorizable" program. Experience suggests that few programs are completely non-vectorizable, but there is a distinct class of programs where MIMD parallelization is simpler or more natural than vectorization.

Dusty Deck Programs

An idea of the best that can be expected from the pipelined MIMD architecture can be obtained by analysis of an easily parallelized program with a simple structure. The heart of this benchmark is a numerical integration to compute the Gamma function. The integral is computed by applying Simpson's rule to sufficiently short intervals. Parallelization is done by data decomposition in which the total interval, 0 to $2\times MM$, is divided into MM integrations over length two intervals, which are done in parallel; MM is taken as 50. The length two intervals are further subdivided into MS subintervals so the amount of work to be done in one parallel chore is proportional to MS, which is on the order of 1000. Processes interact only by adding the contribution of a subinterval to a shared sum and in updating a shared loop index to get the next chore. Self scheduling allows the number of active processes to vary without changing the program. A simple data dependency analysis would allow this parallelization to be done automatically.

The variation in execution time versus the number of parallel processes is shown in Fig. 6. The graph shows the execution time as a function of the number of active processes both using the local memory interface and with it disabled. The graph exhibits several features. First there is the $1/N_p$ reduction in execution time for small values of N_p as new processes make efficient use of the execution pipeline. This decrease in execution time bottoms out as the pipeline becomes full. The simple 8 step instruction pipeline is effectively extended by the effects of the SFU and the divider, so that the $1/N_p$ effect does not level abruptly at $N_p = 8$. Superimposed on the above described curve is the effect of scheduling MM = 50 chores on N_p processes. Since all chores are the same size, the scheduling is best when N_p divides 50 evenly.

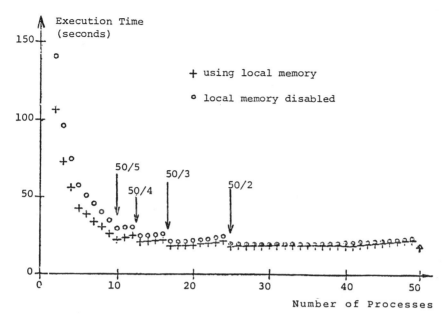

Figure 6: Execution Time for Numerical Integration.

Since both local memory interface and switch are pipelined at a 100 ns step rate, their performance is expected to be similar if the pipeline is full. The switch turnaround, however, is about 2 μsec as compared to 800 ns for the local interface. Thus, the execution times should differ significantly for small numbers of processes, where parallelism is wasted in waiting for memory turnaround but not when the number of processes is large enough to keep either pipeline full. The slowdown resulting from disabling the local memory interface is about 30% for small N_p and decreases to 5% as N_p becomes large enough to fill the pipelines. The results clearly show that a major change in pipeline length has little influence on performance when the number of processes is sufficiently large.

The data, combined with the simple structure of the program, make it possible to eliminate the scheduling effects and compute the speedup $S(N_p)$ which would be obtained in running a job consisting of N_p chores on N_p processors [14]. If N_p processes share the pipeline perfectly, i. e. a process waits only for its own instructions to complete, then $S(N_p) = N_p$. A smaller value of S indicates that, although N_p processes are queued for the pipeline, only S of them occupy actual processing stages simultaneously.

The curves of Fig. 7 indicate that, when the local memory interface is being used for the majority of references, no further benefit is obtained by using more than 18 processes. The flat asymptotic behavior indicates that there are no empty pipeline slots into which instructions from additional processes can be inserted once the asymptote is reached. These 18 processes execute as if 11.8 of them were able to run entirely

15

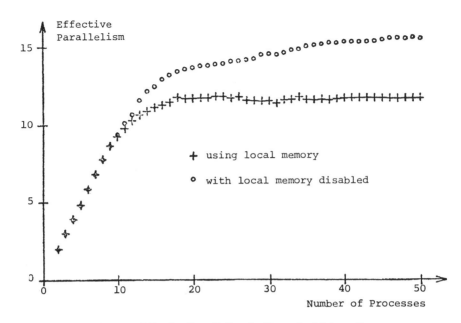

Figure 7: Effective Parallelism in Numerical Integration.

in parallel. With the local memory interface disabled, all memory requests are forced through the switch, thus increasing the pipeline length so more processes are required to keep the pipeline full. Explicit interaction between processes occurs only twice for each execution of the large loop over MS, so the interaction observed is almost entirely a result of hardware utilization by the processes.

One might suspect that the strictly synchronous behavior of the local memory interface would result in a very sharp knee in the local memory enabled curve of Fig. 7 at $N_p = 8$. If all memory references were local, then only the divider would depart from 8 step, 100 ns per step pipelining. In fact, the store indexed (STOX) instruction cannot use the local memory interface and must go through the switch. By actual count, 25% of the instructions in the inner loop are STOX so a substantial amount of switch traffic exists even though all data memory is accessible via the local memory interface. Since STOX has a 2400 ns turnaround, one can estimate effective parallelism with fully loaded pipelines using the instruction count information. Three quarters of the instructions use an 8 step pipeline while one quarter share a 24 step pipe. Thus, the asymptotic speedup should be the weighted average of the pipeline lengths, or 12. This compares favorably with the value of 11.8 obtained from Fig. 7. The close agreement makes it abundantly clear that when N_p is large an effective instruction completion is occurring every 100 ns. The pipelines are thus as fully utilized as is possible with the given instruction mix.

The previous example represents a best case in which the program consists of one loop such that loop body instances for different values of the index can be done completely in parallel. It has been shown [18] that data dependencies between instances of a loop body can be analyzed to extract parallelism in an MIMD environment. To obtain an idea of the degree of parallelism which can be obtained by this technique in the HEP pipelined MIMD environment, a typical sequential Fortran subroutine was parallelized by applying mechanical techniques to each of its loops and synchronizing to perform the loops in order. The program treated is a subroutine of 40 Fortran statements from the MA28 sparse matrix package of the AERE, Harwell, England [25]. The purpose of the subroutine is to sort a sparse matrix, given as a list of corresponding value, row index and column index triples, so that it is stored by column.

The program consists of five disjoint loops performed sequentially, where all loops are simple except the fourth which is nested to depth two. The first loop is an initialization with independent loop body instances and is parallelized by pre-scheduling the work over the available processes. The second counts elements in each column using a shared vector of counts. This loop can also be pre-scheduled by using full/empty to synchronize each count. The probability of simultaneous access, and hence synchronization delay, on a specific count is low. The third loop is a one step recurrence and is parallelized by an algorithm suggested by Ladner and Fisher [26]. A more thorough treatment of parallelizing general recurrences is given by Gajski [27]. The fourth loop does the actual in-place sort. The data dependencies between instances of the outer loop body are more difficult to analyze but probably within reach of an automatic parallelizer. Full/empty synchronization on the array being sorted and on the column counts suffices to allow instances of the outer loop body to be distributed over multiple processes. Since the execution time of the inner loop is data dependent, self scheduling is more effective than pre-scheduling in this case. The fifth loop involves the shifting of a vector and can be parallelized by pre-scheduling blocks of adjacent elements over processes.

When the parallelized version of this process was executed with 20 processes a speedup of 4.8 over the sequential version was measured for a sparse matrix with 5000 non-zeros and 400 columns. This is between the order 12 speedup which the previous example leads one to expect from completely independent loop body instances and a speedup of less than two which was independently measured [14] for the recurrence. This one, carefully analyzed example is typical of other mechanistic parallelizations of sequential benchmarks which have been done for HEP and suggests that automatic parallelization of programs for a single PEM system will obtain speedups on the order of three to six.

Dense Linear Systems Programs

Work using the HEP as a test bed for MIMD algorithms to solve linear systems, both by direct methods [28] and iteratively [29], has previously been reported. Here we consider two applications which do not use new algorithms but reorganizations of sequential algorithms which are suitable to the MIMD environment. Both applications involve LU decomposition, and both MIMD versions have the structure in which an arbitrary number of processes are forked at the beginning of the computation, share the work equally and join to a single stream when the computation is complete. One application is a full matrix decomposition subroutine from the LINPACK linear algebra package [30]. The other is essentially a dense band LU decomposition arising from a partial differential equation on a rectangular grid with red-black numbering.

Both applications afford a comparison between the HEP and the CRAY-1. The CRAY-1 is a pipelined SIMD computer which includes a high speed scalar arithmetic unit in addition to the vector unit. It is implemented with high speed Emitter Coupled Logic (ECL), has a minor cycle clock period of 12.5 ns and uses 64 bit words. The HEP pipelined MIMD machine is implemented with lower speed ECL logic, has a minor cycle clock period of 100 ns and also uses 64 bit words. Up to 16 PEMs can be included in a HEP system but the results here are based on a single PEM system.

The full matrix decomposition is the SGEFA subroutine from LINPACK. This program has been studied in the CRAY-1 pipelined SIMD environment by Dongarra [31], who also implemented and timed the routine on numerous other computers [32]. Parallelization for HEP was straightforward and resulted in a worker subroutine executed by an arbitrary number N_p of processes. The worker subroutine computes a local maximum over $1/N_p$ of the potential pivots, synchronizes to obtain a global maximum and reduces $1/N_p$ of the remaining rows using the pivot row determined. Although the organization of the code differs from that for the CRAY-1, the operations corresponding to different elements of a column are potentially done in parallel while operations on elements of a row are done in sequence, as in the vector version. The HEP program was run with N_p going from one to twenty in steps of one. The same order 100 test matrix was used as was used by Dongarra in the CRAY-1 measurements. The best execution time of 1.24 seconds occurred for $N_p = 17$ processes and corresponds to 0.53 MFLOPS (million floating point operations per second). The compiler used was completely non-optimizing and independent estimates indicate that a compiler capable of ordinary common subexpression collapse and loop invariant removal would produce HEP code which ran faster by a factor of three. Thus, a better performance number to use for comparison of the architectures is probably 1.6 MFLOPS. The empirical probe into the degree of parallelization based on the execution time model of Equation 1 indicates that 97% of the code is parallelized.

Dongarra obtained 14.3 MFLOPS for the fastest Fortran version of SGEFA on the CRAY-1. Assembly code kernels for the basic vector operations gave better performance. This performance exceeds that estimated for a single PEM HEP system running a similar compiler by a factor of nine. An estimate of the fraction of the code which is vectorized is not as easy to obtain as the degree of MIMD parallelization is from the HEP measurements. Dongarra reports speedups for the order 100 test case run with two different compilers with vectorization both off and on. One gave a speedup of 5.9 while the other gave 3.3. The speedup on HEP in going from $N_p = 1$ to $N_p = 17$ processes was 6.9. It should be noted that Dongarra refers to hand coded assembly language programs for the CRAY-1 which perform an order of magnitude better than Fortran routines. This sort of improvement in HEP performance is not attainable by hand coding but only by adding more PEMs to the system.

The second application in this section has a more complex structure and comes from the solution of a sparse system of linear equations arising from the partial differential equation model of an oil reservoir. The red-black numbering scheme is used on the points of a Cartesian grid to obtain a linear system with the specialized form:

$$\begin{bmatrix} I & A \\ B & I \end{bmatrix} \begin{bmatrix} X_1 \\ X_2 \end{bmatrix} = \begin{bmatrix} R_1 \\ R_2 \end{bmatrix} .$$

As a result of this structure, it is only necessary to solve the system

$$(I - BA)X_2 = R_2 - BR_1$$

with one half as many equations and then find X_1 from $X_1 = R_1 - AX_2$. The system is strongly diagonally dominant, so that pivots may be taken from the diagonal during the decomposition.

The original matrix is stored in a sparse form with each column represented by a pair of vectors, one with nonzero values and the other with corresponding row numbers. The structure of $(I - BA)$ is such that LU decomposition can be done with banded matrix techniques rather than those required for random sparsity. It is, however, beneficial to track the envelope of the band rather than to use a constant vector length corresponding to the maximum bandwidth. The numerical problem is thus a mixture of an easily vectorized banded dense matrix decomposition with a less vectorizable random sparse matrix multiply.

The Gauss elimination algorithm is organized somewhat differently for the SIMD and MIMD environments. The vector version [33] works down the band with a moving window on the active portion of the L matrix, simultaneously doing elimination and forward substitution, so the portion of L behind the pivot may be discarded. The elimination operations are done column-wise, using a single column working vector. Columns of the U matrix are put on a push-down stack as they are completed for access in reverse order during back substitution. This storage format is ideal for the back substitution, which uses the "column sweep" [34] method.

The MIMD version of the algorithm assigns different processes to different rows in the elimination, so that, as in the SIMD case, the operations which are executed in parallel correspond to different rows. Since synchronization is not as precise in the MIMD algorithm, simultaneous operations do not necessarily correspond to elements of the same column. The moving window on L is retained, but the working column vector is replaced by a window of working rows covering the active portion of the band. The U matrix is pushed onto the stack by row, corresponding to the fact that a single process is responsible for operations using a row of U during back substitution. Synchronization is tied to the availability of data using the full/empty property of memory cells in HEP, rather than appearing in process control structures such as critical sections. Self-scheduling processes are used to execute a single program. Each process obtains a unit of work, or chore, performs the chore and returns to look for more work. Four types of chores exist:
  - Construct a row of the modified problem $(I - BA)X_2 = R_2 - BR_1$.
  - Scale a completed pivot row, and stack this row of U.
  - Reduce a non-pivot row by a multiple of the pivot row.
  - Do back substitution for one row of U.
Only one control structure is used for process synchronization. This is a barrier type synchronization to prevent any process from proceeding to the back substitution until all have finished the forward phase.

Results reported here are from a data set consisting of a 515 equation system obtained from a $10 \times 10 \times 5$ reservoir model grid. The half bandwidth of $(I - BA)$ was 60 which implied good utilization of the CRAY-1 vector registers. By actual count on the SIMD version of the algorithm the number of floating point operations was 725,030. Dr. Donald Thurnau [33] designed and ran the SIMD version on the CRAY-1 obtaining an execution time of 0.066 seconds. With vectorization turned off, a CRAY-1 execution time of 0.233 seconds was obtained. These correspond to rates of

11.0 and 3.1 MFLOPS respectively. Comparing this factor of 3.5 speedup under vectorization with the speedups of from 3.3 - 8.4 which Dongarra obtained with vectorization turned on in timings of four LINPACK routines suggests that the sparse structure of part of this problem makes the code somewhat less vectorizable than the full matrix LINPACK code.

The MIMD version of the algorithm was run on a single execution unit HEP with results shown in Fig. 8. The optimal number of processes was 13, giving an execution time of 2.09 seconds, corresponding to 0.35 MFLOPS. The non-optimizing Fortran compiler was also used here. In order to get a fair estimate of results with a realistic compiler, the techniques of common subexpression collapse and loop invariant removal were applied by hand to the generated object code. This gave a 3 to 1 reduction in the

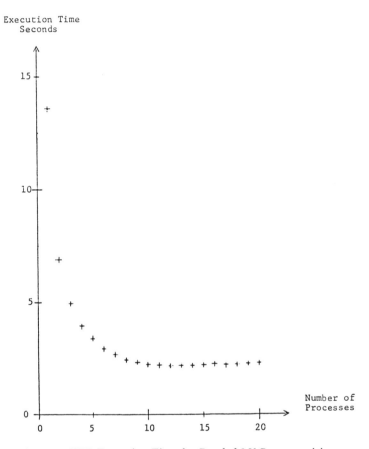

Figure 8: HEP Execution Time for Banded LU Decomposition.

20

number of instructions executed, corresponding to an execution time of 0.70 seconds, or 1.04 MFLOPS. The degree of parallelization estimate from the model of Equation 1 gives 98%, and the speedup in going from 1 to 13 processes was 6.5.

The ratio of the CRAY-1 to HEP clock speeds is 8 to 1 while the ratio of the MFLOP rate for similarly optimized code is 11 to 1. The degree of vectorization versus degree of parallelization estimates indicate that this moderately sparse matrix oriented code may parallelize somewhat better in the MIMD environment. The high degree of parallelization given by the empirical probe on HEP indicates that the code could be executed on a system with several execution units with very little loss in efficiency. No change in the code is required to execute it on a multiple unit system.

Programs which Vectorize Poorly

There are many algorithms important to scientific applications which, while clearly containing operations which may be executed in parallel, do not involve vectors. Some of these algorithms can be transformed so that vector operations are introduced, but the transformation may require global analysis, the transformed program may be quite obscure and the amount of parallelism introduced may be small. In such cases, it may be better to parallelize over multiple instruction streams. Parallel algorithms for two graph theoretic problems have been developed and tested on HEP and previously reported in the literature. They are the shortest path [35] and minimum spanning tree [36] problems. Here we focus on algorithms which were originally developed for sequential machines and which have been programmed for the MIMD environment by exploiting the opportunities for multiple process execution already present in the design.

A large number of computationally expensive scientific applications are based on the solution of large sparse systems of linear equations. The largest program for which the author has produced and analyzed an MIMD version is the MA28 package [25],[37] of Fortran subroutines for in-core LU decomposition and solution of sparse unsymmetric linear systems. The package was parallelized under the self imposed constraints of retaining the numerical properties and user interface of the original package. Retaining the user interface had the additional effect of constraining the storage space used, since all arrays with problem dependent size are supplied by the user. Execution time statistics for the sequential version of the package [38] indicate that most of the time is spent in reduction of non-pivot rows and in the search for a pivot using the Markowitz criterion [39]. The techniques required to parallelize these sections gave good indications of both the possibilities and problems in parallelizing sparse LU decomposition.

Non-pivot row reduction can be done in parallel by multiple processes despite the non-vector logic needed to handle differing patterns of non-zeros in the pivot and non-pivot rows. However, fill-in imposes the requirement for a dynamically allocated storage scheme. MA28 uses a segmented memory approach with rows assigned to segments. In the MIMD environment, such a scheme requires synchronized capture of free space and an eventual pause by all processes for storage compaction. While compaction itself occurs infrequently enough that it does not influence performance, the synchronization code required to allow for it represents a significant overhead. A more static allocation scheme such as paging or a hash table would be better for the MIMD environment.

To speed the sequential Markowitz search, a set of linked lists of rows and columns ordered by number of non-zeros is maintained. Assigning different rows or columns to different processes for the search incurs the overhead of synchronizing this somewhat complex shared data structure. In fact, enclosing accesses to the structure in critical sections limits potential parallelism to about six simply on the basis of the critical to non-critical code ratio. It would be worthwhile to search a few more rows or columns in parallel to reduce the complexity of the shared structure.

In forward and back substitution, the MA28 package solves systems both for the original matrix and its transpose. Both solutions are equally efficient in the sequential environment but require different storage schemes for the LU factors to make parallel forward and back substitution efficient. In the substitution phase it is fairly clear that the limited parallelism available from the hardware makes it inefficient to apply one of the highly parallel recurrence solvers [19] which increases the total number of operations significantly.

Timing data for the LU decomposition phase of the package is shown in Fig. 9 for an order 515 system with 3220 non-zeros. There is a maximum speedup of 5.5 in going from one to 15 processes, and the least squares fit of Eq. 1, indicated by the solid curve in the figure, gives 86% as the degree of parallelization. An interesting point in interpreting the numerical results is that, because several elements may be equally good pivots according to the Markowitz criterion, different pivots may be chosen with different numbers of processes. Thus the goal of maintaining the exact numerical characteristics of the sequential algorithm is not only disturbed by effects such as the non-associativity of floating point operations but also by choice of the pivot sequence.

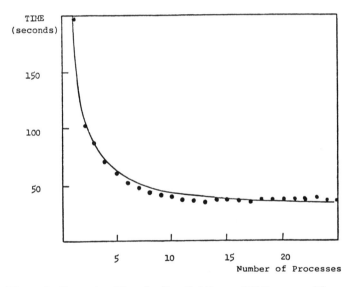

Figure 9: Execution Time for Parallel Sparse LU Decomposition.

One further program deserves mention in this section on non-vectorizable algorithms. This is an adaptive quadrature originally designed by D. H. Grit and J. R. McGraw [40] based on an algorithm of Rice [41] and modified by the author to take maximum advantage both of the HEP hardware and of the Fortran run-time system. The computation is in the form of a binary tree in which an approximation and error estimate are applied to a subinterval at each node of the tree. If more accuracy is required, the subinterval is divided in two, and the same algorithm is applied to each new interval. Since the number of available processes is limited, it is not possible to assign every subinterval to a separate process, but a program which gives away subtrees of the computation when processes are available to do them can be designed and executed by one or many processes with the same numerical results.

A plot of execution time versus number of processes for a moderately complex integrated function has a form similar to graphs already presented. The interesting thing is the speedup. With a maximum tree depth of 14 and 5969 partitions of the original interval, the degree of parallelization is empirically estimated at 99% and the speedup in going from one to 19 processes is 11.0 when run on a HEP system having a small processor to memory switch and including single stream lookahead. When run on this system, the "ideally" parallelizable Simpson's rule integration program previously discussed gives a maximum speedup of only about 9 because the lookahead and small switch makes the single stream execution faster by about 25%. The fact that the adaptive quadrature program speeds up by more than a "perfectly" parallelizable program is apparently a result of the backtracking work which must be done by a single process in handling the whole tree. The fact that multiple processes reduce this backtracking makes it beneficial to use more processes than are actually necessary to keep the MIMD pipeline full.

Performance of a Multi-PEM System

Several performance measurements were made on a Denelcor HEP system located at the U. S. Army's Ballistic Research Laboratory, which provided the research funding which led to the HEP computer. We have attempted to understand the extent to which the performance results apply to the shared memory computational model in general and that to which they are specific to the HEP system. The system consists of four PEMs sharing a memory of four non-interleaved modules by way of a high concurrency switching network. The system will thus support up to 200 user processes in a shared-memory MIMD environment. The pipelined approach limits the actual hardware parallelism available to between 60 and 80 over the total system.

The smallest "kernel" on which detailed measurements were made was matrix multiply. This simple kernel is often used as a probe for performance of vector machines, and it is instructive to study it on a multiprocessor. Its synchronization structure is so simple that the information obtained from it primarily relates to hardware limits.

Several performance measurements were made on a Gaussian elimination algorithm with partial pivoting derived from the code of the SGEFA subroutine in the LINPACK [30] package of linear algebra routines. This is, of course, not an algorithm which favors the MIMD over the SIMD environment, but it has several advantages for the measurement of performance. It has been implemented on many vector machines [31] and thus provides a point of comparison. The parallelism appears at a low enough level to make the interpretation of results with respect to algorithm structure fairly unambiguous. Finally, the partial pivoting imposes enough sequentiality on the execution to make process synchronization a significant factor in performance.

A parallel version of point Successive Over Relaxation (SOR) was developed and measured in detail on the simple model problem of Laplace's equation on a square region [42]. The method was then used in a more realistic form to compute stream function vorticity in a driven cavity. The heart of the parallel SOR algorithm is a producer/consumer synchronization on the values being relaxed. The measurements thus give an indication of the performance costs of this type of synchronization.

Hardware Structure and Performance Limits

The structure and performance of a single PEM, discussed above, is used in understanding the new measurements. Each of the four PEMs in the HEP system at BRL has a degree of parallelism in the pipelined execution units of about 12. A single process uses lookahead to overlap 1.25 to 1.5 instructions in an average mix. This implies that on a single PEM a program may be expected to speed up by no more than 7.5 to 9.5 over single stream execution. The instruction issuing mechanism limits the aggregate instruction rate over all processes in one PEM to 10 MIPS (million instructions per second). The four PEM system thus has an upper bound on the instruction rate of 40 MIPS, imposed by the processor hardware. To obtain 10 MIPS per PEM, there must be enough processes so that one of them is always ready to issue an instruction at every minor cycle, and the processes must not wait on each other for synchronization. In this ideal case, one could expect a program running on four PEMs to give a speedup of 30 to 38 over the same program executing in single stream.

The above numbers only reflect the processor (PEM) limits. The memory also limits performance as a result of the finite reference bandwidth per module. The system has four memory modules which are not interleaved on address. The lack of interleaving arises from an interest in maximizing the utilization of one memory module by an associated PEM in the few process per PEM case. The memory modules are attached to the PEMs through a pipelined switch. The actual configuration of the BRL system is shown in Fig. 10. All paths in a non-overlapping set of paths through the switch can carry 10 million messages per second (MMPS) simultaneously, and each module can service references coming from the switch at this rate. In addition, each memory module has a second port with bandwidth of 10 MMPS connected to only one of the four PEMs. This port, called the Local Memory interface, can not be used by instructions which use the full/empty state of memory cells for synchronization, or by indexed write instructions.

The purpose of the Local Memory interface is to speed up a program having only one or a few processes running on a single PEM and using data memory in a single module associated with that PEM. This and the instruction lookahead feature combine to make the run time of a single process program very sensitive to detailed memory allocation and to instruction mix in the inner loop. This means that speedup over single stream execution, which would otherwise be a candidate for a system independent measure of parallel algorithm performance, is influenced by a number of very system dependent features. The least squares fit to a simple parallel execution time model, described above, is less sensitive to special features used to enhance single stream performance.

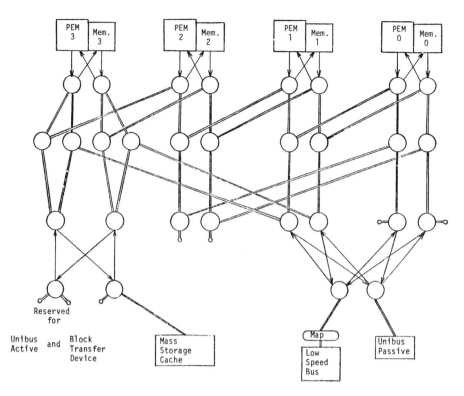

Figure 10: Configuration of a Four PEM HEP System.

As a result of the simplicity of the matrix multiply, most of the information it yields reflects the hardware configuration and capabilities of the four PEM system. The general characteristics of the execution time versus number of processes curve are the same as for several of the one PEM programs. The roughly $1/P$ decrease in execution time levels off at between 50 and 70 processes, with incremental changes resulting from scheduling a fixed number of chores over an incomensurable number of processes. However, there is some interesting fine structure. Fig. 11 shows a portion of the time versus processes curve for a 200×200 matrix multiply. Processes were pre-scheduled over the rows of the first matrix, and scheduling effects can be seen at $50 = 200/4$ and $67 = 200/3$ processes. The strong correlation between groups of four successive points seems clearly related to the distribution of processes across the four PEMs. In the inner product loop for this program there are two floating point and two memory reference instruction out of a total of seven. If the processors ran at the full maximum of 40 MIPS, this ratio would imply a memory request rate and floating point rate equal to 11.43×10^6 per second. The maximum floating point rate measured for the 200×200 matrix multiply was 10.58 MFLOPS with 100 processes, which is within 8% of the

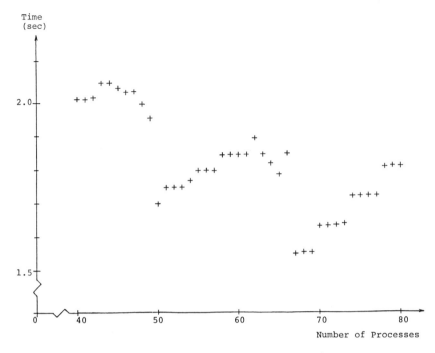

Figure 11: Multiplication of 200×200 Matrices.

limit. Adding the local memory interface bandwidth for one PEM to the 10 MMPS bandwidth of the switch to memory module interface, we find that the required memory bandwidth can be supplied by one memory module in this case.

More floating point speed can be obtained by unrolling the inner product loop. This also increases the number of messages per second to the memory. The 200×200 matrix multiply with inner product loop unrolled to depth four was run both with all data in one memory module and with the two matrices in different memory modules. The system performance indicator (SPI) unit in the HEP is capable of counting floating point, memory reference and other instructions. Combining SPI count differences with elapsed time allowed floating point, memory reference and total instruction rates to be measured. With data in a single memory module, the maximum rate attainable was 29.9 MIPS with 93 processes, while with two modules being used, the maximum was 38.8 MIPS with 100 processes. The numbers of memory reference and floating point instructions in the inner loop were again equal and were each 8/19 of the total in the loop. The measured memory reference rates were 12.7 MMPS using one memory module and 16.4 MMPS using two. Thus, the memory bandwidth is clearly holding down the processor speed in the one module case. The fact that the memory reference rate is very close to 8/19 of the instruction rate in both cases shows that the inner loop does dominate the measurements, as expected.

26

To observe the effects of the hardware limits on the Gaussian elimination program, the inner loop kernel was extracted from the program and all synchronization was removed. This kernel was optimized, up to but not including loop unrolling. In this form, the HEP instruction set gave a loop body with two floating point instructions, three memory references and three other instructions for indexing and branching. Thus the 40 MIP instruction rate limit translates to 10 MFLOPS and 15 MMPS. With the entire matrix in one memory module only one PEM could use the local memory interface. One of the three references in the loop was an indexed write, further limiting the use of local memory.

When the unsynchronized kernel was run on four PEMs with the matrix in one memory module, the speed increased as the number of processes was increased from one to 80, as shown in Fig. 12. At 80 processes, the instruction rate limited at about 30 MIPS, restricted by the single memory module bandwidth limit of about 12 MMPS (taking into account the additional local memory bandwidth). With no simple way to interleave memory modules available, the next best thing was to split the matrix across the boundary between two modules. Since the matrix was stored by column and accessed by row, this distributed the references fairly evenly over the two modules. The instruction rate versus number of processes curve for this case is shown

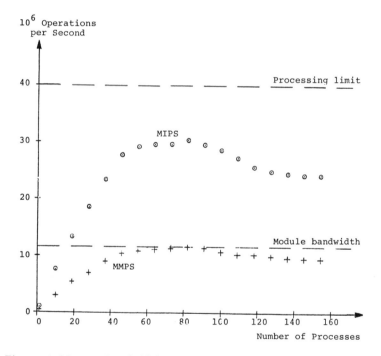

Figure 12: Memory Bandwidth Limitation on the Unsynchronized Kernel

27

in Fig. 13. It shows an instruction rate which increases uniformly, becoming asymptotic to 40 MIPS. The memory reference rate becomes asymptotic to 15 MMPS, well below the 20 MMPS limit for two memory modules.

The one and two memory module measurements of the unsynchronized kernel show up another feature of the four PEM system. It was mentioned earlier that the pipelined switching network uses a "hot potato" routing algorithm, with no message queueing in the switch nodes. The 30 node switch as a whole forms a dynamic queue for blocked messages. When the switch becomes full, routing conflicts degrade its performance in delivering messages to the correct destination. The unsynchronized kernel in one memory model shows a distinct decrease in the instruction rate with number of processes after the limiting memory bandwidth is reached. This is a result of switch filling as more references are issued than the memory module can service. The curve for two memory modules, on the other hand, becomes quite flat at the 40 MIPS instruction rate maximum.

Algorithm Structure and Synchronization

A version of the full matrix Gaussian elimination routine SGEFA from LINPACK was written to run with up to 200 processes spread over four PEMs. Since the routine

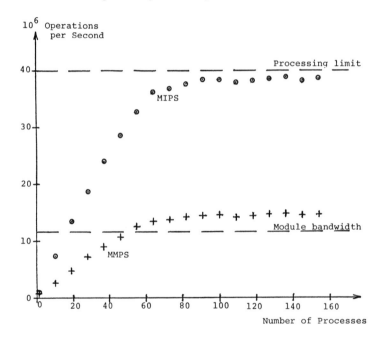

Figure 13: Effect of Removing the Bandwidth Limit

does partial pivoting, the processes must synchronize with each other at least once per pivot. In fact, the synchronization is somewhat more extensive and is summarized in Fig. 14. Three different synchronization mechanisms are used. Enclosing the entire elimination is a FORK-JOIN pair to spawn the processes on all PEMs at the outset and to wait for their completion at the end. For simplicity, input and output is done before the FORK and after the JOIN. Within the multiprocess section, processes wait on each other by means of a "barrier" synchronization. The pseudo-code form of the barrier is:

barrier (code section)

The semantics of this construct are that all processes enter the barrier, one unique process executes the code section after all have arrived and then all are allowed to exit. The barrier can be viewed as a (JOIN; code section; FORK) with the preservation of each process' local execution environment across the JOIN-FORK. The third mechanism used is the standard critical section.

Three barriers are encountered for every pivot, and the restriction of the computation to single stream which occurs for each is expected to lead to some performance degradation. The critical section will have little effect until the number of processes times the critical section length exceeds the length of the parallel code section containing it. The size of the submatrix below the pivot is decreasing, and it will become smaller than the number of processes available to do the reduction at some point. Since the processes reduce only full rows, some will then become idle. The loss of efficiency from this cause grows with the number of processes and decreases with increasing matrix size. Since the FORK-JOIN pair encloses the loop, the synchronization overhead caused by it is minimized.

Many of the synchronization overhead features predicted in the above paragraph can be measured using the above mentioned SPI unit of the HEP. This unit counts instructions executed on behalf of a task, dividing them into the categories of floating point, memory reference and others. As shown in Fig. 15, the unsynchronized row reduction kernel runs asymptotic to about 9.5 MFLOPS as the number of processes increases, while the performance of the full SGEFA program on an order 500 matrix peaks at 7.5 MFLOPS with 73 processes. This 21% reduction is almost completely

```
                    FORK
        pivot_loop:
                    Search part of column for local maximum.
                    Critical section (update global maximum).
                    Barrier (record pivot).
                    Swap part of pivot row into position.
                    Barrier (take reciprocal of pivot)
                    Reduce a part of the non-pivot rows.
                    Barrier (next pivot, reset maximum).
                    Repeat pivot_loop until last pivot.

                    JOIN
```

Figure 14: Synchronization Structure of the Gaussian Elimination

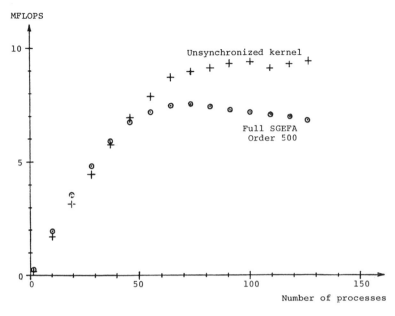

Figure 15: Performance of the Synchronized SGEFA Program

accounted for by the reduction in the total instruction execution rate, which is 32 instead of 40 MIPS. Thus the amount of extra code executed for synchronization is small compared to the waits which occur. The plot of the MFLOP rate versus matrix order in Fig. 16 shows that, while the rate is still rising at order 500, the curve is beginning to flatten. A numerical estimate of the efficiency loss resulting from idle processes while small submatrices are reduced gives less than 1% at order 500.

In the course of developing an optimized Gaussian elimination program, a number of incremental changes were made which gave some detailed insights into the improvements possible over standard HEP Fortran code. Some changes also permitted calculation of the synchronization overheads in the final code. By far the most significant improvement, an execution time decrease of 59%, resulted from optimizing the row reduction inner loop, up to but not including loop unrolling. This is merely a result of the fact that the Fortran compiler used did no optimization.

Of more interest were some of the changes in the barrier synchronization. The initial implementation counted processes entering the barrier and blocked them with a single full/empty cell until the last process had arrived. The compiled code for this implementation amounted to about 20 instructions per process. Since four PEMs can generate memory reference retrys at four times the rate that a single memory module can handle them, it was suspected that switch congestion made this implementation inefficient on the four PEM system. An alternate implementation of the barrier, which suspended processes as they arrived and used the last one to restart them, executed about 100 instructions per process but reduced execution time by 20%, verifying the

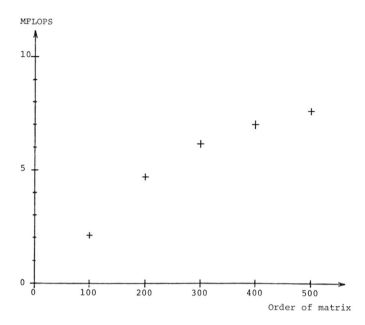

Figure 16: Speed Versus Size of Matrix for SGEFA

memory contention effect. A subsequent improvement in the process suspending barrier halved the number of instructions executed per process and improved execution time by 11.8%. This allowed the determination of the fraction of execution time occupied by barrier synchronization. In the final SGEFA program about 14% of the time is spent in barrier synchronization.

Finally, another difference in process management was measured. Two methods of dividing work among multiple processes are pre-scheduling, in which each process does a predetermined fraction of the work, and self-scheduling, in which processes cooperatively obtain a new unit of work to be done when the last is complete. The program was run with row reduction both pre- and self-scheduled. In the pre-scheduled version, each of P processes reduced every Pth row while in the self-scheduled version, each process empties a shared row index, adds one and refills it in a short critical section. If processes run the loop body in differing amounts of time, self-scheduling tends to even the work load. This actually happens in the SGEFA program because processes on different PEMs access given memory modules in different amounts of time, even though the amount of work per row reduction is constant. On the other hand, self-scheduling introduces a critical section which, although it is short, degrades performance for large numbers of processes. Measurements showed that the change from pre-scheduled to self-scheduled row reduction:
  - reduced execution time 12.5% for 10 processes;
  - did not change it for 48 processes and
  - increased it by 3% for 73 processes.

31

This indicates that balancing the work load in this case is only effective with small numbers of processes. Since the work load imbalance arises from differences in memory access, this is probably a result of the fact that round-trip memory access time only influences run time when the memory pipeline is not kept full. The increased execution time for large numbers of processes arises from conflict over the short critical section required for self-scheduling.

An overall measure of the fraction of a program which can be executed in parallel can be obtained empirically for programs which can be run with varying numbers of processes. The essential measurement is the speedup over single stream execution of the same code. When a single PEM version of the SGEFA program was run on an order 100 matrix, the maximum speedup was 6.9 with 14 processes. The four PEM version gave a maximum speedup of 25.4 with 64 processes on an order 500 matrix. The measurements keep the ratio of the matrix order to number of processes roughly constant and should lie at comparable positions on the increasing speed versus matrix size curves. The four PEM speedup is a factor of 3.68 larger than the single PEM speedup. If the program is assumed to consist of a strictly sequential portion plus a portion which can be executed in parallel by any number of processes with efficiency one, then these numbers can be used to estimate that 95% of the code is in the parallelizable portion.

In the SGEFA measurements, we found that about 14% of the time was spent in barrier synchronization. This is a sizeable fraction of the 20% difference between the speed of the unsynchronized kernel and that of the full SGEFA program. The rest is probably accounted for by pivot selection and row swapping, which does not match the floating point speed of the kernel. Other forms of synchronization less costly than the barrier might be used to reduce the overhead, but this leads to a fairly complicated Gaussian elimination algorithm. In the iterative solution of linear equations by the SOR method, however, the barrier is not the natural synchronization method. There, the producer/consumer synchronization on the new and old values of variables in an iteration is both natural and sufficient to produce a working algorithm. Measurements on a multiprocessor version of SOR give an idea of how little overhead synchronization can impose.

An algorithm was written to implement the point SOR method applied to a two dimensional field of unknowns in the natural rowwise order. The example considered first was the solution of Laplace's equation with Dirichlet boundary conditions on a square region. The updating of the point in row i and column j is represented by the equation:

$$f_{i,j}^{(n+1)} = \frac{\omega}{4}\left(f_{i,j+1}^{(n)} + f_{i,j-1}^{(n+1)} + f_{i+1,j}^{(n)} + f_{i-1,j}^{(n+1)}\right) + (1-\omega)f_{i,j}^{(n)}. \tag{5}$$

The multiprocessor version of the rowwise sequential update allows different processes to sweep different rows, updating the columns in natural order, as shown in Fig. 17. This guarantees that $f_{i,j-1}^{(n+1)}$ and $f_{i,j+1}^{(n)}$ will be used to produce $f_{i,j}^{(n+1)}$. If the process sweeping row i waits until $f_{i-1,j}^{(n+1)}$ has been produced before using it to produce $f_{i,j}^{(n+1)}$, then the dependencies between rows imposed by the natural ordering are satisfied. Thus, it is possible to build a parallel algorithm using multiple processes to sweep multiple rows simultaneously and still compute the same sequence of iterates $f_{i,j}^{(n)}$ which would be produced by a rowwise sequential sweep. The producer/consumer synchronization between rows $i-1$ and i is sufficient to manage the algorithm. A barrier synchronization between complete updates of the field points is not very costly in terms of

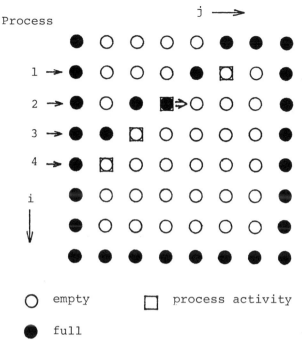

Figure 17: Organization of the Multiprocess SOR Sweep

performance, but it is also unnecessary. It is straightforward to start sweeping rows for iteration $n+1$ as soon as processes become available even though the sweep for iteration n is not entirely complete.

In the HEP Fortran realization of this algorithm, multiple copies of a single subroutine are created after the boundary conditions have been established. The asynchronous field variables along the $I=1$ boundary are set full and the rest of the field set empty. The values, as opposed to the states, of the interior variables are set to the initial solution guess. The subroutine contains code of the form shown in Fig. 18. Each process obtains a row number I and updates it in cooperation with the others by means of an asynchronous variable. Within the inner sequential loop over columns, the VALUE function is used to obtain the value at a field point without observing or altering its full/empty state. Only for the point (I-1,J) is the wait for full and set empty synchronization performed to prevent the process sweeping row I from overtaking the one sweeping row I-1. To determine convergence, a global error norm, $ERNM, is cooperatively updated by the processes. The result of executing this program to solve a 100 by 100 interior field on one PEM for a varying number of processes is the curve of Fig. 19. This curve matches the execution time model of Eq. 4 very well. The rising tail beyond 25 processes is a result of the critical section required to update the error norm. It disappears almost entirely when processes keep a local error norm and update the global one only on completion of a row.

33

```
          WO4 = W*0.25
          OMW = 1.0 - W
          ...
11        I = $II
          $II = I + 1
          IF (I .GT. IL-1)  GO TO 33
          ...
          DO 22  J = 2, JL-1
          TF = WO4*(VALUE($F(I,J+1)) + VALUE($F(I,J-1)) + VALUE($F(I+1,J))
     +          + $F(I-1,J) ) + OMW*VALUE($F(I,J))
          $ERNM = AMAX1( ABS(TF - VALUE($F(I,J)) ), $ERNM)
          $F(I,J) = TF
22        CONTINUE
          GO TO 11
33        CONTINUE
```

Figure 18: HEP Fortran Code for an SOR Process

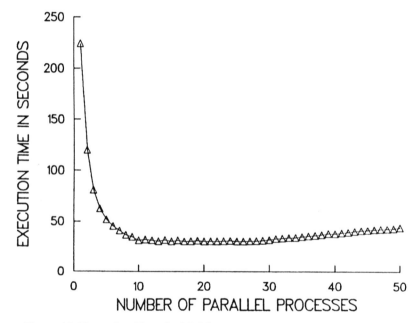

Figure 19: Execution Time for Multiprocessor SOR on a 100 by 100 Field

When the code was hand optimized, it was possible to determine that, out of 19 instructions in the inner loop, eight were floating point operations. Executing the optimized code on four PEMs yielded a speed of about 17 MFLOPS when measured with the SPI unit. Multiplying by the inverse of the inner loop floating point ratio gives the maximum 40 MIPS rate of which a four PEM system is capable. Thus, for this algorithm, the fully synchronized program attains a speed virtually identical to that which could be achieved by running the program kernel with no synchronization.

It is interesting to consider the limit of a very large number of processes performing the rowwise sweeps of Fig. 17, with multiple iterations being in progress simultaneously. The pattern of updates of field points over time resembles that of a multi-color point SOR method [43]. This subject has been pursued [44] and gives rise to a broad class of multi-color SOR methods which are guaranteed to have the same convergence properties as rowwise sequential updating. The multi-color methods are just as useful on vector computers as on multiprocessors.

Program Structure in a Shared-Memory MIMD Machine

Some general observations on the optimal program structure for execution in a shared-memory MIMD environment can be deduced from the detailed measurements reported above. With speedups on the order of 25 available, only 50% efficiency is obtainable when 4% of the code is sequential. The first principle for obtaining the fastest execution of an applications program is thus to have parallel processes running as much of the time as possible. The issue of multiprogramming might influence this but is not of concern here. This implies that multiple processes should be forked as near to the beginning and joined as near to the end of the program as possible. Barriers are essential to synchronization in the absence of JOINs but also introduce sequential code. The barrier is more efficient than the JOIN-FORK pair because process environments need not be allocated or released, and local variables retain their values across a barrier. Thus, the program structure advocated is a body of code executed by multiple processes, established at the outset and not terminated until the end. All sequential code appears inside barrier synchronizations in this model. With programs of this structure, the issue of efficient parallel execution reduces to the efficiency of synchronization mechanisms.

Within a parallel environment, the DOALL construct [18] is meaningful. To implement the DOALL, either pre-scheduling or self-scheduling of the work is possible. Self-scheduling is good when conditionals in the loop body yield different execution times for different instances of the loop body. Self-scheduling can be done without any knowledge of the number of processes being used but introduces a critical section into the loop to update the shared loop index. Using pre-scheduling to implement DOALL requires one (the compiler perhaps) to have some knowledge of the parallel environment. The number of processes must be known, and each process must have a unique identifying index between one and this number. Despite the logical simplicity of self-scheduling, even a three instruction critical section to copy, update and restore the loop index requires a loop body of 192 or more instructions for efficient execution with 64 processes, according to the execution time model of Eq. 4. A parallel execution environment, with number of processes and a unique index available to each process, seems desirable.

Some comments can also be made with regard to synchronization based on data and that based on control structures. The primary hardware level synchronization mechanism in the HEP is the full/empty memory cell, a data based mechanism. The advantage of data oriented synchronization is that it tends to be distributed over multiple items, with few processes contending for the same item simultaneously. For example, the four PEM program using SOR to solve Laplace's equation on a 100 by 100 grid ran at essentially the maximum possible 40 MIPS rate synchronizing on the individual matrix elements. However, the use of data synchronization to implement barrier by blocking processes on memory access was seen in the SGEFA measurements to be much worse than using the control oriented operations of process suspension and start up. This shows that, if many processes compete for a single data item with the HEP type of shared memory, serious memory contention and loss of switch throughput can occur. The environmental parameters needed to analyze this situation are not connected directly to the number of processes executing but have to do with hardware configuration and are better left in the domain of the operating system.

Conclusions

Parallel implementations of a broad range of scientific applications on the HEP pipelined MIMD computer have been presented. The fairly flat asymptotic behavior of execution time versus number of processes in all cases suggests that the pipelines in the machine are fully utilized for more than 15-20 processes per PEM, and, where the application is simple enough to determine instruction count, this suggestion is borne out. A key issue in the performance of a parallel applications program is the fraction of the total processing which can be spread across parallel hardware units. An empirical probe of the degree of parallelization indicates that from 86%, in the case of the sparse matrix package, to 98%, in the case of banded LU decomposition, of the code can be executed in parallel. A simple execution time model, incorporating a hardware limit on parallelism and a critical section approximation to synchronization overhead, seems to fit the HEP pipelined MIMD performance quite well.

Simple, automatable techniques for parallelizing existing Fortran programs for MIMD machines are possible and succeed in much the same cases as those in which automatic vectorization is successful. Distinctly better results can be obtained, however, by a global analysis of the algorithm, perhaps involving a change in the basic data structures used or in the method used to synchronize parallel processes.

The pipelined MIMD architecture is, as expected, not as effective on problems dominated by long vector operations as is a pipelined SIMD approach, but, assuming a common underlying technology, there is probably no more than a factor of two difference in Fortran produced code. A high degree of parallelization is found in the MIMD versions of dense linear systems programs, so that the efficiency of the SIMD architecture probably arises from hardware support for sequencing through the elements of vectors and from the highly predictable resource utilization pattern in the parallel operations. MIMD parallelism is also applicable to codes which do not vectorize well. Sparse linear systems solution is an important example of a computationally expensive application class in this category. In cases where the sequential formulation involves backtracking, a parallel implementation which reduces it may reduce the total computation performed as well as the execution time, as was the case with adaptive quadrature.

Memory module bandwidth limits and associated congestion in the processor to memory switch can be observed when data is confined to a single memory module. Interleaving modules on address would be a solution to this problem. In fact, in the four PEM system, dividing the data between just two memory modules gave more than enough bandwidth to eliminate the observed speed limitations in all cases measured. One source of contention for a single memory can arise from the use of a shared full/empty variable to implement flow of control oriented synchronization. Alternative implementations which reduce the memory contention have always been found to be possible.

Finally, the performance investigations on the HEP have led to some insight into the qualitative structure of algorithms which are efficient in the shared memory, MIMD computational model. General characteristics seem to be to FORK processes early in the program and JOIN them near the end, using explicit synchronizations to handle precedence constraints. Distributing synchronizations so that each process interacts with a limited number of others is also valuable where possible.

REFERENCES

[1] Flynn, M. J., "Some Computer Organizations and Their Effectiveness," *IEEE Trans. on Computers,* pp. 948-960 (1972).

[2] Dennis, J. B., "The Varieties of Data Flow Computers," *Proc. of the First Intn'l Conf. on Distributed Computing Systems,* pp. 430-439 (1979).

[3] Bouknight, W. J., Denenberg, S. A., McIntyre, D. E., and Slotnick, D. L., "The Illiac IV System," *Proc. IEEE,* pp. 369-379 (1972).

[4] Russell, R. M., "The Cray I Computer System," *Comm. of the ACM,* vol. 21, no. 1, pp. 63-72 (1978).

[5] Flanders, P. M., Hunt, D. J., Parkinson, D. and Reddaway, S. F., "Efficient High Speed Computing with the Distributed Array Processor," *Symp. on High Speed Computer and Algorithm Organization,* University of Illinois, Academic Press (1977).

[6] Batcher, K. E., "STARAN Parallel Processor System Hardware," *Proc. of the Natl. Computer Conf.,* pp. 405-410 (1974).

[7] Batcher, K. E., "Design of a Massively Parallel Processor," *IEEE Trans. on Computers,* pp. 1-9 (Sept. 1980).

[8] Shoor, R., "CDC 205 Runs 800 Million Operations/Sec," *Computerworld,* pp. 1-2 (June 9, 1980).

[9] Satyanarayanan, M., *MULTIPROCESSORS: A Comparative Study,* Prentice-Hall, Englewood Cliffs, N. J. (1980).

[10] Wulf, W. R., Levin, R. and Harbison, H., *Hydra/C.mmp: An Experimental Computer System,* McGraw-Hill, New York (1980).

[11] Katsuki, D., Elsam, E. S., Mann, W. F., Roberts, E. S., Robinson, J. G., Skowronski, F. S. and Wolf E. W., "Pluribus: An Operational Fault-Tolerant Multiprocessor," *Proc. IEEE,* vol. 6, no. 10, pp. 1,146-1,159 (1978).

[12] Gilliland, M. C., Smith B. J. and Calvert, W., "HEP - A Semaphore-Synchronized Multiprocessor with Central Control," *Proc. of the 1976 Summer Computer Simulation Conf.,* Washington, D. C., pp. 57-62 (July 1976).

[13] Smith, B. J., "A Pipelined, Shared Resource MIMD Computer," *Proc. of the 1978 Intn'l Conf. on Parallel Processing,* Bellaire, MI, pp. 6-8 (August 1978).

[14] Jordan, H. F., "Performance Measurements on HEP - A Pipelined MIMD Computer," *Proc. of the 10th Annual Intn'l Symp. on Computer Architecture,* Stockholm, Sweden (June 1983).

[15] Jordan, H. F., "Experience with Pipelined Multiple Instruction Streams," *Proc. IEEE,* Vol. 72, No. 1, pp. 113-123, January 1984.

[16] Kuck, D., Kuhn, R., Leasure, B. and Wolfe, M., "The Structure of an Advanced Vectorizer for Pipelined Processors," *Proc. of COMPSAC 80, the 4th Intn'l Computer Software and Applications Conf.*, Chicago, IL, pp. 709-715 (October 1980).

[17] Allen, J. R., and Kennedy, K., "PFC: A Program to Convert Fortran to Parallel Form," *Proc. of the IBM Intn'l Symp. on Parallel Processing*, Rome (March 1982).

[18] Padua, D. A., Kuck, D. J. and Lawrie, D. H., "High-Speed Multiprocessors and Compilation Techniques," *IEEE Trans. on Computers*, vol. C-29, no. 9 (Sept. 1980).

[19] Heller, D., "A Survey of Parallel Algorithms in Numerical Linear Algebra," *SIAM Review*, vol. 20, pp. 740-777 (1977).

[20] Andrews, G. R. and Schneider, F. B., "Concepts and Notations for Concurrent Programming," *Computing Surveys*, Vol. 15, No. 1, pp. 3-43 (March 1983).

[21] Dennis, J. B. and Van Horn, E. C., "Programming Semantics for Multiprogrammed Computations," *Commun. ACM*, Vol. 9, No. 3, pp. 143-155 (March 1966).

[22] Conway, M. E., "A Multiprocessor System Design," *Proc. AFIPS Fall Jt. Computer Conf.*, Vol. 24, Spartan Books, Baltimore, MD, pp. 139-146 (Nov. 1963).

[23] Jordan, H. F. and Sawyer, P., "A Multi-microprocessor System for Finite Element Structural Analysis," *Trends in Computerized Structural Analysis and Synthesis*, A. Noor and H. McComb, Jr., Eds., Pergamon Press, pp. 21-29 (1978).

[24] Jordan, H. F., "Parallelizing a Sparse Matrix Package," *Report CSDG 81-1*, Computer Systems Design Group, Elec. Eng. Department, Univ. of Colorado, Boulder (December 1981).

[25] Duff, I. S., "MA28 - A Set of FORTRAN Subroutines for Sparse Unsymmetric Linear Equations," *AERE Report R.8730*, H. M. Stationery Office, London (1977).

[26] Ladner, R. E. and Fisher, M. J., "Parallel Prefix Computation," *Journal of the ACM*, vol. 27, no. 4, pp 831-838 (Oct. 1980).

[27] Gajski, D. D., "An Algorithm for Solving Linear Recurrence Systems on Parallel and Pipelined Machines," *IEEE Trans. on Computers*, pp 190-206 (March 1981).

[28] Lord, R. E., Kowalik, J. S. and Kumar, S. P., "Solving Linear Algebraic Equations on a MIMD Computer," *Proc. of the 1980 Intn'l Conf. on Parallel Processing*, IEEE Computer Society Press, pp 205-210 (1980).

[29] Kowalik, J. S. and Kumar, S. P., "An Efficient Parallel Block Conjugate Gradient Method for Linear Equations," *Proc. of the 1982 Intn'l Conf. on Parallel Processing*, IEEE Computer Society Press, pp 47-52 (1982).

[30] Dongarra, J. J., Bunch, J. R., Moler, C. B. and Stewart, G. W., *LINPACK Users Guide*, SIAM Publications, Phil., PA (1979).

[31] Dongarra, J. J., "Some LINPACK Timings on the CRAY-1," *Proc. of the 1978 LASL Workshop on Vector and Parallel Processors*, pp 58-75 (1978).

[32] Dongarra, J. J., "Performance of Various Computers Using Standard Linear Equations Software in a Fortran Environment," *ANL Tech. Memo.* (1983).

[33] Thurnau, D. H., Scientific Software Corp., private communications, (1982).

[34] Kuck, D. J., "A Survey of Parallel Machine Organization and Programming," *ACM Computing Surveys,* vol. 9, no.1, pp 29-59 (March 1977).

[35] Deo, N., Pang, C. Y. and Lord, R. E., "Two Parallel Algorithms for Shortest Path Problems," *Proc. of the 1980 Intn'l Conf. on Parallel Processing,* pp 244-253 (1980).

[36] Deo, N. and Yoo, Y. B., "Parallel Algorithms for the Minimum Spanning Tree Problem," *Proc. of the 1981 Intn'l Conf. on Parallel Processing,* pp 188-189 (1981).

[37] Duff, I. S. and Reid, J. K., "Some Design Features of a Sparse Matrix Code," *ACM Trans. on Math. Software,* vol. 5, no. 1, pp 18-35 (March 1975).

[38] Duff, I. S., "Practical Comparison of Codes for the Solution of Sparse Linear Systems," *Sparse Matrix Proc., 1978,* Duff, I. S. and Stewart, G. W., Eds., SIAM, pp 107-134 (1979).

[39] Markowitz, H. M., "The Elimination Form of the Inverse and its Application to Linear Programming," *Management Science,* vol. 3, pp 255-269 (1957).

[40] Grit, D. H. and McGraw, J. R., "Programming Divide and Conquer on a Multiprocessor," *Report UCRL-88710,* Lawerence Livermore National Laboratories (May 1983).

[41] Rice, J. R., "Parallel Algorithms for Adaptive Quadrature III - Convergence," *ACM Trans. on Math. Software,* vol. 2, no. 1, pp 1-30 (March 1976).

[42] Patel, N. R. and Jordan, H. F., "A Parallelized Point Rowwise Successive Over-Relaxation Method on a Multiprocessor," accepted for publication in *Parallel Computing* (1983).

[43] Adams, L. M. and Ortega, J. M., "A Multi-color SOR Method for Parallel Computation," *Proc. 1982 Intl. Conf. on Parallel Processing,* Bellaire, MI, pp. 53-58 (August 1982).

[44] Adams, L. M. and Jordan, H. F., "Is SOR Color-blind?" *Rept. No. 84-14,* ICASE, NASA Langley Res. Ctr., Hampton, VA (May 1984).

1.2   THE ARCHITECTURE OF HEP

BURTON SMITH
Denelcor, Inc.
Aurora, Colorado

1.   INTRODUCTION

The HEP computer system is a parallel shared memory supercomputer. Unlike other supercomputers, however, it has no vector instructions. Instead, it achieves its speed through the application of many scalar instruction streams to a single problem. The synchronization primitives implemented by the HEP hardware make it possible to achieve extremely tight coupling among the instruction streams; the resulting flexibility makes the HEP architecture effective for a very broad class of computations. In addition, the unique design of the HEP processors overcomes the significant memory access delays that accompany large configurations. The HEP was designed to be a general purpose computer system, able to achieve high performance on essentially any computational problem. This section describes its important architectural attributes.

2. BACKGROUND

The spectrum of general purpose computing is representing an increasingly narrow speed range, which now extends roughly from 1 million to 20 million instructions per second. As integrated circuits continue to improve in density, speed, and cost, it is becoming harder to differentiate among microcomputers, minicomputers, and mainframes. Meanwhile, the fastest of the general purpose machines are becoming limited by the infamous "Von Neumann Bottleneck".

There is general agreement that major architectural innovations for higher speed must be in the direction of increased parallelism. It seems that every computer manufacturer, and every university with an interest in hardware, has a project underway in parallel architecture. It is not agreed by any means, however, that these more highly parallel computer systems will be as "general purpose" as their predecessors have been. The major source of disagreement seems to stem from uncertainty about the amount of parallelism that is ultimately available in the problems we solve with computers.

The appropriate measure for the amount of parallelism in a computer program is just the time average of the number of operations or instructons that are executed simultaneously. It is certainly not the average rate at which those operations or instructions are executed, because the shorter execution times of the more parallel parts of the program bias the average. This popular misconception is exploited in brainteasers: "If I travel half the distance to work at 20 km. per hour and the remainder at 100 km. per hour, what is my average speed for the trip?" The answer is of course not 60 km. per hour but 33.3, which explains why most of us dislike stop-and-go traffic so much; our brains are taking time averages rather than speed averages and are not deceived. This observation has come to be called "Amdahl's Law" [1], and underlies most of the informed skepticism about parallel architectures.

Whatever the future reveals about the general applicability of parallel processing, it has become clear that vector instructions alone are insufficiently flexible to avoid the dreary consequences of Amdahl's Law. Significant speed improvements through parallelism will only be possible if we can apply that parallelism to all of our computations. This implies that operating systems, input/output facilities, compilers, linkers, all must be parallel. The consequences for the computer industry are mind-boggling; new approaches are required not just in architecture but also in languages, compiler technology, operating systems, numerical analysis, software engineering, and artificial intelligence. A revolution is beginning in the way we compute, and it will make progress only to the extent that general purpose parallelism is available in existing computer architectures.

The next evolutionary step in parallel architecture is the MIMD computer. The acronym "MIMD" stands for "Multiple Instruction stream, Multiple Data stream" in a taxonomy developed by Flynn [2]. Machines of this type are able to execute multiple instructions simultaneously to carry out a single computation. The general idea is that a number of processors cooperate with each other in dividing up the work; typically, they communicate by sharing memory, by exchanging messages, or a combination of these two methods.

It is likely that other architectural ideas will eventually replace the MIMD approach; most notable among these are several "dataflow" proposals [3,4,5]. A dataflow computer executes instructions based on what data are available or needed rather than on program counters. To use an anthropomorphic metaphor, dataflow is a responsive, communications-intensive way to organize a team of workers, whereas in MIMD computers the workers are driven by rigid schedules and may spend lots of time waiting for each other if the schedules are unrealistic. The truth is that MIMD computers can be programmed to be quite flexible and responsive in allocating their time to computations, but dataflow provides still more flexibility and responsiveness, and therefore more potential parallelism.

3. KEY PROBLEMS IN MIMD ARCHITECTURE

As Arvind and Iannucci have pointed out [3], there are several difficult problems that confront the architect of an MIMD computer. The first of these is the problem of memory latency. If the computer contains a significant number of processors and each is fast enough so that its cycle time is limited by the speed of light, then the physical size of the whole computer will make most of the memory a significant distance away from any one processor. That is, several instruction times will be needed to access most of the memory if it is to be shared. Competition by several processors for the same memory at the same time only makes the problem worse. Many architects have given up trying to solve this problem and use only messages, prohibiting shared memory entirely and surrendering flexibility and responsiveness; others allow shared memory but make local copies of the data in caches. This solution exchanges the latency problem for another one, namely how to maintain consistency when one or more of the copies is written. A third approach, used in the HEP and in dataflow architectures, will be described below.

A second problem facing the MIMD architect is how to synchronize efficiently. Parallel processes must be able to wait for each other without having to execute lots of extra instructions or waste time in other ways, and without significantly affecting the other processes that are running in parallel and not waiting. The use of traditional methods like interrupts limits the synchronization rate to once every few hundred instructions; primitives like test-and-set which wait busily and thereby can avoid exchanging processes in the processor are better, but these approaches usually waste instructions to accomplish waiting. The best ideas are those which somehow keep the waiting processes fully ready to continue execution once the wait is over, and use the processor for something else in the meanwhile. The HEP and the dataflow architectures can synchronize as often as once per instruction using this technique.

A third problem in MIMD architecture is how to avoid bottlenecks or other shortcomings which inhibit the amount of parallelism that can be attained, thereby limiting the number of processors that is practical. It is likely that as time passes we will learn how to use more parallelism and become increasingly able to exploit more ambitious MIMD systems. Changing an architecture, especially the instruction set, to correct bottlenecks in parallelism is especially unpleasant because it destroys software compatibility. It is very important that an MIMD architecture be not just today's fast computer, but also a stable foundation for the development of tomorrow's better and more highly concurrent software.

Accompanying the problems facing the MIMD architect are two significant opportunities. An MIMD computer can be modular in its computing power; more processors can be employed by those users that can take advantage of them. This feature is particularly attractive if additional processors can be installed in the field. Also, a system will be more available for useful work if one can logically replace failed processors or other components. Thus the reduced system reliability that accompanies large numbers of processors can be compensated for, at least in part.

4. PIPELINED INSTRUCTION INTERPRETATION

There is a widespread misconception about the meaning of the adjective "pipelined" when applied to a computer architecture. It certainly does not mean vector instructions are present; in fact, it implies nothing whatsoever about instructions. Pipelining is just a technique to increase the utilization of a section of hardware by turning it into an "assembly line" and giving it new tasks to do before the tasks it is currently working on are finished. It is possible whenever hardware can be designed to process data in sequential stages, and is profitable whenever there are a few independent and sufficiently similar tasks to be done. Pipelining can therefore be exploited in an architecture when parallelism is present in some part of instruction execution.

If multiple processes are executed by a single processor, almost all of the hardware can be pipelined. This is in fact the way a HEP processor is organized. Each of the program counters fetches an instruction from memory and travels with it through the stages of the pipeline until execution of the instruction is complete and the program counter has been incremented. This technique improves the utilization of the hardware because of the noninterference of the processes. Each instruction is executed independently of the others in the pipeline, so the pipeline can be kept full with relative ease and the instruction rate is limited only by logic speeds.

A variable number of processes can be provided for by using a hardware queue to extend the pipeline so that it can hold more program counters. The approach actually used in HEP is to store the program counters in a memory and enqueue the addresses rather than the program counters themselves. Instructions are available to user programs for creating and destroying processes. These facilities make several additional things possible. First, the number of instruction streams can be varied to suit the changing parallelism in a program, and this can be done without changing the number of processors, without interrupts, and without busy waiting. Second, a processor can take over the work that was previously executing in another processor, so that failures are not necessarily catastrophic even for partially completed computations. This sort of adaptability is analogous to that obtained in vector pipeline architectures, which have little or no trouble dealing with different vector lengths.

By far the most important benefit that results from having a queue of processes is that memory latency in a shared memory system can be hidden through the use of parallelism. It is only necessary that the pipeline include the shared data memories and the network that interconnects them with the processors. As long as the queue can keep the instruction pipeline busy, memory references do not cause the processor to wait any more than the other instructions do. In this situation, the queue shrinks and grows as the memory references become more or less frequent in the course of the program. Unlike the vector pipeline case, there is no fixed over-head which reduces parallelism here. The result is that the speed of a HEP processor depends on parallelism but not on the physical size of the system; that is, speed is directly proportional to the amount of hardware if the program is sufficiently parallel.

5. PROCESS SYNCHRONIZATION

There is a "folk theorem" in parallel processing to the
effect that most synchronization methods are equally
powerful. More precisely, if efficiency and fairness
considerations are set aside, any of a large class of
synchronization methods can be used to simulate the others. For example, a programmer using a (primitive) MIMD
computer could use test-and-set loops to implement critical sections, which could then be used to implement
semaphores. Semaphores might then implement messages
between processes, which might form a basis for still
higher level synchronization methods. Any of these
could be used to reimplement the original test-and-set
loops.

Since most synchronization methods are sufficiently
powerful, any selection should also be based on usefulness and performance. The best approach is to choose a
method that will accomodate algorithms requiring very
intensive synchronization and communication. A one-word
message facility is especially attractive for this purpose because it directly communicates a value from one
process to another. Using this method, processes can
cooperate even in the evaluation of a single scalar
arithmetic expression, which is as intimate as we can

expect processes to be. The other synchronization methods presumably do not need to be so efficient because they will be used less frequently; they can therefore be implemented using the one-word messages.

The HEP implements one-word messages by adding a single bit, the full/empty bit, to every location in the register set and every location in the shared data memory. Control bits present in every instruction can be used to make read operations wait for the full state and then set empty; writes can be made to wait for empty and then set full. In other words, any writable storage location can be used to transmit a one-word message. If a location is not in the requested state the instruction is not executed; the program counter is left unmodified and the instruction is reattempted when its process makes its next trip through the pipeline.

To avoid wasting instruction cycles for data memory references, the HEP has a second queue located between the instruction pipeline in the processor and the pipelined interconnection network that leads to the data memories. When unsuccessful attempts to access the memory return to the processor, they are reinserted in this second queue so that they can be retried later without reexecuting the instruction. As long as the instruction pipeline stays full, the processes waiting for memory access have not slowed down the processor; in fact, keeping these waiting processes in the memory pipeline actually speeds up the rest of the processes to compensate. Thus, the way HEP conceals memory latency has a synergistic effect on the cost of this kind of synchronization.

The HEP has no interrupts, but it has something better, namely parallel processes. External asynchronous devices can send or receive messages and synchronize with HEP processes (or each other) simply by filling or emptying memory locations. Either direct memory access or memory-mapped input/output can be used. Latency is very low because a waiting process immediately resumes execution in the processor once the wait is over. Low repetition rate external events are handled without busy waiting by a minicomputer attached to the interconnection network. The minicomputer looks like a memory to the processors, except that incoming memory references are removed from the pipelined switch and reinserted when the awaited event occurs. The elegance of this consistent approach to process synchronization is due largely to synergy between the queue driven pipelines and the simple implementation of one-word messages.

6. MODULARITY

Most of the modularity in the HEP system results from the design of its pipelined interconnection network. Pipelining insures that the network's physical size does not limit its bandwidth, but also makes possible a very high degree of configuration flexibility so that various numbers of processors, memories, and other components can be added, even to an already installed system. The network is made up of nodes, each of which has a set of tables that are used to steer the memory references through the network. The time required to access these tables appears only as additional memory latency; even so, signals travel through the network, logic and all, at one fifth the speed of light. Since the tables are writeable, faulty links between nodes or even the nodes themselves can be programmed out of the system. As long as the system components remain connected by the network, the system is usable in spite of the failures. This high degree of reconfigurability, together with the variable number of instruction streams made possible by pipelining, allows the removal of failed processors from the system and the transferral of their instruction

streams to a working processor in the midst of program
execution.

7. CONCLUSIONS

The HEP computer system contains several ideas which
combine in a synergistic way to provide solutions to
important problems in MIMD architecture. Future MIMD
and dataflow systems will elaborate further on these
ideas, and in so doing will eventually bring about the
widespread use of parallel processing in the mainstream
of general purpose computing.

8. REFERENCES

1. Gene Amdahl, "The Validity of the Single Processor Approach to Achieving Large-Scale Computing Capabilities", AFIPS Conference Proceedings
30 (1967), pp. 483-485.

2. M.J. Flynn, "Some Computer Organizations and
Their Effectiveness", IEEE Transactions on Computers C21 (Sept. 1977), pp. 948-960.

3. Arvind and R.A. Iannucci, "A Critique of Multiprocessing von Neumann Style", Proceedings of
the 10th Symposium on Computer Architecture
(1983), pp. 426-436.

4. J.B. Dennis, "Data Flow Supercomputers", IEEE
Computer 13 (Dec. 1980), pp. 48-56.

5. D.D. Gajski, D.A. Padua, D.J. Kuck, and R.H.
Kuhn, "A Second Opinion on Data Flow Machines
and Languages", IEEE Computer 15 (Feb. 1982),
pp. 58-69.

PART 2

PERFORMANCE

2.1 PERFORMANCE CHARACTERIZATION OF THE HEP

R.W. HOCKNEY
Reading University, U.K.

2.1.1 INTRODUCTION

The problem of characterizing the timing behaviour of a computer as complex as the Denelcor HEP is very difficult, and there is no entirely satisfactory method. On the one hand, if every facet of the architecture is taken into account, the number of parameters used in the description (perhaps 100 or so) is so large that the timing formulae become unmanageable. In the limit of this approach, one is engaged in a cycle-by-cycle simulation of the timing behaviour which necessarily must be performed on a computer. Of course, the best simulator of the HEP is the HEP itself, and in the final analysis, if one wishes to know how long a job will take on the HEP, one must actually run the job on the HEP. On the other hand, an analyst designing algorithms for a machine needs a much simpler characterization that captures the essense of the timing with the least possible number of parameters, and provides algebraic timing formulae that can be easily manipulated and minimized. There is an obvious correlation between the number of parameters and the accuracy of the description, so that any description which minimizes the number of parameters so as to obtain a simpler description, inevitably compromises the accuracy. However simplified descriptions can still be useful in suggesting which algorithms are likely to be the most successful on a particular machine, and in comparing the timing behaviour of widely different computer architectures. Having selected some competing algorithms on this simplified basis, they should then be programmed on the HEP (if one is available) to determine the best.

In the approach that is developed below, we define a general model that describes many algorithms. The execution time of an algorithm is described in terms of two timing parameters characterizing the programming environment (both hardware and software), and three operations counts characterizing the algorithm. Although this is a coarse description, it is probably the least complex description that can give meaningful results. Measurements are then described using a simple benchmark, that give the values of the timing parameters and how they vary with the number of instruction streams in a HEP program.

2.1.2 Two-Parameter Characterization

The timing of algorithms on computers with a single instruction stream (SIMD computers) has already been characterized by two parameters (Hockney and Jesshope 1981; Hockney 1982, 1983, 1984b). An SIMD algorithm is modelled as a sequence of vector operations each obeying the timing relation

$$t = r_\infty^{-1}(n + n_{\frac{1}{2}}) \tag{1}$$

where

t is the execution time for a single vector operation
of length n

r_∞ is the <u>asymptotic performance</u> for infinitely long
vectors, usually measured in millions of floating-
point operations between pairs of numbers per second
(Mflop/s)

$n_{\frac{1}{2}}$ is the <u>half-performance length,</u> that is to say the
vector length required to achieve half the asymptotic
performance.

Summing a sequence of such operations, one obtains the time, T, for an SIMD algorithm

$$T = r_\infty^{-1}(s + n_{\frac{1}{2}}q) \qquad (2)$$

where

  s is the number of floating-point operations between
     pairs of numbers in the algorithm

  q is the number of sequential vector operations
     comprising the algorithm

In deriving equation (2) we have assumed that the parameters r_∞ and $n_{\frac{1}{2}}$, which describe the computer timing behaviour, are constants for the computer and independent, for example, of the type of arithmetic operation being performed. This is rarely exactly true, but frequently approximately so. Fortunately, it is a good representation of the HEP, because all operations, except division, take eight clock periods. Again we see the conflict between accuracy which would demand separate values of r_∞ and $n_{\frac{1}{2}}$ for each type of arithmetic operation, and manageability which demands the same values of r_∞ and $n_{\frac{1}{2}}$ for all operations. In what follows we assume that an appropriate average value of the parameter pair $(r_\infty, n_{\frac{1}{2}})$ can be used. This is the nature of this two-parameter model of computation.

In equation (2) the algorithm is described by the two operations' counts (s, q) and the computer by the parameter pair $(r_\infty, n_{\frac{1}{2}})$. The operations' counts (sometimes called the computational complexity) will usually be non-linear functions of the problem size (e.g. matrix dimension or mesh size), and the counts will differ between different algorithms for solving the same mathematical problem.

In comparing two alternative algorithms (denoted by superscript (1) and (2)) on the same computer, one may ask for the conditions when the two algorithms have the same time of execution. Equating equation (2) for the two algorithms one obtains the condition

$$n_{\frac{1}{2}} = \frac{s^{(1)} - s^{(2)}}{q^{(2)} - q^{(1)}} \tag{3}$$

The RHS of equation (3) depends only on the operations' counts of the algorithms, and is usually a non-linear function of the problem size. Equation (3) shows that the best choice between the two algorithms depends on the relative size of the non-linear RHS and the $n_{\frac{1}{2}}$ of the computer. We note particularly that the best choice of algorithms does not depend on the value of r_{∞} (which affects both algorithms by the same factor) nor does it depend on the startup time in seconds for a vector operation which is given by the ratio $n_{\frac{1}{2}}/r_{\infty}$. In this model of computation, the choice of algorithm depends only on the parameter $n_{\frac{1}{2}}$ and the operations' counts of the algorithms through equation (3). This dependence can be nicely represented by an "Algorithmic Phase Diagram" that divides the parameter plane of (problem size vs $n_{\frac{1}{2}}$) into regions where each algorithm has the least execution time. The formula for the "Equal Performance Line" between the regions is equation (3). Such algorithmic phase diagrams have been given for the solution of tridiagonal systems of linear equations (Hockney 1981, 1982) and for the solution of Poisson's equation (Hockney 1983).

The extension of the above methodology to MIMD computing with multiple instruction streams, requires a different model of computation. However we will still limit the characterization of

the computer (including its software environment) to two parameters.
In any MIMD program there will be a critical path, the time of
execution of which is the time of execution of the whole program.
In some cases the critical path is obvious (there may only be one path),
and in other cases it may be very difficult to determine or even be
data-dependent and therefore unknown until run-time. However to
proceed further with a timing analysis, we must assume that the
critical path is known.

Along the critical path, the program is modelled as a sequence
of parallel work segments, in each of which the work is divided
between several logically independent (i.e. not communicating)
instruction streams. These instruction streams may be implemented
as separate processes in a single PEM of the HEP, or be executed in
separate processors in a multi-microprocessor architecture or a
multi-PEM HEP. From the point of view of the computational model,
all these cases are treated with the same analysis, simply as
separate instruction streams. The essence of the parallel work
segment is that the computation is synchronized before and after
each segment. That is to say, all the work in a segment must be
completed before the next segment can begin. The time to execute
a segment is therefore the sum of the time to execute the longest
of the instruction streams plus the time to synchronize the multiple
instruction streams.

It is often said with truth that the penalty for MIMD computation
is the cost of synchronization, and we will use the second of the
MIMD timing parameters, $s_{\frac{1}{2}}$, to measure this overhead. This is
analogous to the use of the parameter $n_{\frac{1}{2}}$ in the SIMD
computational model, because the penalty for SIMD computation is

the vector startup time, and $n_{\frac{1}{2}}$ measures the magnitude of this overhead
in terms of how many floating point operations could have been
performed in this time. With this philosophy in mind, we define the
time, t, for the ith parallel work segment to be

$$t = r_\infty^{-1}(s_i/E_i + s_{\frac{1}{2}}) \tag{4}$$

where

    s_i is the number of floating-point operations between

        pairs of numbers (henceforth called the amount of

        work) in the ith work segment

    E_i is the efficiency of process utilization in the ith

        work segment

    r_∞ is the asymptotic (or maximum possible) performance

        in Mflop/s as before

    $s_{\frac{1}{2}}$ is the synchronization overhead measured in equivalent

        floating-point operations

In equation (4) the value of both r_∞ and $s_{\frac{1}{2}}$ will depend on the number
of instruction streams or processor used. For example, if there
are p processors the r_∞ in equation (4) is p times the asymptotic
performance of one processor. The value of $s_{\frac{1}{2}}$ also depends on the
type of synchronization and the efficiency of the software tools
provided for synchronization. We obtain values below for both
FORK/JOIN and BARRIER synchronization in HEP FORTRAN.

    The efficiency E_i in equation (4) takes into account the fact
that some processors may finish before others and therefore be
forced to remain idle by the synchronization mechanism until all
other processors have finished. If all the processors take the same

length of time then $E_i = 1$, and we have the same functional form as equation (1) for SIMD computation. This is perfect scheduling of the work between the parallel instruction streams of a segment. In all but the simplest problems, however, some processor will become idle and the scheduling will be less than perfect. In this case $E_i < 1$. The efficiency is, in fact, the same as that defined by Kuck (1978).

The time, T, for an MIMD algorithm is calculated by summing equation (4) for each parallel work segment along the critical path, giving

$$T = r_\infty^{-1}(s/\bar{E} + s_{\frac{1}{2}}q) \tag{5}$$

where

q is the number of parallel work segments along the critical path of the algorithm

$s = \sum_{i=1}^{q} s_i$ is the total amount of work along the critical path

$\bar{E} = s/(\sum_{i=1}^{q} s_i/E_i)$ the average efficiency of process utilization along the critical path of the algorithm

For algorithms that fit into the above computational model, we see that the programming environment (computer hardware, system software and compiler facilities) is described by the parameter pair $(r_\infty, s_{\frac{1}{2}})$, and the algorithm itself is described by the triplet $(s, q, \bar{E})$. As in the case of SIMD computing the value of r_∞ cancels when comparing the performance of two MIMD algorithms on the same computer. That leaves the value of $s_{\frac{1}{2}}$ as the computer parameter that determines the choice of the best MIMD algorithm.

Low values of $s_{\frac{1}{2}}$ mean low synchronization overhead, so that $s_{\frac{1}{2}}$ is a good quantitative figure of merit to use in comparing the relative importance of this overhead in two different computer systems. By measuring the synchronization overhead in terms of the amount of work that could have been done in the time taken for synchronization (rather than measuring it in seconds), the value of $s_{\frac{1}{2}}$ determines the importance of the overhead in a floating-point calculation. In particular, if the amount of work in a work segment $s_i = s_{\frac{1}{2}}$ (and $E_i = 1$), equation (4) shows that half the time is used for useful calculation and half on synchronization overhead, resulting in an average calculation rate of half the maximum (i.e. a rate of $\frac{1}{2}r_\infty$). The parameter $s_{\frac{1}{2}}$ is therefore the yardstick that should be used to judge whether it is worth splitting-up a job between several instruction streams. If we wish an average performance greater than half the maximum, then the amount of work within a work segment must exceed $s_{\frac{1}{2}}$ floating-point operations. In general, if we consider a simple case of one work segment with perfect scheduling ($E_i = 1$) and an amount of work s, then the average performance is

$$r = s/t = r_\infty/(1 + s_{\frac{1}{2}}/s) \qquad (6)$$

Because the cost of communication between instruction streams is often high in MIMD systems, values of $s_{\frac{1}{2}}$ tend to be quite large, often several hundred or thousand floating-point operations. It is important, therefore, to divide an MIMD algorithm into large independent blocks of code which are given to different instruction streams, thereby achieving very large values of s. This is called parallelization at the outermost level of a program, and often means the parallel execution of different cases of the outermost DO-loop. If one achieves $s \gg s_{\frac{1}{2}}$, equation (6) shows that the average performance r approaches the maximum of r_∞. This philosophy of programming is in sharp contrast to SIMD programming, in which it is the innermost DO-loops of a program that are parallelized by being replaced with vector instructions.

2.1.3 The (r_∞, $s_{\frac{1}{2}}$) Benchmark

The objective is to design a simple benchmark test which will measure the two parameters (r_∞, $s_{\frac{1}{2}}$) of an MIMD computer. We wish to choose a problem without data dependencies, so that it can be computed with unit efficiency ($\bar{E} = 1$). The simplest case is the element-by-element multiplication of two vectors of length s, in which the work is divided between p instruction streams (which henceforth, using the terminology of HEP, we refer to as processes), and in which s is a multiple of p. The work is to be computed as a single parallel work segment, and the code timed must include the synchronization of the processes. If the execution time, t, is measured as a function of s, the parameters can be obtained by fitting the best straight line to the results, using the generic form

$$t = r_\infty^{-1}(s + s_{\frac{1}{2}}) \qquad (7)$$

If t is plotted against s, then r_∞ is the inverse slope of the best straight line through the experimental measurements, and $s_{\frac{1}{2}}$ is the negative intercept of the line with the s axis.

In choosing a vector operation spread over several instruction streams as a benchmark for measuring the parameters (r_∞, $s_{\frac{1}{2}}$), we do not wish to imply that it would be sensible to compute a vector operation in this way in an actual HEP program. We have already explained that an MIMD program is most sensibly parallelized at the outmost DO-loops, rather than the innermost DO-loops that represent vector operations. A program consisting of a single DO-loop is chosen as the benchmark, only because it is the simplest problem to analyse which has a variable amount of arithmetic and no data-dependencies.

The HEP FORTRAN code for the (r_∞, $s_{\frac{1}{2}}$) benchmark using FORK/JOIN synchronization is given in Fig. 1. All the arithmetic work is performed by the subroutine DOALL which contains the DO-10 loop for the element-by-element multiplication of two vectors. The vector length NS (replacing the variable s in the discussion above) starts at 1 and is doubled up to 16384. For each vector length the work is divided between NPROC processes or instruction streams (replacing the variable p in the text). The DO-30 loop CREATES NPROC-1 processes, and the last process is initiated by the CALL DOALL statement. This completes the FORK of the FORK/JOIN synchronization logic. The control program then waits on the statement DUMMY=$DONE because $DONE is initially set to the empty state and cannot be read until it becomes full.

Synchronization is achieved by the three asynchronous variables $ISTART, $KOUNT and $DONE which are initially set to empty by the PURGE statement. $KOUNT is then set to NPROC and counted down by one as each of the NPROC processes executing the DOALL routine finishes its work. This occurs immediately after the DO-10 loop in the subroutine DOALL. All but the last of the processes to finish will find its local register variable I non zero, and the asynchronous variable $DONE will not be touched. However the last process to finish finds I = 0 and sets $DONE = 1.0 with its state full. The

```
      COMMON/SYNC/$ISTART, $KOUNT, $DONE, NPROC, NS
      COMMON/DATA/A(16384), B(16384), C(16384)
      DIMENSION ISPY(5)

      NS = 1
50    CONTINUE
      DO 20 NPROC = 1, 20
      PURGE $ISTART, $KOUNT, $DONE
      $KOUNT = NPROC
      $ISTART = 1
      CALL SETSPY

      DO 30 I = 1, NPROC-1
      CREATE DOALL
30    CONTINUE
      CALL DOALL
      DUMMY = $DONE

      CALL SPY(ISPY)
      TIME = 1.0E-7*FLOAT(ISPY(1))
      WRITE (6,100) NS, NPROC, TIME
20    CONTINUE

      NS = 2*NS
      IF (NS.LE.16384) GOTO 50
      STOP

      SUBROUTINE DOALL
      COMMON/SYNC/$ISTART, $KOUNT, $DONE, NPROC, NS
      COMMON/DATA/A(16384), B(16384), C(16384)
      REGISTER INTEGER I
      I1 = $ISTART
      $ISTART = I1 + 1

      DO 10 I = I1, NS, NPROC
      C(I) = A(I)*B(I)
10    CONTINUE

      I = $KOUNT-1
      $KOUNT = I
      IF (I.EQ.0) $DONE = 1.0
      RETURN
      END
```

Fig. 1 HEP FORTRAN program for the $(r_\infty, s_{\frac{1}{2}})$ Benchmark using FORK/JOIN
        synchronization

control program is then able to read the variable $DONE and the program proceeds. This is the JOIN of the FORK/JOIN synchronization.

The asynchronous variable $ISTART is used to ensure that each of the NPROC processes performs a different part of the NS floating-point multiplications which are to be performed. The first two instructions of DOALL read the value of $ISTART (initially set to 1) into a local variable, I1, and increment its value by one. Since an asynchronous variable is shared by all processes, each process takes its turn to access $ISTART, and therefore takes a different value into its local variable I1. In fact, each process will take a different integer from the range 1 to NPROC into its variable I1. Since I1 is the starting index for the DO-10 loop within DOALL, each process will therefore perform a different set of elemental operations, in an interleaved fashion. The process that has I1 = 1 computes elements with indices (1, NPROC + 1, 2*NPROC + 1, etc.), that which picks up I1 = 2 computes elements with indices (2, NPROC + 2, 2*NPROC + 2, etc.) and so on.

Timing is performed by the system routines SETSPY and SPY, which respectively start and read the timer into the array ISPY. ISPY(1) is the time in clock periods of 100 ns between the calls to SETSPY and SPY, and TIME is the time in seconds. For each value of vector length NS, the control program varies the number of processes from 1 to 20 in the DO-20 loop, and prints the time as a function of vector length and number of processes. For simplicity we have omitted from Fig. 1 statements at the beginning to initialize the arrays A and B with values, and FORMAT statements.

Figure 2 gives the control program for the $(r_\infty, s_{\frac{1}{2}})$ Benchmark using BARRIER synchronization. The subroutine DOALL remains

70

```
      COMMON/SYNC/$ISTART, $KOUNT, $DONE, NPROC, NS
      COMMON/DATA/A(16384), B(16384), C(16384)
      DIMENSION ISPY(5)

      NS = 1
50    CONTINUE

      DO 20 NPROC = 1, 20
      PURGE $ISTART, $KOUNT, $DONE
      $KOUNT = 0
      DO 30 I = 1, NPROC
      CREATE DOALL
30    CONTINUE
40    IF(WAITF($KOUNT).LT.NPROC) GOTO 40
      CALL SETSPY

      $ISTART = 1
      DUMMY = $DONE

      CALL SPY(ISPY)
      TIME = 1.0E-7*FLOAT(ISPY(1))
      WRITE (6, 100) NS, NPROC, TIME
20    CONTINUE

      NS = 2*NS
      IF(NS.LE.16384) GOTO 50
      STOP
```

Fig. 2 HEP FORTRAN program for the $(r_\infty, s_{\frac{1}{2}})$ Benchmark using BARRIER
        synchronization. The subroutine DOALL is the same as in
        Fig. 1

unchanged. In this case the processes are assumed already to have been created. This occurs in the DO-30 loop, which CREATES NPROC processes, each executing the subroutine DOALL. Each instruction stream then waits on the instruction I1 = $ISTART within DOALL, because the variable $ISTART is in the empty state and cannot be read. When the control program passes statement 40 the timer is started, $ISTART is set to 1 and is given the full state. This enables all the processes to proceed by reading $ISTART in turn as described above. The control program then waits on the statement DUMMY = $DONE because $DONE is empty, until the last process sets $DONE = 1 and gives it the full state. The timer is then called and the results printed. In this case the variable $DONE is being used as the shared <u>barrier variable</u>, and the statement DUMMY = $DONE acts as a barrier that cannot be passed until all processes have finished. BARRIER synchronization clearly has less timing overhead than FORK/JOIN synchronization because it does not include the cost of initially creating the processes.

2.1.4 Measurements of $(r_\infty, s_{\frac{1}{2}})$

The theoretical timing of the $(r_\infty, s_{\frac{1}{2}})$ Benchmark has been considered in detail by Hockney (1984a), and a brief summary of some measurements given by Hockney and Snelling (1984). We give here a full discussion of all results.

Figure 3 shows the timing diagram for the benchmark for the case of p = 15 processes. Process number 1 is the control process which executes the main program at the top of Fig. 1. This CREATES in sequence processes 2 to 15, each of which executes a copy of the

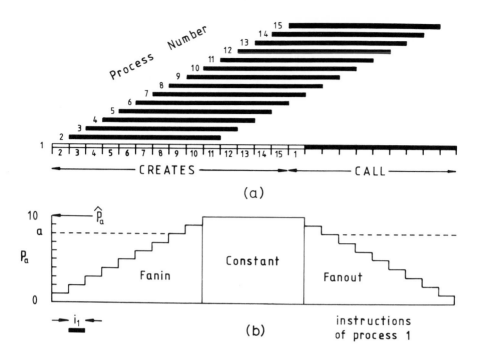

Fig. 3 Timing of the (r_∞, $s_{\frac{1}{2}}$) Benchmark for FORK/JOIN synchronization.
(a) The division of the work between 15 processes. Solid line
is work performed by each process using subroutine DOALL.
Open lines are instructions used to CREATE and CALL processes
in the control process 1. Instructions vertically above
each other are in the process queue at the same time.
Horizontal axis is the number of instructions in process 1,
in units of the number of instructions needed to CREATE a
process, i_1. (b) The number of active processes, p_a, showing
the Fanin, Constant and Fanout phases. The integral under the
dotted line (or the solid line if it is higher) is
proportional to the time to complete the benchmark.

subroutine DOALL, and finally the control program itself calls the
subroutine DOALL. Thus 15 instruction streams have been initiated,
each of which is obeying in its own time the instructions of
subroutine DOALL. The horizontal axis in Fig. 3 is marked out in
units of the number of instructions executed by the FORTRAN CREATE
or CALL statement. The solid black lines are the instructions of
the body of the subroutine DOALL, that is to say the initial and
final instructions for synchronization using $ISTART and $KOUNT,
and the instructions of the DO-10 loop which perform the useful
arithmetic. Instructions lying vertically above each other in
Fig. 3(a) are in the process queue of the HEP at the same time,
and the number of active processes, p_a, is shown below in Fig. 3(b).
This is the number of process tags in the process queue and increases
stepwise as the p processes are started in sequence. This is the
Fanin phase. Eventually, if the number of processes created, p,
is sufficient, a steady-state results in which a process finishes
as a new process is created, and the number of active processes in
the process queue remains constant. This is the Constant phase.
Finally the processes die one-by-one as they finish their work
(i.e. execute their RETURN statement), and the number of active
processes decays stepwise until all are finished. This is the
Fanout phase.

Our attention is directed at the value of p_a because this
determines the time interval between the execution of successive
instructions in any process. If $p_a \leqslant a$ the number of segments in
the instruction pipeline (a = 8 on HEP) then the interval between
instructions of any process is $\Delta t = a = 8$ clock periods. If $p_a > a$,
however, the interval between instructions in a process is $\Delta t = p_a$
clock periods, because the process tags form a circular queue with

74

only one process tag for each process. Since process number 1 CALLs
the subroutine DOALL last, and each process takes the same time,
process number 1 will finish last. We can, therefore, determine
the time for the benchmark by calculating the time for process
number 1. This time in clock periods is the area under the dotted
line in Fig. 3(b), or the solid line if this is higher, giving

$$t = \tau \int \max(a, p_a) \, di \tag{8}$$

where

    i is the number of instructions in process number 1

       (the abscissa of Fig. 3)

    τ is the clock period (100 ns on HEP)

    t is the time for the benchmark

In evaluating equation (8) we use the following notation:

i_1 - number of instructions per FORTRAN CREATE or CALL statement

i_2 - number of instructions for synchronization in subroutine
    DOALL (using variables \$ISTART and \$KOUNT)

i_3 - average number of instructions per floating-point operation

i_4 - number of instructions for DO-loop setup and control
    within subroutine DOALL

$i_5 = i_2 + i_4$ - number of instructions for sync/setup

$i_6 = i_5 + \frac{s}{p} i_3$ - number of instructions executed within the
    subroutine DOALL.

$j_1 = i_1/i_3$ - equivalent number of floating-point operations per
    FORTRAN CREATE

$j_5 = i_5/i_3$ - equivalent number of floating-point operations per
    sync/setup

75

a - effective length of the HEP instruction pipeline (a variable parameter to be chosen, not necessarily 8)

p - number of processes CREATed or CALLed

p_a - number of active processes in the process queue

$\hat{p}_a$ - maximum number of active processes in the process queue.

There are two cases to consider depending on whether the instruction pipeline becomes full or not. If the number of active processes never exceeds the length of the instruction pipeline ($\hat{p}_a < a$) the pipeline is never full and the interval between instructions is always $\Delta t = \tau a$. The time to execute the benchmark is the same as the time to execute process number 1, which is

$$t = (i_1 p + i_5 + \frac{s}{p} i_3)a\tau \qquad (9)$$

where the first term is the time to create the p processes, the second term is the time for the synchronization and DO-loop control instructions, and the third term is time for process 1 to perform its share of the arithmetic, that is to say s/p floating-point operations out of the total of s operations. Comparing equation (9) with the generic form

$$t = r_\infty^{-1}(s + s_{\frac{1}{2}}) \qquad (10)$$

we find

$$r_\infty = \frac{p}{a}\frac{\tau^{-1}}{i_3} \quad , \quad s_{\frac{1}{2}} = p(j_1 p + j_5) \qquad (11)$$

Thus if the pipeline is never full, we expect to find the asymptotic performance increasing linearly with the number of processes, and $s_{\frac{1}{2}}$ increasing quadratically with p.

If however the pipeline is full sometime during the benchmark ($\hat{p}_a > a$), then one must take into account that the time between instructions is no longer constant ($\Delta t = p_a \tau$), and thus varies with the number of active processes. Evaluating the sums and comparing with the generic form (10), we obtain

$$r_\infty^{-1} = \frac{\tau^{-1}}{i_3} \quad , \quad s_{\frac{1}{2}} = a(a-1)j_1 + (j_1 + j_5)p \qquad (12)$$

For this case of the full pipeline, one finds that the asymptotic performance is constant independent of the number of processes, and that $s_{\frac{1}{2}}$ varies linearly with p.

The pipeline becomes full sometime during the benchmark if more than p = a processes are created, and there is sufficient work to keep them busy long enough. The latter condition is expressed by

$$s > s_1 \quad \text{where} \quad s_1 = p\{(a-1)j_1 - j_5\} \qquad (13)$$

If there are fewer than 'a' processes then clearly the pipeline can never be filled, but also if there is insufficient work for each process, the processes die out too quickly to sustain more than 'a' active processes.

The above predictions are well substantiated by the benchmark measurements. Figure 4 shows a typical plot of measured time, t, against amount of arithmetic, s, for a constant number of processes p. The measured points indicated by the open circles form a good straight line. In this example the inverse slope of the line gives r_∞ = 1.7 Mflop/s, and the negative intercept with the s axis gives $s_{\frac{1}{2}}$ = 828. Figure 5 shows the result of many such measurements of (r_∞, $s_{\frac{1}{2}}$) for different values of p, the number of processes created.

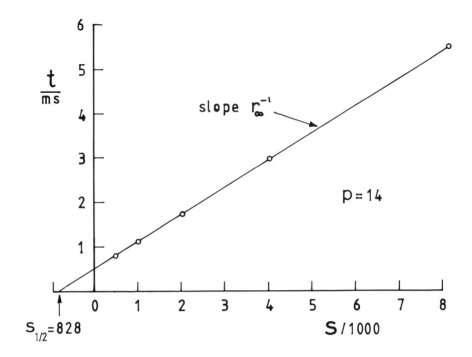

Fig. 4 Typical experimental measurement of r_∞ and $s_{\frac{1}{2}}$. Time, t, is plotted as a function of amount of arithmetic, s, for a constant number of processes, p. Open circles are experimental measurements. The inverse slope of the best straight line (solid) is r_∞, and the negative intercept with the s-axis is $s_{\frac{1}{2}}$.

As predicted by equations (11) and (12) we find a quadratic increase of $s_{\frac{1}{2}}$ with p until the pipeline is filled, followed by a slow linear increase. The values of r_∞ show as expected a linear increase of asymptotic performance until the pipeline is filled, followed by a constant value. The solid line is a fit of the theoretical equations (11) and (12) to the measured results, using the following values

$$a = 12, \ i_1 = 29, \ i_3 = 6, \ i_5 = 49 \qquad (14)$$

One might wonder why the empirically determined length of the instruction pipeline is a = 12, when there are only 8 segments in the instruction pipeline of the HEP. This is because the data and results in the benchmark are stored in main memory, and not in the PEM registers. Consequently the memory reference instructions are 'waved-off' into the SFU to await the arrival of the requested data from the Data Memory Module. This effect has been ignored in our timing analysis, but can be approximately taken into account by slightly lengthening the instruction pipeline. Thus 'a' becomes the effective length of the instruction pipeline, and a = 12 seems to be a good value.

It is clear that the best operating point for this benchmark is to choose p = 12 because this gives the minimum synchronization overhead, $s_{\frac{1}{2}}$, for the maximum of r_∞. Taking the optimum situation we find that for FORK/JOIN synchronization

$$r_\infty = 1.7 \ \text{Mflop/s} \ , \ n_{\frac{1}{2}} = 820 \qquad (15)$$

Alternatively we can consider the time of the benchmark as a function of p, for a constant amount of arithmetic, and ask what is

the optimum number of processes to create, p_{opt}. It is clear
from Fig. 5 that p_{opt} = a, because if p > a the synchronization
overhead $s_{\frac{1}{2}}$ increases without any further increase in r_{∞}. This is
also seen very clearly if we plot t as a function of p for constant s,
as is done in Fig. 6. We see a very rapid decrease in execution
time as p increases up to p_{opt} = a, after which the execution time
increases slowly. The theoretical analysis shows that for p < p_1 and
p > p_2 the pipeline is never full, where

$$p_1 = a \quad \text{and} \quad p_2 = \frac{s}{(a - 1)j_1 - j_5} \tag{16}$$

and the time varies as

$$t = a \left(\frac{s}{p} + j_1 p + j_5\right) i_3 \tau \tag{17}$$

To the left of p_1, the pipeline is never full because not enough
processes have been created. To the right of p_2, the pipeline is
never full because the amount of arithmetic, s, is insufficient to
keep eight processes active, out of the many more that have been
created.

Between p_1 and p_2 the pipeline is full, and the time varies
linearly with the number of processes created.

$$t = \{s + (j_1 + j_5)p + a(a - 1)j_1\} i_3 \tau \tag{18}$$

In Fig. 6 the solid lines are a fit of the theoretical curve (17)
for p < a and (18) for p > a to the measured results, using the
parametric values given in (14).

The condition for filling the pipeline and choosing the optimum
number of processes to create is shown in Fig. 7. The (p, s) plane

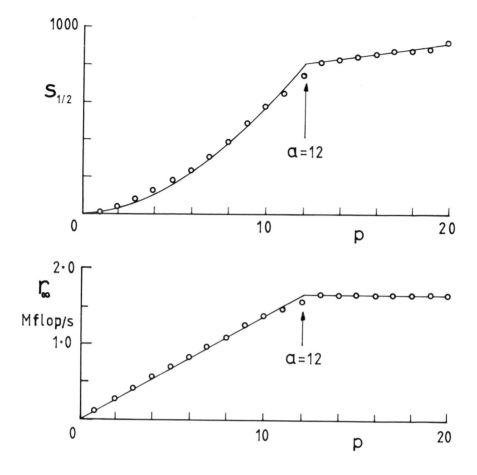

Fig. 5   Measured values of r_∞ and $s_{\frac{1}{2}}$ for different numbers of processes

created, p.   Open circles are the observed values and the

solid line is a theoretical fit using equations (11) and (12)

with the parameters (14).   The parameter 'a' is the effective

length of the HEP instruction pipeline.   Note the quadratic

variation of $s_{\frac{1}{2}}$ with p for p < a and the linear variation

for p > a.   The best operating point is at $p = p_{opt} = a$.

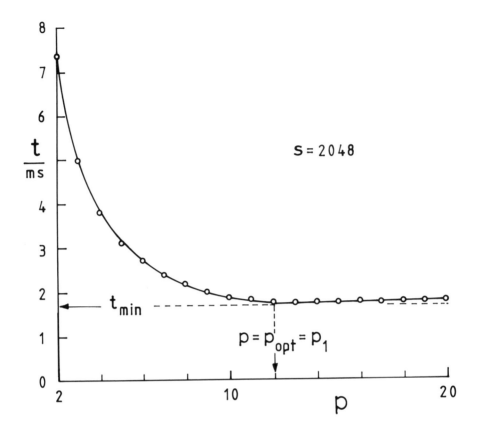

Fig. 6   Time, t, as a function of the number of processes created, p,
         for a constant amount of arithmetic, s, showing the minimum
         execution time, t_{min}, for $p = p_{opt} = p_1$ processes created.
         Open circles are measured values and the solid line is the
         theoretical result of equation (17) and (18) with the
         parameters (14).

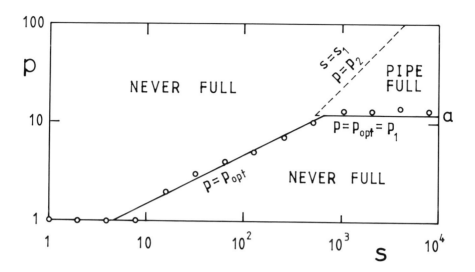

Fig. 7 The optimum number of processes to create, p_{opt}, as a function of the amount of arithmetic, s. The (p, s) plane is also divided into regions in which the HEP instruction pipeline is never full, or full at sometime during the benchmark. The straight lines are drawn from equations (16) and (19) using the parameters (14). Open circles are the observed values. Note that both axes are logarithmic.

is divided into regions when the pipeline is filled (shaded) and never filled (unshaded) by the lines $p = p_2$ and $p = p_1$. The optimum value of p is given by

$$p_{opt} = \sqrt{\frac{s}{j_1}} \quad s < s_3 = a^2 j_1 \qquad (19)$$

if the pipeline is never full, and

$$p_{opt} = a \quad s > s_3$$

if the pipeline is filled. The solid line is the theoretical value of p_{opt} using the parameters given in (14) and the open circles are the measured values.

One may also consider the minimum time obtained when $p = p_{opt}$, as a function of the amount of arithmetic, and this is shown in Fig. 8. The theoretical analysis, drawn as the solid line, shows

$$t_{min} = (2\sqrt{sj_1} + j_5)ai_3\tau \, , \, s < s_3 \qquad (20)$$

when the pipe is never full, and

$$t_{min} = \{s + a(aj_1 + j_5)\}i_3\tau \, , \, s > s_3 \qquad (21)$$

when the pipe is full.

The $(r_\infty, s_{\frac{1}{2}})$ Benchmark results using BARRIER synchronization are shown in Fig. 9. The theoretical solid curves use the parameters

$$a = 13, \, i_1 = 5, \, i_3 = 6, \, i_5 = 40 \qquad (22)$$

The best operating point will be at p = 13 with the values

$$r_\infty = 1.67 \text{ Mflop/s} \, , \, s_{\frac{1}{2}} = 230 \qquad (23)$$

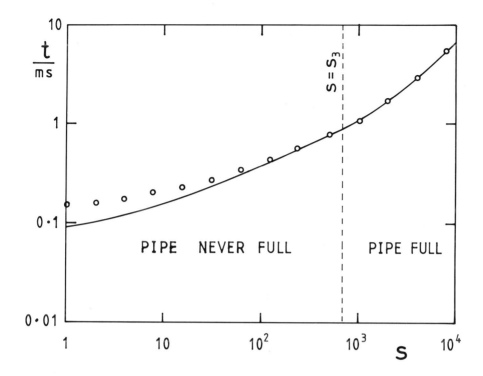

Fig. 8   The minimum time, t, obtained when $p = p_{opt}$ as a function
of the amount of arithmetic, s. Open circles are the
measured values and the solid line is the theoretical
result from equations (20) and (21) using the parameters
(14). For $s > s_3$ the HEP pipeline is full sometime
during the benchmark, whereas for $s < s_3$ the pipeline
is never full.

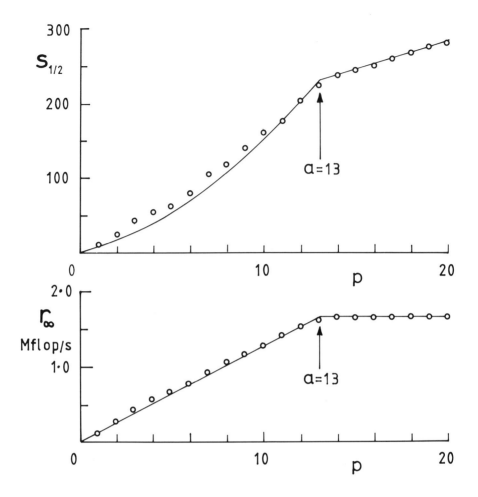

Fig. 9   Measured values of r_∞ and $s_{\frac{1}{2}}$ for BARRIER synchronization
as a function of the number of processes created, p.
The optimum operating point is when the number of processes
created, p, equals the effective HEP pipeline length,
a = 13. Open circles are measured values, and the solid
line is the theoretical result from equations (11) and
(12) using the parameters (22).

As expected the synchronization parameter $s_{\frac{1}{2}}$ is substantially less than
that obtained using FORK/JOIN synchronization because the processes are
not recreated at the beginning of each parallel work segment in BARRIER
synchronization.

The values of r_∞ obtained above apply to a situation in which all
variables are stored in the main data memory of the HEP, a situation
which we refer to as "memory-to-memory operation". This is a worst
case from the performance point of view because no use is being made
of the registers within the PEM. Nevertheless it represents a
situation that is likely to be representative of many FORTRAN jobs that
do not make much use of the built-in FORTRAN functions. At the other
extreme one can consider a benchmark that makes extensive use of the
registers and represents a best-case situation of "register-to-register"
operation. The benchmark chosen replaces the DO-10 loop of the
subroutine DOALL in Fig. 1 by the following

```
        DO 10 I = I1, NS, NPROC
        IF (A(I), LE, 0.0) THEN
                C(I) = SIN(A(I))*EXP(B(I))                    (24)
        ELSE
                C(I) = COS(A(I))*EXP(B(I))
        ENDIF
```

In this benchmark the evaluations of the series approximations for the
SIN, COS and EXP functions takes place in the registers, and ensures
that a large amount of register-to-register arithmetic takes place for
every reference to main memory for the quantities A(I), B(I) and C(I).
The benchmark is also designed to demonstrate the ability of an MIMD
computer to compute concurrently programs that include data dependent

conditional statements. In this case some processes will be computing
the sine function and others the cosine depending on their particular
value of A(I).

The timing measurements have been repeated for this register-to-
register benchmark with the following results:

$$
\begin{array}{lll}
\text{FORK/JOIN} & r_\infty = 4.8 \text{ Mflop/s}, & s_{\frac{1}{2}} = 710 \\
\text{BARRIER} & r_\infty = 4.8 \text{ Mflop/s}, & s_{\frac{1}{2}} = 1900
\end{array}
\tag{25}
$$

It is clear that in this benchmark the average number of instructions
per floating-point operation, $i_3 \approx 2$, compared with $i_3 = 6$ for the
previous memory-to-memory case. However, because the rate of production
of useful floating-point operations, has been increased 3 fold, the
importance of the fixed synchronization overhead is proportionately
increased. The range of (r_∞, $s_{\frac{1}{2}}$) values given in equations (15), (23)
and (25) probably encompass the performance to be expected from the
HEP. Actual applications are expected to give values between these
limiting cases.

2.1.5 Conclusions

A two-parameter timing model has been defined for MIMD computation
which is particularly suitable for the HEP, and the values of the
two-parameters (r_∞, $s_{\frac{1}{2}}$) have been measured using a simple benchmark.
The theoretical analysis of the benchmark gives results in good
agreement with the measured values. The parameter, $s_{\frac{1}{2}}$, measures
the importance of the synchronization overhead and can be used to
include quantitatively the cost of synchronization in a HEP program,
and also to compare quantitatively the magnitude of the

synchronization overhead of the HEP with that of other machines. Now
that quantitative values are available for the synchronization overhead,
it is to be hoped that algorithm designers will include this overhead
in their estimates of algorithm execution time.

Acknowledgment

The author wishes to acknowledge the invaluable assistance of
Mr. D.F. Snelling of Denelcor, Inc. in obtaining the data upon which
this paper is based, and for many penetrating discussions on the
architecture and timing of the Denelcor HEP. Without his assistance
this paper could not have been produced.

REFERENCES

Hockney R.W. and Jesshope C.R. (1981), Parallel Computers -
Architecture, Programming and Algorithms, Adam Hilger, Bristol
(distributed in North and South America by Heyden & Son, Philadelphia).

Hockney R.W. (1982), "Characterization of Parallel Computers and
Algorithms", Comput. Phys. Commun., vol. 26, 285-291.

Hockney R.W. (1983), "Characterizing Computers and Optimizing the
FACR(ℓ) Poisson-Solver on Parallel Unicomputers", IEE Trans. Comput.,
vol. C-32, 933-941.

Hockney R.W. (1984a), "Performance of Parallel Computers",
in High-Speed Computation, J. S. Kowalik (ed.), Springer-Verlag,
Berlin, 159-175.

Hockney R.W. (1984b), "The $n_{\frac{1}{2}}$-Method of Algorithm Analysis" in
PDE Software: Modules, Interfaces and Systems, B. Engquist and
T. Smedsaas (eds.), Elsevier Science Publ., North-Holland,
Amsterdam, 429-444.

Hockney R.W. and Snelling D.F. (1984), "Characterizing MIMD Computers:
e.g. the Denelcor HEP", in Parallel Computing 83, M. Feilmeier,
G.R. Joubert, and U. Schendel (eds.), Elsevier Science Publ.,
North-Holland, Amsterdam, 521-526.

Kuck D.J. (1978), "Computers and Computation", Wiley, New York.

PART 3

PROGRAMMING AND LANGUAGES

3.1. A BRIEF SURVEY OF IMPLICIT PARALLELISM DETECTION

KARL J. OTTENSTEIN
Dept. of Mathematical and Computer Sciences
Michigan Technological University
Houghton, Michigan 49931

This section briefly surveys compiler methods for the automatic detection of implicit program parallelism for a multiprocessor such as the HEP. Such detection is obviously important for source languages that have no constructs for explicitly expressing parallelism (e.g., FORTRAN '77). It can also be important if a language does permit the expression of parallelism. For example, the constructs available in the language for specifying parallelism may not allow an appropriate granularity for the target machine. Furthermore, the existence of these constructs does not guarantee their most advantageous use. The complexity of program dependence patterns is such that it is possible for a programmer to accidentally declare processes that race or deadlock, or to miss opportunities for parallelism. Maintenance is an issue as well: a program might be modified in such a way that the original explicit process partitioning is no longer as good as it might be. Regarding portability, if the source program is tailored to a particular architecture and is moved to another with

This material is based on work supported by the National Science Foundation under Grants DCR-8203487, DCR-8404463 and DCR-8404909. HEP time was made available by Argonne National Laboratory.

different process creation, synchronization and communication costs, the process partitioning and synchronization specified by the programmer may no longer be appropriate or efficient. These anamolies and inefficiencies should be eliminated or called to the programmer's attention when possible (the general problem is NP-complete), yet it is the analysis required to detect implicit parallelism that might detect them.

Should languages that allow the expression of parallelism be used, then, if compiler complexity will be the same as for sequential languages? Even for sequential languages, should conventional imperative languages be used, or are functional languages more appropriate? These are open human factors problems. There seem to have been no studies that have examined the appropriate degree of control over parallelism to permit in a language and what the best method of parallelism expression is in terms of psychological complexity and resulting software reliability.

The balance of this section is organized as follows. First, work in the area of compiler techniques specifically applicable to multiprocessors is reviewed broadly. We then summarize a few specific transformations. Next, intermediate program representations for use by the compiler are briefly discussed. We conclude with a discussion of some open problems.

3.1.1. Background

A difficulty in searching the literature in this area is the varying level at which different researchers analyze programs for parallelism. For example, a paper may claim to solve the problem of detection of implicit parallelism, yet what it really addresses is the scheduling of straight-line code for a pipelined architecture. Most work in translation for parallel architectures has been done at the University of Illinois by David Kuck along with his students and colleagues: U. Banerjee, S.-C. Chen, R. Kuhn, D. Lawrie, B. Leasure, Y. Muraoka, D. Padua, R. Towle, M. Wolfe and others [13,35-41,52,53,61]. Additional dependence analysis research has been performed at Rice University by Ken Kennedy, J.R. Allen and others [3-6,33] and at Michigan Tech and IBM Yorktown by K. Ottenstein, J. Ferrante and others [20-23,48-50]. Most of the Illinois and Rice work has been aimed at "vector" machines. That of Padua [52,53] is specifically directed towards multiprocessors, as is some of the Rice, Michigan Tech and IBM work. Padua's work shows that the kind of dependence analysis used for vectorization is immediately applicable to detecting parallel sections of code for multiprocessing.

An excellent survey of multiprocessing was given by Baer in 1973 [12]. As noted there, Bernstein [15] first saw the need to perform dependence analysis to delimit sections of code that could be scheduled concurrently[1]. Others, such as Ramamoorthy and Gonzalez [55], built analyzers to recognize some implicit parallelism. Baer summarizes the methods and results of a few of these attempts, aimed primarily at locating independent program regions. A more current survey is threaded through a recent book by Hwang and Briggs [30].

In 1972, Kuck et al reported the results of a study of parallelism in a sample of small FORTRAN modules [35]. They performed tree height reduction, including Muraoka's distribution algorithms, and statement subsumption to obtain bushier trees and additional concurrency. Loop distribution was done to obtain independently iterating loops from a loop containing several statements and scalar expansion was performed, replacing scalar references with new vector references to break scalar dependences and allow further loop iteration concurrency. (Scalar expansion increases the storage requirements of a program. It thus presents storage management problems [45,63].) Given the specific assumptions made on the number of loop iterations and the costs of certain computations, this study suggested that enough parallelism could be found in the sample of FORTRAN programs to merit their execution on a multiprocessor. Theoretical

---

[1]Using a term invented by the Blue CHiP Project at Purdue [58], these code sections will be called "proclets" here.

speedups of 1.2 to 17 were estimated using up to 100 processors; Kuck estimated that an "ordinary" FORTRAN program could reasonably utilize 16 processors. A later paper in 1974 gave similar results, also on small modules [36].

During this same period, several commercial compilers were producing vector code from FORTRAN. These, too, relied on an analysis of subscripting patterns in loops for more precise dependence knowledge [42,43,54]. Kuck surveyed the maturing analysis techniques in 1976 [37,38]. Arnold [8] reports results comparing three later vectorizers: Kuck and Associates' KAP (Kuck Analyzer Package), Pacific Sierra Research's VAST (Vector and Array Syntax Translator) and the CDC Cyber 200 FORTRAN compiler. KAP almost always produced greater speedups: the vectorized code ran roughly 10 times faster than the unvectorized code. KAP also took about 10 times as long as the other packages to translate the modules. Arnold attributes both of these characteristics to the fact that KAP does a thorough dependence analysis while the other vectorizers operate by pattern matching DO loops. (KAP performed worse on several samples due to vectorizing sections for which the setup costs negated the speedup.)

The mid-70's is also the period during which a radically new approach to multiprocessor organization was being proposed: the data flow machine [9,18,19]. Program dependence patterns are more than an analysis tool here: they are basic to the nature of the machine code and its execution. With instruction level concurrency and possibly thousands of processors, this architecture offers potentially the most parallelism of any. While low-level concurrency is appealing, some [26] feel that it may only be appropriate for scalar operations. Even among the data flow advocates, there is some concern about the efficiency of such fine-grained scheduling. Thus, "block-driven" data flow organizations have been suggested [11,16,57]. This presents the problem of clustering to determine what groups of instructions should constitute a block. (This problem is discussed further in the last section of this survey.)

Jones and Schwarz report the results of experience with the Carnegie-Mellon C.mmp and Cm* projects and the Bolt, Beranek and Neuman PLURIBUS system [31]. As most other work[2] on multiprocessors reports theoretical or simulated results, this survey is of particular interest even though it does not address the issue of compilers for multiprocessors in any depth. Synchronization costs were found to be a minor factor [46], as Kuck had hypothesized [52]. Cm* has increasing reference times for local, intracluster and intercluster memory references. As

---

[2]until most recently. See the later chapters of this book, for example.

expected, the degree of data locality was seen to affect the degree of parallelism on that machine. Jones and Schwarz note that a programmer must be aware of these costs, just as in a virtual memory environment a programmer really must consider paging behavior when designing code for performance. This data allocation problem [45,63] is another area that must be addressed by algorithms extracting parallelism from sequential code.

Several recent commercial developments should be mentioned here. Additional vector processors have been introduced both here and abroad, yet there is little public information to suggest that their vectorizing compilers use any new techniques. Several prototype multiprocessors are being constructed, notable examples being the NYU Ultracomputer [27] and the Livermore Midas system [44]. The Denelcor HEP, and the ELXSI System 6400 are the first commercial multiprocessors with nontrivial numbers of processors. Neither of these machines yet has a "parallelizing" compiler, a reflection not of available technology, but of newness to the marketplace. The ELXSI machine was designed as a high performance multiprogrammed business machine without the intention of running many processes cooperating on a single task [47]. The HEP, as discussed in Chapter 1, is programmable through conventional languages with the user responsible for the parallel implementation of his code. While we suggest that a "parallelizing" compiler would be appropriate for a machine such as the HEP for the variety of reasons mentioned at the start of this section, the HEP can be utilized as delivered. The CDC CyberPlus system [56], on the other hand, _requires_ a sophisticated compiler to schedule the 15 functional units addressed by each 240-bit instruction on each processor. As with the ELI 512 (extremely long instruction) machine [24], Fisher's microcode compaction-derived technique of trace scheduling [25] is used to gather operations into instructions [56].

The effect on compiler design of this difference between HEP and CyberPlus instruction scheduling is worthy of comment. On a HEP PEM, pipelining is dynamic, available instructions being scheduled onto functional units by the hardware at runtime. Total unit utilization may be lower than in a CyberPlus processor, but the compiler is freed from dealing with parallelism at the instruction level. Only the larger grain issue of finding reasonably sized independent sequences of instructions (proclets) must be addressed on the HEP -- currently by the user, but perhaps in the future by the compiler. The CyberPlus approach may yield higher performance because of better functional unit utilization and the ability to schedule synchronous activities, but the compiler's task is much harder.

Experience will tell which design, both hardware and (as it matures) software, achieves better performance.

3.1.2. Transformations

This section briefly discusses a few of the transformations that need to be considered in targeting code for a multiprocessor such as the HEP. All transformations and issues examined by others in the context of vectorization are relevant to work in multiprocessing, as mentioned previously. Wolfe [63] gives an overview and comparison of methods for array subscript analysis as well as a variety of (primarily vectorizing) transformations. A more recent thesis by Allen [5] discusses dependence analysis for subscripted variables in great detail and gives numerous applications in the context of a vectorizing compiler.

We assume the following two phase approach for a "parallelizing" compiler. First (top down and machine independent), break the sequential program into as many proclets as possible, on a control region basis. Next (bottom up and machine dependent), cluster the proclets as required by the parameters of the machine at hand to achieve a realistic partitioning of the program into processes. As the detection of scalar proclets is trivial (given an appropriate intermediate program representation), the balance of this section is concerned with array dependences.

Padua [52,53] gives several transformations on loops. He shows how loops may be partitioned into parallel sections by examining distance vectors [42] on array reference dependence patterns. Intuitively, the distance vector for some particular array dependence edge gives the integer span for each subscript between two references. Thus, a dependence edge from a definition A(I) to a use A(I-3) would have a distance vector of <3>. (All examples that follow are from Padua's thesis [53].)

A total partition is possible if all iterations of a loop may be run in parallel. Such a loop is:

```
    DO 10 I=1, M
        A(I) = B(I) + C(I)
 10 CONTINUE
```

An example of a partial partition (loop splitting) is the transformation of:

```
    DO 20 I=3, M
        A(I) = A(I-2) + 1
 20 CONTINUE
```

into:

```
Process 1:                      Process 2:

    DO 21 I=3,(M-1)/2*2+1,2          DO 22 I=4,M/2*2,2
        A(I) = A(I-2) + 1               A(I) = A(I-2) + 1
 21 CONTINUE                     22 CONTINUE
```

Given a loop with several array references and several

dependences with different distance vectors, Padua notes
that the loop may be split into g independent loops, where g
is the greatest common divisor of the dependence distances.
For example, the loop

```
      DO 30 I=7, N
        B(I) = A(I-3) + B(I-3)
        A(I) = B(I-6) + A(I-6)
   30 CONTINUE
```

can be partitioned into three proclets, each executing the
two statements with different index sets:

```
      Process 1:  I = 7, 10, 13, ...
      Process 2:  I = 8, 11, 14, ...
      Process 3:  I = 9, 12, 15, ...
```

A technique called **alignment** shifts the indices in one or
more statements to increase the greatest common divisor of
the dependence distances and hence obtain more partitions.
Loop interchange (discussed in more detail in [5,33,63])
reverses the order of nested loops when profitable and
possible. This transformation can lead to improved
partitioning. For example,

```
      DO 40 I=2, MI
        DO 50 J=1, MJ
          A(I,J) = A(I-1,J) + 1
   50     CONTINUE
   40 CONTINUE
```

is independent in J and sequential in I. By reversing the
loops, we obtain MJ independent proclets.

Padua gives examples of where software pipelining can be utilized to achieve speedups on multiprocessors. (He uses semaphores for synchronization; these may be easily approximated using asynchronous variables on the HEP.) He shows how the loop

```
    DO 60 I=2, N
        A(I) = (B(I) + A(I-1)) * 2
        D(I) = A(I)**2 + 1
        C(I) = C(I-1)**2 + D(I)
60 CONTINUE
```

can be transformed into three proclets, each of which is a loop over I containing one of the assignment statements. The processes synchronize on the production of A(I) and D(I). Alternatively (and not realistically for the HEP), there could be N-1 proclets, each consisting of the three statements for some fixed value of I and synchronizing as required by the A(I) -- A(I-1) and C(I) -- C(I-1) dependences. Wolfe also discusses pipelining, showing how index set shifting can expose parallelism, particularly when combined with loop interchanging [63]. He notes that the result is equivalent to the well-known wavefront method.

Allen and Kennedy [6,7] suggest code replication as an additional method of breaking loop dependences. They give the following example on which alignment cannot be applied:

```
        DO 100 I=2, N
           A(I) = B(I) + 10
           C(I) = A(I) + 5
           D(I) = C(I) + A(I-1)
    100 CONTINUE
```

Note that A(I-1) refers to values computed within the loop for every iteration except the first. Allen and Kennedy break the A(I-1) -- A(I) dependence by introducing a temporary variable:

```
        DO 100 I=2, N
           IF (I .GT. 2) THEN
              T = B(I-1) + 10
           ELSE
              T = A(I-1)
           ENDIF
           A(I) = B(I) + 10
           C(I) = A(I) + 5
           D(I) = C(I) + T
    100 CONTINUE
```

All iterations of the loop are now independent. The first iteration of the loop should be peeled [22] off and scalar propagation and subsumption applied to the resulting code. This gives us:

```
        A(2) = B(2) + 10
        C(2) = A(2) + 5
        D(2) = C(2) + A(1)
        DO 100 I=3, N
           A(I) = B(I) + 10
           C(I) = A(I) + 5
           D(I) = C(I) + B(I-1) + 10
    100 CONTINUE
```

The header code thus obtained is independent of any of the iterations.

105

An interesting aspect to breaking a sequential process into proclets is that many transformations are the inverse of common compiler optimizations [34] and should be inverted after analysis is complete. Consider two examples: induction variable substitution and loop distribution.

<u>Induction variable substitution</u> [33,40] replaces references to loop co-indices with appropriate references to a single loop index. This is an essential step in the process of determining array reference dependences. As an example, substitution would convert

```
      I = 5
      DO 20 J = 1, 10
         A(J) = A(I)
         I = I + 5
   20 CONTINUE
```

into the equivalent

```
      DO 20 J = 1, 10
         A(J) = A(J*5)
   20 CONTINUE
```

in order for subscript analysis to determine that only "old" values of A are referenced in the loop and that hence all iterations can be executed in parallel. This is the inverse of the <u>reduction in strength</u> transformation commonly applied to sequential programs to remove "expensive" operators (like the multiplication above) from loops. Reduction in strength should be applied <u>after</u> analysis here since the resulting code will be faster whether run in parallel or sequentially.

Thus, we invert a conventional optimization to assist analysis and then apply the original optimization on each sequential proclet remaining. The result of applying induction variable substitution, followed by loop distribution and then reduction in strength may produce different auxiliary induction variable patterns. (In the example shown, however, the original code will result.)

Loop distribution (splitting) and loop fusion [41] provide another example where both a transformation and its inverse are useful. Loop distribution might first be applied to split loops into independent proclets. If in the clustering phase it is determined that some of the split loops (or other similar loops) should all be assigned to the same process, loop fusion would then merge them together into a single loop, eliminating the overhead of multiple loop headers and tests.

3.1.3. Intermediate Program Representation

A critical issue in producing any translator, much less one targeted for a multiprocessor, is the choice of the intermediate program form [17,51] on which the analysis and transformation algorithms will operate. Much related work has been done over the past eight years in the area of dependence-based program forms; this is surveyed briefly in a recent report [22]. The dependence graphs used in the Illinois Parafrase vectorizer [40,52] are designed for hierarchically analyzing dependence relations in programs for vectorization. This representation has been used by commercial vectorizers as well. Allen [5] has introduced several related concepts, including the differentiation between loop independent and loop carried dependences. The program dependence graph (PDG) [22,23] was conceived specifically for program optimization, accomodating standard optimizations as well as including the kinds of dependence information originated in the Parafrase system. The PDG abstracts both control and data dependences of a program, aiding many multiprocessing transformations.

As an example of the advantage of the PDG control dependence representation, consider the conventional control flow graph in Figure 1. Two sequential loops are followed by a conditional that contains a loop nest on one branch. (The statements are represented here by nodes labeled Si.) Figure 2 gives the corresponding PDG control dependence subgraph. All statements (operators) are successors of region nodes that summarize the conditions required for execution. These regions, labeled Ri, are defined by predicates. "Entry" is the condition for execution of the program, and is a distinguished node in every PDG. Note the difference in structure between these two graphs. The PDG

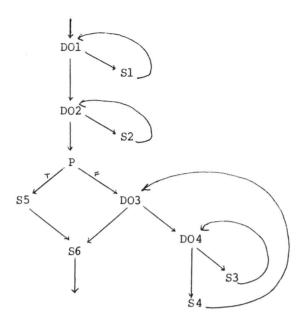

Figure 1 - A Control Flow Graph

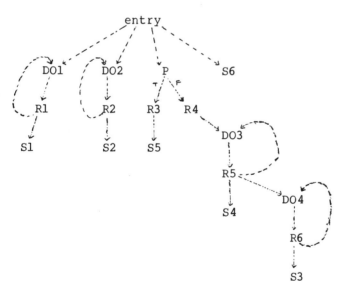

Figure 2 - PDG Control Dependence Subgraph

subgraph shows that the two initial loops, the conditional, and the final statement _may_ be independent of each other. As far as control information is concerned, <u>this</u> <u>may</u> <u>be</u> <u>the</u> <u>case</u>. Data dependences are what will impose any sequencing on these regions. The implied organization given by the conventional control flow graph is limiting to conventional optimization (because it hinders the rearrangement of large sections of code as done in [20]) as well as parallelism extraction. The graphs used in the Parafrase system are eventually transformed [41,52] to have similar abstraction advantages.

The complete PDG for a program consists of the control dependence subgraph and a cyclic data dependence subgraph, where all nodes in the latter are successors of appropriate region nodes in the former. The data dependence subgraph is built in two phases. First, data flow analysis [1] is performed to determine the definitions which reach each basic block. Then, the subgraph is constructed by linking basic block DAG's (directed acyclic graphs [1]) together using that information. A distinguished node "undefined" is a data dependence predecessor of all nodes which might reference an uninitialized variable. I/O is represented by treating file names similarly to array names. Complete details are given elsewhere [22] with additional examples in [21,50]. The PDG may be viewed as a partially functional representation of an imperative program. As such, the renaming transformation required by Parafrase/PFC to break dependences among scalars is totally unnecessary as "renaming" is automatic by construction. Some of the advantages of functional languages cited by Arvind [10] thus accrue even for an imperative source.

Parafrase and the Rice PFC vectorizer [3] use a statement-oriented intermediate form. In Parafrase, the internal structure of statements is represented with syntax trees [13]. The dependences denoted with edges between statements in those forms are similarly denoted between nodes in the PDG where necessary: output, anti, true and control dependence. The control abstraction in the PDG is one of its major advantages. It facilitates the location of parallel regions in a program as well as the performance of major restructuring transformations such as code motion, loop interchange, loop fusion, loop splitting, loop unrolling and procedure integration[3]. A major advantage of the PDG is that the need to convert control dependence [4,52] is eliminated and vectorization is sometimes reduced to simple path questions [22,62]. The data dependence

----

[3]Procedure integration [2] is the in-line expansion of a procedure body at a call site. Optimization of the procedure code for the specific parameters passed can yield fewer dependences and increase the opportunities for parallelism. If no benefits can be gained, the procedure call may be restored.

representation facilitates the detection of fine-grained parallelism.

The PDG represents programs at the operator, rather than the statement level. Regions may be abstracted when desired by posting summary information. Automatic renaming of scalars, mentioned above, is one benefit of the operator-level representation. Other cases where operator-level dependences are important include the following:

(1) expression factoring. Vectorization can be improved with knowledge of the exact operands causing dependences since subexpressions can be factored out of statements [63]. Wolfe notes that associativity, commutativity and distributivity can be applied, if possible and stable, to rearrange expressions for better vectorization. This can aid multiprocessing as well.

(2) analysis in the presence of embedded function calls. Consider the following with functions f, g, p and q:

$$x = f(a) + g(b)$$
$$y = p(a,r) * ...$$

If both **f** and **g** are expensive and side-effect free, it may become important to schedule them concurrently. Suppose that **p** references **a** and sets **r** as a side effect. The side effect computation may be more critical to clustering operations into proclets than the multiplication in the assignment to **y**; if so, the call should be factored out into the process that references **r**.

(3) procedure integration [2]. Expanding a procedure at a call site requires operator-level knowledge for parameter substitution and optimization, all of which can yield fewer dependences and greater parallelism.

(4) induction variable substitution. This transformation, discussed in the previous section, is simplified by having all definitions and uses linked explicitly as is done in the PDG. The reduction in strength algorithm presented in [49] can be readily inverted for use with

the PDG. Figure 3(a) shows the PDG after loop
induction variable detection [20] has been performed
and I has been converted to a **DO** operator with an
unknown upper bound and annotated as a co-index. Only
data dependences are shown. Where the strength
reduction transformation propagates linear functions of
the induction variable up, splitting **DO** operators and
producing multiple loop indices, induction variable
substitution merges co-indices and pushes the linear
function down into the loop as seen in Figure 3(b).

(5) data flow machines. It is fairly easy to produce code
from a PDG for a low-level asynchronous data flow
machine.

3.1.4. Open Problems

Two important areas have received little attention:
clustering and debugging support. The PDG is a low-level
representation of a program where operator nodes may be
viewed as processes and edges represent communication. This
level is appropriate for a data flow machine, but not for
other multiprocessor architectures. Clustering is the
process of grouping operators (of differing execution costs)
together in such a way that the intercluster communication
costs are minimized and the resulting clusters can be
optimally scheduled onto the available processors without
excessive process creation costs. (Clustering is clearly
NP-complete, so we must rely on heuristics.) As soon as a
cluster becomes larger than a basic block (i.e., some
control structure becomes part of the cluster) or includes a
procedure call, the static paths of the dependence graph no

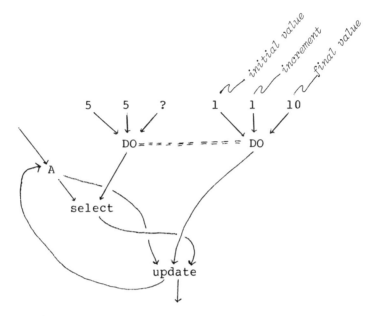

(a) Initial PDG Data Dependence Subgraph

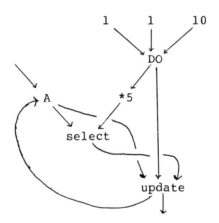

(b) Revised Indexing Streams

Figure 3 - Induction Variable Substitution

longer provide enough information to determine cluster execution costs. Dynamic properties must be known, with better results achievable with better estimates.

Clustering is a bottom up view of program "parallelization". A top down view would be of partitioning the graph or high-level language program. Low-level information is required for most of the transformations mentioned earlier, yet the high-level organization of a program could well guide the clustering process. Heuristics for parallelization might thus involve a combination of clustering and partitioning.

An additional constraint when clustering for the HEP is the limit on the maximum number of processes that can be active at one time. Berman and Snyder [14] note the mapping problem of running a parallel algorithm with a certain number of processes on a machine with fewer processors. One possibility with the HEP is to not consider the fixed limit on processes while clustering, but instead to view a HEP process as a virtual processor onto which proclets are mapped. The HEP handles so many scheduling functions in hardware that the only way to do controlled scheduling may be with the "self-scheduling" concept of Jordan [32] or the "ask for" concept of Lusk and Overbeek (elsewhere in this book). Viewing a HEP process as a virtual processor, the idea here is for a free "processor" to request another job from some pool of tasks.

Compile-time debugging support is an issue addressed by Taylor and Osterweil [59,60] who describe how data flow analysis can assist in detecting program synchronization anamolies. Little seems to have been done with run-time debugging support. Given the major restructuring done by a "parallelizing" compiler, how is a program fault (e.g., divide by zero) detected in some particular process linked back to a location in the source code for presentation to the user? Techniques for debugging optimized sequential code may be of help. Hennessy [28] discusses the issues in that area. Zellweger [64] presents some techniques useful for certain control flow transformations that might be extended into a parallel context.

3.1.5. Programming Environment

Allen and Kennedy [6,7] are examining the problem of building an interactive programming environment [29] for developing parallel programs. Their experience with vectorization showed that there were many times when loops were vectorizable, but their compiler did not have enough information available to vectorize the loops safely. While some researchers are considering the use of assertion statements to aid transformation, this work at Rice suggests

116

that the compiler should interact appropriately with the user to aid transformation. Their specific focus is on loop transformations such as Padua's with a target machine similar to the NYU Ultracomputer. One of the novel ideas about the project is the retention of interprocedural data flow information to assist transformation.

Others have suggested interactive optimizing compilers in the past, but few have been developed. It seems clear that the complexity of parallelization is such that user interaction during the transformation process is essential. An integrated software development environment as suggested by Allen and Kennedy is a good way of providing that interaction with a consistent user interface for development, testing and debugging.

REFERENCES

1. Aho, A. V. and J. D. Ullman, Principles Of Compiler Design, Addison-Wesley Publishing Company, 1977.

2. Allen, F. E. and J. Cocke, A Catalogue of Optimizing Transformations, in Design and Optimization of Compilers, R. Rustin (editor), Prentice-Hall, 1971, 1-30.

3. Allen, J. R. and K. Kennedy, PFC: A Program to Convert FORTRAN to Parallel Form, MASC Tech. Rep. 82-6, Dept. of Math. Sciences, Rice Univ., March 1, 1982.

4. Allen, J. R., K. Kennedy, C. Porterfield and J. Warren, Conversion of Control Dependence to Data Dependence, in Conf. Rec. Tenth ACM Symp. on Princ. of Prog. Lang., Austin, Texas, Jan. 24-26, 1983, 177-189.

5. Allen, J. R., Dependence Analysis for Subscripted Variables and its Application to Program Transformations, Ph.D Thesis, Rice University, Houston, April 1983.

6. Allen, J. R. and K. Kennedy, A Parallel Programming Environment, CS Tech. Rep. #3, Computer Science Department, Rice University, August 1984.

7. Allen, J. R. and K. Kennedy, Interactive Transformation of Programs for Execution on Parallel Machines, Presentation at the Workshop on Operating Systems and Environments for Parallel Processing, Los Alamos, August 7-9, 1984.

8. Arnold, C. N., Performance Evaluation of Three Automatic Vectorizer Packages, in *Proc. 1982 Int. Conf. on Parallel Processing*, Bellaire, Mich., August 1982, 235-242.

9. Arvind, K. P. Gostelow and W. Plouffe, The (Preliminary) ID Report: An Asynchronous Programming Language And Computing Machine, Tech. Rep.-114, Department of Information and Computer Sciences, University of California, Irvine, May 10, 1978.

10. Arvind, Decomposing A Program for Multiple Processor Systems., MIT LCS Comput. Struc. Group Note 42, October 1979.

11. Babb, II, R. G., Parallel Processing with Large-Grain Data Flow Techniques, *IEEE Computer 17*,7 (July 1984), 55-61.

12. Baer, J. L., A Survey of Some Theoretical Aspects of Multiprocessing, *ACM Computing Surveys 5*,1 (March 1973), 31-80.

13. Banerjee, U., S. Chen, D. J. Kuck and R. A. Towle, Time and Parallel Processor Bounds for Fortran-like Loops, *IEEE Trans. Computers C-28*,9 (Sept. 1979), 660-670.

14. Berman, F. and L. Snyder, On Mapping Parallel Algorithms into Parallel Architectures, in *Proc. 1984 Int'l Conf. on Parallel Proc.*, R. M. Keller (editor), IEEE-CS/ACM, Bellaire, Michigan, August 21-24, 1984, 207-309.

15. Bernstein, A. J., Analysis of Programs for Parallel Processing, *IEEE Trans. Elec. Computers EC-15*,5 (Oct. 1966), 757-763.

16. Chang, T. L. and P. D. Fisher, A Block-driven Data-flow Processor, in *Proc. of the 1981 ICPP*, M. Liu and J. Rothstein (editor), Bellaire, Mich., Aug. 25-28, 1981, 151-155.

17. Chow, F. C. and M. Ganapathi, Intermediate Languages in Compiler Construction - A Bibliography, *ACM SIGPLAN Notices 18*,11 (November 1983), 21-23.

18. Dennis, J. B., First Version of a Data Flow Procedure Language, MAC Technical Memo 61, Laboratory for Computer Sciences, M.I.T., May 1975. Revised Computations Structures Group Memo 93.

19. Dennis, J. B., Data Flow Supercomputers, IEEE Computer 13,11 (Nov. 1980), 48-56.

20. Ferrante, J. and K. J. Ottenstein, A Program Form Based on Data Dependency in Predicate Regions, in Conf. Record of the Tenth Ann. ACM Symp. on Prin. of Programming Languages, Austin, Texas, January 24-26, 1983, 217-236.

21. Ferrante, J., The Program Dependence Graph as a Basis for Node Splitting Transformations, IBM Research Report RC10542, June 7, 1984.

22. Ferrante, J., K. J. Ottenstein and J. D. Warren, The Program Dependence Graph and its Use in Optimization., IBM Research Report RC 10543, May 1984.

23. Ferrante, J., K. J. Ottenstein and J. D. Warren, The Program Dependence Graph and its Use in Optimization [Extended Abstract], in Proc. 6th Int. Conf. on Programming, Toulouse, France, April 17-19, 1984, 125-132. Published as volume 167 of Lecture Notes in Computer Science.

24. Fisher, J. A., Very Long Instruction Word Architectures and the ELI-512, Dept. of Computer Science Report 253, Yale Univ., Dec. 1982.

25. Fisher, J. A., The VLIW Machine: A Multiprocessor for Compiling Scientific Code, IEEE Computer 17,7 (July 1984), 45-54.

26. Gajski, D. D., D. A. Padua, D. J. Kuck and R. H. Kuhn, A Second Opinion on Data Flow Machines and Languages, IEEE Computer 15,2 (Feb. 1982), 58-69.

27. Gottlieb, A., R. Grishman, C. P. Kruskal, K. P. McAuliffe, L. Rudolph and M. Snir, The NYU Ultracomputer - Designing an MIMD Shared Memory Parallel Computer, IEEE Trans. Computers C-32,2 (Feb. 1983), 175-189.

28. Hennessy, J., Program Optimization and Exception Handling, in Conf. Record of the 8th Ann. ACM Symp. on Prin. of Programming Languages, Williamsburg, VA, Jan. 26-28, 1981, 200-206.

29. Howden, W. E., Contemporary Software Development Environments, Comm. ACM 25,5 (May 1982), 318-329.

30. Hwang, K. and F. A. Briggs, _Computer Architecture and Parallel Processing_, McGraw-Hill, 1984.

31. Jones, A. K. and P. Schwarz, Experience Using Multiprocessor Systems - A Status Report, _ACM Comp. Surveys_ 12,2 (June 1980), 121-166.

32. Jordan, H. F., Parallel Programming on the HEP Multiple Instruction Stream Computer, August 20, 1981.

33. Kennedy, K., Automatic Translation of Fortran Programs to Vector Form, Tech. Rep. 476-029-7, Rice Univ. Dept. Of Mathematical Sciences, October 1980.

34. Kennedy, K., Personal communication, September 1981.

35. Kuck, D. J., Y. Muraoka and S. Chen, On the Number of Operations Simultaneously Executable in Fortran-like Programs and their Resulting Speedup, _IEEE Trans. Computers_ C-21,12 (Dec. 1972), 1293-1310.

36. Kuck, D. J., P. P. Budnik, S. Chen, D. H. Lawrie, R. A. Towle, R. E. Strebendt, E. W. Davis, J. Han, P. W. Kraska and Y. Muraoka, Measurements of Parallelism in Ordinary FORTRAN Programs, _IEEE Computer_ 7,1 (Jan. 1974), 37-46.

37. Kuck, D. J., Parallel Processing of Ordinary Programs, in _Advances in Computers_, vol. 15 , M. Rubinoff and M. C. Yovits (editor), Academic Press, 1976, 119-179.

38. Kuck, D. J., A Survey of Parallel Machine Organization and Programming, _ACM Comp. Surveys_ 9,1 (Mar 1977), 29-60..

39. Kuck, D. J., _The Structure of Computers and Computations_, Wiley, 1978.

40. Kuck, D. J., R. H. Kuhn, B. Leasure and M. Wolfe, The Structure of an Advanced Vectorizer for Pipelined Processors, _Proc. IEEE 4th Int. COMPSAC_, Chicago, 1980, 709-715.

41. Kuck, D. J., R. H. Kuhn, D. A. Padua, B. Leasure and M. Wolfe, Dependence Graphs and Compiler Optimizations, in _Conf. Record of the 8th Ann. ACM Symp. on Prin. of Programming Languages_, Williamsburg, VA, Jan. 26-28, 1981, 207-218.

42. Lamport, L., The Parallel Execution of DO Loops, _Comm. ACM_ 17,2 (Feb. 1974), 83-93.

43. Lamport, L., On Programming Parallel Computers, in _Proc. of a Conf. on Prog. Lang. and Compilers for Parallel and Vector Machines_, New York, March 18-19, 1975. Published as ACM SIGPLAN Notices 10, 3 (March 1975) 25-33.

44. Logan, D., C. Maples, D. Weaver and W. Rathbun, Adapting Scientific Programs to the _MIDAS_ Multiprocessor System, in _Proc. 1984 Int'l Conf. on Parallel Proc._, R. M. Keller (editor), IEEE-CS/ACM, Bellaire, Michigan, August 21-24, 1984, 15-24.

45. Mace, M. E. and R. A. Wagner, Globally Optimum Selection of Memory Storage Patterns, IBM Research Report RC 10676, August 10, 1984.

46. Oleinick, P. N., _Parallel Algorithms on a Multiprocessor_, UMI Research Press, 1982. 110 pages [47 pages text]. This is a revision of the author's 1979 CMU Ph.D. thesis.

47. Olson, R., Parallel Processing in a Message-Based Operating System, Presentation at the Workshop on Operating Systems and Environments for Parallel Processing, Los Alamos, August 7-9, 1984.

48. Ottenstein, K. J., _Data-Flow Graphs as an Intermediate Program Form_, Ph.D. Thesis, Purdue University, August 1978.

49. Ottenstein, K. J., An Intermediate Program Form Based on a Cyclic Data-Dependency Graph, CS-Tech. Rep. 81-1, Math and Computer Sciences, Mich. Tech. Univ., October 1981. Under revision.

50. Ottenstein, K. J. and L. M. Ottenstein, The Program Dependence Graph in a Software Development Environment, in _Proc. ACM SIGPLAN/SIGSOFT Symp. on Practical Soft. Dev. Environments_, Pittsburgh, April 23-25, 1984, 177-184. Published as ACM SIGPLAN Notices 19, 5 (May 1984) and ACM Software Engineering Notes 9, 3 (May 1984).

51. Ottenstein, K. J., Intermediate Program Representations in Compiler Construction: A Supplemental Bibliography, _ACM SIGPLAN Notices 19_,6 (June 1984), 25-27.

52. Padua, D. A., D. J. Kuck and D. H. Lawrie, High-Speed Multiprocessors and Compilation Techniques, _IEEE Trans. Computers TC-29_,9 (Sept 1980), 763-776.

53. Padua Haiek, D. A., _Multiprocessors: Discussion of Some Theoretical and Practical Problems_, Ph.D Thesis, Univ. of Illinois, Urbana-Champaign, 1980.

54. Pressberg, D. L. and N. W. Johnson, The Paralyzer: IVTRAN's Parallelism Analyzer and Synthesizer, in _Proc. of a Conf. on Prog. Lang. and Compilers for Parallel and Vector Machines_, New York, March 18-19, 1975, 9-16. Published as ACM SIGPLAN Notices 10, 3 (March 1975) 25-33.

55. Ramamoorthy, C. V. and M. J. Gonzalez, A Survey of Techniques for Recognizing Parallel Processable Streams In Computer Programs, in _Proc. AFIPS Fall Joint Comp. Conf._, vol. 35 , Las Vegas, Nov. 18-20, 1969, 1-15.

56. Ray, W., Cyberplus: A Multiparallel Operating System, Presentation at the Workshop on Operating Systems and Environments for Parallel Processing, Los Alamos, August 7-9, 1984.

57. Requa, J. E. and J. R. McGraw, The Piecewise Data Flow Architecture: Architectural Concepts, _IEEE Trans. Computers_ C-32,5 (May 1983), 425-438.

58. Snyder, L., Introduction to the configurable, highly parallel computer, Purdue University Computer Science Dept. Tech. Rep.-351, May 1981.

59. Taylor, R. N. and L. J. Osterweil, Anomaly Detection in Concurrent Software by Static Data Flow Analysis, _IEEE Trans. Soft. Eng._ SE-6,3 (May 1980), 265-278.

60. Taylor, R. N., A General-Purpose Algorithm for Analyzing Concurrent Programs, _Comm. ACM_ 26,5 (May 1983), 362-376.

61. Towle, R. A., _Control and Data Dependence for Program Transformations_, Ph.D. Thesis, Univ. Of Ill., 1976.

62. Warren, J. D., A Hierarchical Basis for Reordering Transformations, in _Conf. Rec. 11th ACM Symp. Princ. Prog. Lang._, Salt Lake City, Utah, January 1984.

63. Wolfe, M. J., _Optimizing Supercompilers for Supercomputers_, Ph.D. Thesis, Dept. of Computer Science, Univ. of Illinois, Urbana-Champaign, October 1982.

64. Zellweger, P. T., An Interactive High-Level Debugger for Control-Flow Optimized Programs, in _Proc. ACM SIGSOFT/SIGPLAN Soft. Eng. Symp. on High-Level Debugging_, M. S. Johnson (editor), Pacific Grove, Calif., March 20-23, 1983, 159-171. Published as ACM SIGPLAN Notices 18, 8 (August 1983) and ACM Software Eng. Notes 8, 4 (August 1983).

3.2. HEP SISAL: PARALLEL FUNCTIONAL PROGRAMMING†

STEPHEN J. ALLAN and R. R. OLDEHOEFT
Colorado State University
Fort Collins, Colorado

SISAL (Streams and Iteration in a Single-Assignment Language) [McGraw, 1984] is a language designed to express algorithms for execution on machines capable of highly concurrent operation. The principal application area for use of SISAL is numeric computation that strains the limits of current high performance machines.

SISAL, a functional programming language, joins similar languages that display the following characteristics: (1) freedom from side effects, (2) locality of effect, (3) parallelism constrained only by data dependencies, and (4) a single assignment convention [Ackerman, 1982]. These characteristics allow the compiler to easily detect and exploit the parallelism of the underlying architecture and in the program.

Four groups associated with different organizations and with different target architectures cooperated to define SISAL. The organizations (and architectures) are: Lawrence Livermore National Laboratory (Cray vector processors), Digital Equipment Corporation (clusters of VAX processors), the University of Manchester (Manchester data flow machine), and Colorado State University (Denelcor HEP multiprocessor). In addition, investigators have begun preliminary considerations for a distributed version [Sielker, 1984] of SISAL. SISAL owes a great debt to VAL [Ackerman, 1979; McGraw, 1982] and retains its

† This research is supported by ARO Contract DAAG29-82-K-0108.

functional, single assignment character. Yet there are several significant differences from VAL: simplified error types, general recursion, stream data type, and modified iteration forms.

Issues dealing with the implementation of components of the HEP SISAL run time support system such as the stream data type, array handling, process management, and dynamic storage allocation, are discussed in the next chapter.

3.2.1. Overview of Chapter

This chapter presents the major features of the functional programming language SISAL. Sample programs and program segments are included to illustrate the features and the use of the language.

Section 3.2.2 describes several design decisions concerning the language design and some rationale behind those decisions. Section 3.2.3 gives an overview of the language with emphasis on those features that are new and/or unusual. Section 3.2.4 shows two complete SISAL programs and describes them. Section 3.2.5 gives a brief overview of the implementation of the compiler and useful optimizations. Finally, section 3.2.6 discusses possible future directions of the language.

3.2.2. DESIGN PRINCIPLES

SISAL was designed with several goals in mind. Four of these goals are listed below.

1. Promote a wide use of the language in parallel processing research centers.
2. Allow the study of architectural trade-offs inherent in machine design.
3. Provide a vehicle for the developing and the sharing of a pool of benchmark programs.
4. Allow the study of the benefits or lack thereof of a functional programming style.

SISAL is expected to evolve into a general purpose language appropriate for writing programs to run on future parallel computers. In the past, programming languages have reflected a particular architecture on which the language was to run (i.e., FORTRAN, VAL [Ackerman, 1979]). SISAL does not have idiosyncrasies reflecting the particular nature of the application area or target machine. The variety of machines on which SISAL is being implemented tests this premise.

SISAL offers several advantages for use on a multiprocessor system. First, the user need not (and cannot) manage or detect the parallelism in the program. The compiler detects the parallelism in the program (also decides on the amount of parallelism to exploit) and generates calls to run time software that takes advantage of the parallelism and manages it. This allows the user to concern himself only with the expression of the algorithm and not with the expression of parallelism or the implementation of it.

Working in a parallel environment should not increase the time and effort required to arrive at a working program. We know from experience that working with imperative languages such as HEP FORTRAN increases the time and effort needed for program development. An imperative language is one that achieves its primary effect by changing the state of variables by assignment. The user must explicitly manage the parallelism and synchronization, a time consuming and error prone activity. SISAL allows the programmer to ignore these matters.

3.2.2.1. Implicit Concurrency

With the advent of parallel processors, the search of a way control the parallelism of the underlying architecture began. Three different approaches were employed. The first was to design compilers for existing programming languages that extract the parallelism from the program (e.g., vectorizing compilers for FORTRAN); this has been successful [Kuck, 1980]. Yet, imperative programming languages restrict the expression of the algorithm so the inherent parallelism may be hidden.

The second approach was to extend existing programming languages and add features that allow the user to exploit the parallelism in the underlying architecture. These language extensions reflect the underlying architecture, do not reflect the way a programmer thinks, and force the programmer to manage the parallelism.

The third approach was to design a new language that facilitates the use of parallel architectures. These languages give parallel constructs but still require explicit parallelism management.

SISAL programmers concern themselves with expression algorithms, not with exploiting underlying parallel processing activities. The compiler is able to detect the parallelism because the language excludes features that inhibit the detection of parallelism (e.g., aliasing, side effects). However, SISAL does not constrain the user to the point where he is not able to express the algorithm in a convenient manner.

3.2.2.2. Aids for System Design

The syntax of the language is similar to imperative languages such as Pascal. Some functional programming languages have a syntax that is awkward and difficult to read (e.g., LISP, fp [Backus, 1978]). A Pascal-like syntax was chosen since it decreases the amount of time it takes to learn the language and aids in the readability of the program once it is written.

Debugging in a parallel environment is a difficult problem. Tools need to be available to ease the burden on the user. Since the system has complete knoledge of the parallelism, the debugging process will be easier and less time consuming in the SISAL environment.

3.2.3. LANGUAGE FEATURES

This section surveys the major features of SISAL focusing on those features that are interesting and/or unusual. The principle areas of interest in SISAL are data types, values, basic expressions, parallel expressions, sequential expressions, type checking, and error handling. These are discussed in the following subsections.

3.2.3.1. Data Types

The scalar data types included in SISAL are: **integer, real, boolean,** and **character.** Examples of the basic operations on scalar data types are shown below.

$$+, *, =, <, \&$$

The structured data types in SISAL are: **array, stream, record,** and **union** (discriminated union). These are similar to the structured data types in other languages with the exceptions explained below.

Arrays in SISAL differ from languages such as Pascal because the bounds of the array are not part of the type declaration. Array bounds are only known when the array is created; indices are always integers. A declaration appears as shown below.

type Info = **array** [**integer**]

This declares a type Info that is an array with elements of type integer. Note that arrays bounds are not part of the declaration. Multidimensional arrays are constructed as an array of arrays. An example of an array construction using the above declaration follows.

array Info [-1:2; 1:100; 0:150]

This expression creates an array of type Info with a lower bound of -1 and an upper bound of 1. The values of the elements of the array, starting from index -1, are 2, 150, and 100. An array is subscripted in the same manner as in Pascal. Array creation, as shown above, allows concurrency because each expression giving values to the array may be complicated expressions including function references; all may be evaluated in parallel.

Figure 3.2-A shows the standard operations on arrays.

array_fill	Create array initialized
array_limh, array_liml	High/low index
array_size	Number of elements
array_adjust	Shift origin
array_addh, array_addl	Extend upper/lower bound
array_remh, array_reml	Delete element at upper/lower bound
array_setl	Set lower bound
‖	Concatenate

Figure 3.2-A. Array Operations

The above operations are all functions except concatenate which is a binary operation. Notice that these operations show the dynamic nature of arrays.

Streams are a data type not present in most existing programming languages. Streams are similar to arrays and to sequential files. A stream is similar to an array and a file because a group of data is collected to form a single object, known by a single name and each element is of the same type. It is similar to a sequential file because access to elements in the data structure is sequential, i.e., the ith element of the structure can only be accessed after the first i-1 elements have been accessed. There is no possibility of random access to an element in a stream as there is in an array. A stream declaration is shown below.

type Si = **stream** [**character**]

The type Si is a stream and each element of the stream is a character. A stream may be initially constructed as follows.

stream Si ['d', 'b', 'p', 'a']

This creates a stream of type Si with the elements 'd', 'b', 'p', and 'a'. The element 'p' cannot be accessed until elements 'd' and 'b' are accessed.

Figure 3.2-B shows the standard operations on streams.

stream_append	Add element at end
stream_first	Select first element
stream_rest	Select all but first element
stream_empty	Test for empty
stream_size	Number of elements
‖	Concatenate

Figure 3.2-B. Stream Operations

The operations are all function invocations except concatenate which is a binary operation.

Streams allow a new level of concurrency. Streams allow pipelined operation: as soon as the first element of the stream is produced it is available to consumers of the stream. The consumer may have to wait for successive elements of the stream in order to continue. In contrast, arrays must be completely constructed before any consumer can operate on it.

Records in SISAL are much like the record data type in Pascal. The declaration specifies the name and type of each field. Records are accessed as in Pascal, using the dot notation. Consider the following record declaration.

type Interval = **record** [X_low, X_high : **real**]

This declaration defines a type Interval to be a record with two fields, each of type real. A record expression is generated in a manner similar to arrays and streams. The expression

record Interval [X_low : 2.5; X_high : 3.5]

generates a record of type Interval with the fields X_low and X_high having the value 2.5 and 3.5 respectively. The opportunity to exploit concurrency in the generation of record expressions exists since the values of all fields may be computed simultaneously.

The standard record operation, replace, replaces fields with new values. This operation shows concurrency because several fields can be changed at the same time and each change is independent of the others.

The union data type permits discriminated union types as in CLU [Liskov, 1978]. A discriminated union allows a piece of data to have different types of values during the execution of the program. The union declaration

type Result = **union** [none : **null**; more : Interval]

declares Result as a union type that can have two different types during the execution of the program, the **null** type and the type Interval. A **null** data type only occurs in a distinguished union type when in one or more alternatives no data value is required. Each field in the **union** is referred to by a tag name, "none" and "more". At any given point in time an identifier has a tag associated with it and a value of the proper type.

The expression

U := **union** Result [none]

creates a value of type union with a tag of none and assigns it to the identifier U (of type Result). Since the type of the tag "none" is **null**, no data value is required.

The only standard operation for the union data type is a test for the tag of a value. Assume U is defined as shown above. The test "**is** none(U)" returns true while the test "**is** more(U)" returns false.

The union data type can be used to simulate the enumerated data type as defined in Pascal. The tag names are defined and are given the type **null** because only the tags are important in this case. The **is** test can be used to find the tag at a given time as seen above. An example of an enumerated type declaration is

type Enum = **union** [red, green, blue : **null**]

and a tag is given as follows.

union Enum [red]

3.2.3.2. Values

SISAL is a value oriented languages versus most existing languages that are variable oriented. Variable oriented languages associate storage with an identifier. The value of these variables can be repeatedly changed because of the storage associated with the variable. In a value oriented language, all functions and expressions (e.g., **if-then-else**, **for**) return values rather than making changes in storage. These values are then used in other expressions as needed.

SISAL is a single assignment language [Ackerman, 1982; Tesler, 1968]. That is, it requires that once an identifier is bound to a value, that binding remains in force for the entire scope of access to that identifier. The identifier name may be used again in a new scope but the identifier is considered to have a different name. This prevents identifiers from being used as variables.

The single assignment rule has the biggest effect on a structured data type since a structured data type is treated as a single value. Thus operations defined on a structured data type must work on the whole structure (value) at once. When a single element of a structured data type is added, deleted, or changed, the entire structure must be "copied" according to the single assignment rule. More will be said about the impact of this rule in a later section.

3.2.3.3. Basic Expressions and Functions

All constructs (e.g., **if-then-else, for,** functions) in the language produce an expression as a result. The return expression may be a multi-expression, a list of expressions separated by commas. The arity of a multi-expression is the number of expressions in the list. In an assignment, several identifiers may be given values at the same time if the expression returns a multi-expression of the proper arity.

The most basic expression in the language is that made from basic operators, e.g., arithmetic operators. These operations can be combined to form complicated expressions and multi-expressions.

Functions are used in the language to form results and to modularize programs. These are functions in the pure mathematical sense because there are no side effects or global references inside the body of the function. Parameters are always passed by value (or with that effect). Any number of expressions may be returned by a function and these expressions may be of any data type (e.g., array, record). The body of a function is an expression (or multi-expression) of the correct arity. Unlike VAL, SISAL allows recursion as a computational tool.

Figure 3.2-C shows a function header.

function Split (Data : Info **returns** Info, Info, Info)

Figure 3.2-C. Function Header

This header defines a function named Split that has one input parameter (Data) of type Info and returns a multi-expression of arity three, each expression of type Info. Figure 3.2-D shows the result of a function invocation assigning three values returned from the function Split.

L, Middle, R := Split(Data)

Figure 3.2-D. Multi-expression Assignment

In this example the results of Split are assigned to the identifiers L, Middle, and R respectively and each identifier has the type Info.

Let-in expressions are used to introduce a new scope and introduce new identifiers. This is similar to a block in PL/I or Algol. The **let-in** expression allows the user to define new identifiers, give them values, and evaluate an expression within their scope. The **let-in** expression consists of a declaration part and a return part. The declaration part appears after **let** and is used to introduce new identifiers. The return part follows **in** and is an expression.

Figure 3.2-E shows an example of a **let-in** expression.

```
let
    L, Middle, R := Split( Data )
in
    Quicksort( L ) || Middle || Quicksort( R )
end let
```

Figure 3.2-E. **Let-in** Expression

Three new identifiers L, Middle, and R of type Info are created in the declaration part. No explicit declaration of the types of these identifier is given because the type can be deduced from the types of expressions returned from the function Split. The expression returned from the **let-in** is the expression following **in**. The value retuned above is of type Info.

Function invocations and **let-in** expressions introduce new scopes. This gives the programmer the opportunity to define new identifiers (or reuse identifier names previously used) and assign new values to the identifiers. The scope of each identifier introduced in a **let** block is the entire block less any inner constructs that reintroduce the same identifier. However, an identifier must not be referenced before its own definition.

All scopes for identifiers not introduced in a given **let** block pass into that block. Hence, if the scope of an identifier (introduced by an outer construct) includes a **let** block and that identifier is not reintroduced, it may be referred to freely within the block. When a scope is exited, these identifiers and their values become inaccessible. The scoping rules are much like Pascal with the exception that in looking for the definition of an identifier the search stops on a function boundary. Nothing from the environment outside the function may be imported into the current environment except through the use of parameters.

135

3.2.3.4. Parallel Expressions

The **for** expression allows the user to express a computation that can be done in parallel if the SISAL system wishes. This implies there are no data dependencies among the iterations in the loop. A **for** consists of a loop controlling expression, a body, and a result expression.

The expression controlling the loop has one of three forms: execute the body of the loop for (1) each element of an array, (2) each element of a stream, or (3) each integer in a range. The loop controlling expression also allows multiple indices. There are two forms for multiple indices, (1) **dot** or (2) **cross**. **Dot** produces an inner, or dot, product range of index expressions. For example,

$$\text{I \textbf{in} 1,10 \textbf{dot} J \textbf{in} 11,20}$$

defines the set of ten index pairs [1,11], [2,12], [3,13], etc. The index range formed by **cross** is the Cartesian, or outer, product of the index expressions. For example

$$\text{I \textbf{in} 1,10 \textbf{cross} J \textbf{in} 11,20}$$

defines an index range consisting of the tuples [i,j], where $1 \leq i \leq 10$ and $11 \leq j \leq 20$.

The optional body of the **for** expression calculates any temporary values used in the return expression.

The return expression returns any number of the following values: scalar values (**value of**), array values (**array of**), and stream values (**stream of**). Scalar values can also use reduction operators (e.g., **sum**) that are performed on the collection of values in a sequence. The associativity order of the reduction operator may be specified by using **left, right**, and **tree**.

Figure 3.2-F shows an example of a **for** expression.

```
for E in Data
returns
  array of E when E < Data[1]
  array of E when E = Data[1]
  array of E when E > Data[1]
end for
```

Figure 3.2-F. **For** Expression

The loop controlling expression is "E **in** Data". The type of Data is Info (array of integers). The loop is executed once for every element in the array Data and E takes on the value of each of those elements. The body of the **for** expression is empty. The result expression is everything following **returns**. The expression returned in this example is a multi-expression of arity three, each an array of integers (type Info). The **when** clause indicates that a value is appended to the array when the boolean expression following the **when** is true. This boolean may be negated by using **unless** instead of **when.**

As an example of the use of a reduction operator consider the code segment Figure 3.2-G.

```
for S in InStream
returns
  value of sum S
end for
```

Figure 3.2-G. Reduction Operator

InStream is a stream of integers. The expression controlling the loop is "S **in** InStream" and the identifier S takes on the value of each element in InStream. The body of the loop is empty. The result expression is a single scalar value that is the sum of each element in the stream.

3.2.3.5. Sequencing Expressions

There are several sequential expressions available in SISAL. These include **if-then-else, for initial,** and **tagcase.**

The **if-then-else** expression is similar to an if-then-else statement in Pascal. The boolean expression is tested, and depending on the result of the test, either the **then** or the **else** part of the expression is evaluated. Both branches of the **if-then-else** must return expressions of the same type and arity. Consider the example in Figure 3.2-H.

$$
\begin{aligned}
S := \ &\textbf{if } T < \text{Maxt} \\
&\quad \textbf{then } \text{Filter(stream\_rest(\textbf{old} S), T)} \\
&\quad \textbf{else } \text{stream\_rest(\textbf{old} S)} \\
&\quad \textbf{end if}
\end{aligned}
$$

Figure 3.2-H. **If-then-else** Expression

The **if-then-else** expression executes the **then** branch or the **else** branch depending on the result of the boolean expression (T < Maxt). Each branch returns an expression type stream (assuming Filter and stream_rest are functions that return a stream expression). The resulting stream is assigned as the value of S, that is of type stream.

The **for initial** expression is for sequential iteration. The **for initial** expression consists of a declarations and initialization part, loop termination test, body of the loop, and resulting expression.

New identifiers are introduced and initialized in the declaration and initialization part of the loop. These are the only identifiers used in successive iterations and **old** (to be explained later) only applies to these identifiers.

138

The loop is terminated with a pre- or post-testing condition. The condition is pre-tested if the test is placed before the body of the loop and post-tested if the test is placed after the body of the loop. The termination test can use positive logic (**while**) or negative logic (**until**).

The **for initial** loop is a sequential loop and so one must access values of identifiers defined in previous iterations. This is done using the reserved word **old**. "**old** identifier" indicates that the previous value of identifier is wanted rather than the value assigned on the current iteration of the loop. If values are needed from earlier iterations a sequence of **old**s is used.

The result expression returns the same types of values as described in the **for** expression (scalars, arrays, streams).

Consider the example segment shown in Figure 3.2-I.

```
for initial
  I := 3
while I < Limit
repeat
  I := old I + 2
returns
  stream of I
end for
```

Figure 3.2-I. **For-initial** Expression

The declaration part of this iterative loop declares the identifier I and initializes it to 3. The loop termination condition is "**while** I < Limit". The loop continues to iterate as long as the value of I is less than the value of Limit. The position of this test shows that it is a pre-testing condition. If a post-testing condition is wanted, the termination condition is placed just before the **returns**. If

until is used instead of **while** the condition for loop termination is the loop iterates as long as the condition is false. The body of the loop is the expression between **repeat** and **returns** (or a termination clause). The result expression appears after **returns**. This loop generates a stream of odd integers starting with 3 and terminating with Limit (if Limit is odd). The value of I from the previous iteration is accessed using **old**.

The **tagcase** expression permits access to information bound to an identifier whose type is **union**. This expression looks much like a case statement in Pascal. The **tagcase** consists of an expression and a body. The expression contains the identifier on which the **tagcase** is executed. The tag of the identifier is tested and the appropriate branch in the body is executed. The body contains cases for tags with expressions returned and a default condition (**otherwise**) that is executed if the tag is not specified in the body. Each case in the body of the **tagcase** must return an expression of the same type and same arity.

Figure 3.2-J shows how an enumerated type might be tested. The declarations are as shown in section 3.2.3.1.

```
tagcase U
  tag red: 3
  tag green: 4
  otherwise: 5
end tagcase
```

Figure 3.2-J. **Tagcase** Expression

U is of type Enum. Depending on the tag of U the value 3, 4, or 5 is returned as the result expression of the **tagcase**. The **otherwise** is used when the tag of U is neither red nor green. The type of each expression is the same, integer.

140

3.2.3.6. Type Checking

Type checking is performed in the SISAL translator by testing that the type of each expression or subexpression matches the type required by the context in which it appears. The type of the operation is easily determined from the operators and elementary terms.

The rules for conformance of two types are as follows. Two basic type specifications conform if they are identical. Two type specifications conform if they are the same type. Two array or two stream specifications conform if their base types conform. Two record or two union type specifications conform if their correspondingly named component types or constituent types conform; the order in which they are listed must be the same. A defined type name conforms to the type specification appearing on the right hand side of its definition.

3.2.3.7. Error Handling

Exceptions are handled in SISAL through special error elements in each data type. The element **undef** indicates that some form of arithmetic error prevented the desired execution flow. Arithmetic errors that could produce this value include: overflow, underflow, divide by zero, array subscript out of bounds, etc. The error element **broken** indicates that some form of control flow error prevented the generation of the desired results. Control flow errors include: conditional expressions whose boolean expression produces an error value, iterations whose termination boolean expression produces an error value, etc.

Figure 3.2-K shows the test for errors.

is undef	Test for **under**
is broken	Test for **broken**
is error	Test for all errors

Figure 3.2-K. Error Tests

The user cannot define his own error values.

3.2.4. EXAMPLES IN SISAL

This section shows two sample programs written in SISAL, a quicksort function and a function to generate prime numbers. Following each program is a discussion of the program.

3.2.4.1. Quicksort

% In QUICKSORT, one takes the first item, Data[1], in the array Data
% and uses it to divide the rest of the list into sublists L (left)
% and R (right) such that all items in L are less than Data[1] and
% all items in R are greater than Data[1]. All items equal to Data[1]
% are put into Middle. Finally all sublists have only one
% item and are ordered. The sublists are ordered by concatenating
% the sublists to obtain a sorted list.

type Info = **array** [**integer**]

function Quicksort (Data : Info **returns** Info)

  function Split (Data : Info **returns** Info, Info, Info)

    for E **in** Data
    returns
      array of E **when** E < Data[1]
      array of E **when** E = Data[1]
      array of E **when** E > Data[1]
    end for

  end function % Split

  % Quicksort body

  if array_size(Data) < 2
  then
    Data
  else
    let
      L, Middle, R := Split(Data)
    in
      Quicksort(L) || Middle || Quicksort(R)
    end let
  end if

end function % Quicksort

3.2.4.2. Discussion of Quicksort

The Quicksort function takes an input parameter of type Info, array of integers, and returns an expression of type Info of the same length with the values sorted in ascending order. The result of the Quicksort function is the expression returned from the **if-then-else** expression in the body of the function.

Quicksort first checks if the size of Data is less than two, if it is, Data is already sorted (there is only one element) and Data is returned as the value of the function. If the size of Data is greater than or equal to two, the array is split into three arrays by the Split function (explained later). The three arrays returned by Split are sorted by recursive calls to Quicksort, concatenated together to form a single array, and returned as the value of the Quicksort function.

The function Split takes an input array and returns three arrays. On every iteration through the loop (the body of Split), a value is placed into one of the three arrays. At the termination of the loop, the three arrays are returned as the result of the function (some may be empty). The first of these arrays contains those values in the Data array that are less than the first value of the Data array. The second array contains those values that are equal to the first value of the Data array and the third array contains those values that are greater than the first value of the Data array.

3.2.4.3. Sieve of Eratosthenes

% Generate all prime integers up to a limiting value
% using the Sieve of Eratosthenes.
type Si = **stream** [**integer**]
global Sqrt (Q : **real returns real**)

function Sieve (Limit : **integer returns** Si)

  function Integers (Limit : **integer returns** Si)
  % Produce a stream of 3, 5, 7, 9, ..., Limit
    for initial
     I := 3
    while I < Limit
    repeat
     I := **old** I + 2
    returns stream of I
    end for
  end function % Integers

  function Filter (S : Si; M : **integer returns** Si)
  % Produce a stream of values obtained from the argument stream,
  % excepting those values that are a multiple of M.
    for I **in** S
    returns stream of I **unless** mod(I,M) = 0
    end for
  end function % Filter

% Generate a stream of primes inserting a filter on the stream
% against each prime produced, up to the square root of the last
% value to be considered.
  let
    Maxt : **integer**(Sqrt(**real**(Limit)))
  in
    for initial
     S := Integers(Limit);
     T := 2;
    while not stream_empty(S)
    repeat
     T := stream_first(**old** S);
     S := **if** T < Maxt
       then Filter(stream_rest(**old** S), T)
       else stream_rest(**old** S)
       end if
    returns stream of T
    end for
  end let
end function % Sieve

3.2.4.4. Discussion of Sieve of Eratosthenes

The purpose of the Sieve function is to take an input value (Limit) and generate all prime integers (including 2) up to Limit. The result expression is the expression returned from the **let-in** expression in the body of Sieve. The algorithm used creates a stream of possible prime numbers and then inserts filters into the stream to eliminate multiples of prime numbers already found.

The **let-in** in the body of Sieve first calculates the limiting value above which primes need not be checked, Maxt. This value is then used in the **for initial** loop to test whether filters need to be placed on the stream. The sequential loop executes for each element of a stream of odd integers produced by the function Integers. The first element of the resulting stream is the first value that the identifier T takes on, namely 2. In the body of the loop, the next prime number is taken from the stream (the first element of the stream is always prime). This prime is checked against the threshold (Maxt). If it is less than Maxt, a call to the function Filter occurs (Filter is explained below). If the prime is greater than or equal to Maxt the new value of the stream is the old stream with the first element deleted. The prime number, T, is then placed on the stream returned from the **let-in** expression.

The function Integers generates a stream of odd integers from three up to the limiting input value (if Limit is odd). This is done by sequentially generating a sequence of odd integers and placing them on the resulting stream.

The function Filter produces a stream of values obtained from the argument stream, excepting those values that are multiples of M. M has already been found to be prime.

3.2.5. IMPLEMENTATION ON THE HEP

A current project at CSU is implementing a SISAL programming system on the HEP with the HEP/UPX† operating system. Some details may change in the methods discussed in the implementation as experience is gained. The compiler is implemented using the UNIX‡ operating system. The front-end is implemented using the tools lex [Lesk, 1975] and yacc [Johnson, 1975]. Lex is a tool for generating lexical analyzers and yacc is a tool for generating LALR(1) parsers. The implementation language of the compiler, both front-end and back-end, is C.

The SISAL language is analyzed, parsed, and an internal graph is generated. The output of the front-end of the compiler is a form of a data flow graph called IF1 [Skedzielewski, 1983]. The output is an ASCII file that is a linear representation of the internal graph. This ASCII file is used as input into the optimizer and the back-end of the compiler. The back-end recreates the internal form of the graph and generates the intermediate code for the portable C compiler [Johnson, 1978; Cann, 1984]. This intermediate code file is used as input into the second pass of the portable C compiler that does the actual code generation for the machine.

We decided not to directly generate code for the machine for two reasons. First, it simplifies the back-end. Second, it increases portability. With a few changes the code generator is able to run on any machine running UNIX and using the portable C compiler.

---

† HEP/UPX is a trademark of Denelcor, Inc.
‡ UNIX is a Trademark of AT&T Bell Laboratories.

147

There are a set of machine independent optimizations that are common to the different implementations of SISAL. These run as a separate pass between the front-end and the back-end. An IF1 file is input and an improved version of the IF1 file is output. Such optimizations as invariant code removal from loops and common subexpression elimination are included. Another important optimization that allows the code generator to determine when an array needs to be copied or when it may be changed in place is currently being developed. It is essential to minimize the amount of copying needed. Stream usage must be examined to determine when new streams must be created. The above optimizations are all part of the optimization package.

There are also machine dependent optimizations that must be performed to achieve efficient execution. An example is the movement of function calls to the earliest location in the function where all the parameters are available. This is important in this implementation of SISAL on the HEP because the granularity of parallelism is at the function level and loop body level. The function invocations are done as early as possible to have the results of the invocation available as soon as possible. The compiler may generate parallel calls to handle code segments at these levels. This is discussed further in section 3.3.1.1.

3.2.6. FUTURE DIRECTIONS OF THE LANGUAGE

SISAL is a research language, but it is hoped that the base is there to make it a production language. Several large programs (greater than 5000 lines) have been written in SISAL. The writing of these programs has shown several issues that need to be addressed by the designers of SISAL.

The array operations seem to be awkward and need to be reviewed and improved. There is a need for a VECTOR data structure and a MATRIX data structure that allows the compiler to use contiguous storage for arrays rather than array of arrays. For these data structures, the bounds of the array must be known at compile time.

The unification of the two loop structures is also under consideration. There seems to be no reason for two different loop structures when the compiler is able to detect whether the loop is a parallel loop or a sequential loop.

3.2.7. REFERENCES

[Ackerman, 1979] W. B. Ackerman and J. B. Dennis. VAL -- A value-oriented algorithmic language: preliminary reference manual. Technical Report TR-218, Computation Structures Group, Laboratory for Computer Science, MIT, Cambridge, MA, June 1979.

[Ackerman, 1982] W. B. Ackerman. Data flow languages. *IEEE Computer* 15, 2: 15-25.

[Backus, 1978] J. Backus. Can programming be liberated from the von Neumann style? A functional style and its algebra of programs. *Communications of the A.C.M* 21, 8: 613-641.

[Cann, 1984] D. Cann, et. al. The intermediate form of the portable C compiler. Computer Science Technical Report CS-84-09, Colorado State University, Fort Collins, CO, September 1984.

[Johnson, 1975] S. C. Johnson. YACC - yet another compiler compiler. CSTR 32, Bell Laboratories, Murray Hill, NJ, 1975.

[Johnson, 1978] S. C. Johnson. A portable compiler: theory and practice. *Fifth Annual ACM Symposium on Principles of Programming Languages* (January 1978), pp. 97-104.

[Kuck, 1980] D. A. Kuck, et. al. High-speed multiprocessors and compilation techniques. *IEEE Transactions on Computers* c-29, 9: 763-776.

[Lesk, 1975] M. E. Lesk. LEX - a lexical analyzer generator. CSTR 39, Bell Laboratories, Murray Hill, NJ, 1975.

[Liskov, 1978] B. H. Liskov, et. al. CLU reference manual. Memo 161, Computation Structures Group, Laboratory for Computer Science, MIT, Cambridge, MA, July, 1978.

[McGraw, 1982] J. R. McGraw. The VAL language: description and analysis. *ACM Transactions on Programming Languages and Systems* 4, 1: 44-82 (January 1982).

[McGraw, 1984] J. R. McGraw, et. al. SISAL: streams and iteration in a single-assignment language. Language Reference Manual, Ver. 1.2, Lawrence Livermore National Laboratory M-146.

[Sielker, 1984] H. Sielker, et. al. Issues in implementing SISAL on distributed systems. Computer Science Technical Report CS-84-06, Colorado State University, Fort Collins, CO, June 1984.

[Skedzielewski, 1983] S. Skedzielewski and J. Glauert. IF1 -- An intermediate form for applicative languages. Draft 9, 1983.

[Tesler, 1968] L. G. Tesler and H. J. Enea. A language design for concurrent processes. *Proceedings 1968 Spring Joint Computer Conference* (May 1968), pp. 403-408.

3.3. EXECUTION SUPPORT FOR HEP SISAL†

R. R. OLDEHOEFT and S. J. ALLAN
Colorado State University
Fort Collins, Colorado

In the preceding section we introduced and exemplified the SISAL programming language. In particular, some language features require significant run time support for correct and efficient implementation. The design goals of the run time software are several. First, we maintain accurate adherence to the functional semantics of SISAL. Second, we exploit the parallel execution of programs in ways appropriate to the HEP architecture. Third, the support software is efficient for programs deemed "typical." Finally, the run time support software will continue to execute any legal SISAL program to completion or until exhausting the available data memory. In this section we discuss several areas: mapping program sections onto HEP hardware processes for parallel execution, implementing streams and their interaction with process management, allocating dynamic storage, supporting arrays, and interfacing with the HEP/UPX‡ operating system. The methods discussed here are under development; some details may change as experience is gained. Others may find this software useful as building blocks in their projects.

† This research is supported by ARO Contract DAAG29-82-K-0108.

‡ HEP/UPX is a trademark of Denelcor, Inc.

3.3.1. PROCESSES

In this section we explain the granularity of processes in HEP SISAL and define the process descriptor structure in anticipation of later discussions.

3.3.1.1. Process Definition

The available parallelism in the target HEP architecture influences decisions about process definition and management. A HEP SISAL program runs as a single HEP/UPX process and uses, during a particular execution, a fixed number of hardware subprocesses with which to effect parallel execution. The length of the pipelined function units in PEMs and the intensity with which cooperating hardware subprocesses compete for their use limits the potential speedup over sequential execution. For most SISAL programs it is not necessary to resort to extremely fine-grained (operator level) parallelism to take advantage of available speedup with a limited number of hardware subprocesses.

The run time software is organized as a set of functions, written mostly in C, that processes call to obtain service. This is in opposition to organizing the services as daemon processes that respond to messages from other processes. We chose this course to prevent such servers from becoming bottlenecks to throughput and to prevent them from occupying hardware subprocesses when no work is required of them. The functions themselves must operate on shared data structures. We have tried to minimize the exclusive access required to this data so that other bottlenecks do not reappear. See section 3.3.4 on dynamic storage allocation for examples of these considerations.

The units of parallel execution in HEP SISAL are the function body, a "stripe" of a parallel loop, and a component of a multi-expression. Compiler restructuring transforms the last two cases to function executions, so the first case is the only concern of run time process management. If each function reference were instantiated as a hardware subprocess with data memory empty-full state for synchronization, then a hardware create fault would quickly result when more than the allowed number of subprocesses was attempted. In a slightly more complex version, deadlock would result as parent processes held PSW slots waiting forever for completion of child functions who cannot execute. Deadlock is prevented by requiring that a parent process waiting for value(s) from children relinquish its PSW slot and cease execution. To prevent needless process management, a parent referencing a function will execute the child function synchronously and sequentially if there are no available hardware subprocesses in which to begin asynchronous execution. This "fork-or-call" decision is made dynamically during execution at each reference. The work necessary to "fork" and to "call" are comparable, so there is little extra cost in this approach. The compiler moves function references upward in the code so that, as soon as it is known that a function value will be needed, its parallel execution may commence. Both parent and child have state RUNNING. Later, when a value from a child is needed, the parent will become VBLOCKED and cease execution if the number of currently executing child processes still computing values is nonzero. Each terminating child process decrements this number; the last one may assume the parent's identity and continue its execution.

Functions containing loops that produce or consume streams require more complex management. However, we defer discussing them until later.

3.3.1.2. Data Structures

In this section we briefly summarize the necessary components of the process descriptor data structure. For more detailed discussion along with a commentary on the associated routines see [Booker, 1984]. The major components of a process descriptor are:

parent:	pointer to descriptor of process that instantiated this process
next,last:	pointers for doubly linked lists containing blocked processes
ch_wait:	number of extant child processes
psw:	process state word if not RUNNING
regs:	vector of saved general register contents for non-RUNNING processes
reg_slot:	register set index for RUNNING processes
nr_in_args:	number of function arguments
in_args:	pointers to input argument values
nr_fvalues:	number of function output values
fvalues:	pointers to output value destinations
scratch:	local data memory scratch space
stack:	stack for executing in C run time routines

The use of most of these fields will be apparent after reading the sections below. Some nonexecuting processes have descriptors in residence on a doubly linked list of similar processes; the "next" and "last" fields form these lists. The hardware state of a process that has no hardware subprocess executing on its behalf resides in the fields "psw" and "regs." A contiguous group of registers is available to all the hardware subprocesses of a HEP SISAL program; 16 registers are used by each. A bit map retains the in use/available state of each register set. A process that is to be made RUNNING is supplied with a register set by finding the index of a one-valued bit in the map and multiplying that by 16 to obtain the proper register base address. The index is saved in "reg_slot." When a RUNNING process is to leave that state "reg_slot" gives the position in the bit map to reset to zero so the register set can be re-allocated to another RUNNING process. The "scratch" field is a process-dependent amount of space for values that cannot be maintained in general registers during execution and for items that must have a data memory address for access by other processes. The final field, "stack," is an area used when a process is executing in C code that is part of the run time support system.

There is no explicit process state field. In the discussions below, a process state is reflected by its being in execution or residing on a list of descriptors for processes with the same state.

3.3.2. STREAMS

Section 3.2.3.1 described usage of streams of values in SISAL programs. Here we discuss the data structures for streams and the implementation of operations. We require that both the producer and consumers of a stream be executable simultaneously so the processes of a program can form generalized parallel pipelines. Only a contiguous substream of the stream needs to be extant at any instant because values that have been processed by the slowest stream consumer can be discarded. In this way programs can be executed that produce and consume (finite prefixes of) streams of infinite length.

3.3.2.1. Data Structures

For the greatest flexibility, we have elected to use a dynamically allocated linked list of items for implementing a stream. By recognizing that each stream datum in any stream of any type requires the same amount of space, we can improve the performance of stream operations. Complex data (arrays, for example) occur in streams as pointers to other space. Program initialization includes the allocation of a special pool of space for stream elements and its organization as a free list of identical cells with fields:

value: the datum itself
ref ct: number of consumers yet to use this element
next: pointer to the successor stream element

Producers and consumers can quickly obtain or recycle free cells.

The stream descriptor structure has these fields:

head: pointer to first extant stream element
tail: pointer to last stream element produced
nr_cons: number of consumers of this stream
cb_head: pointer to first blocked consumer process
cb_tail: pointer to last blocked consumer process
pd_proc: pointer to producer process descriptor
eos: end-of-stream signal
cur_size: number of extant stream elements
max_size: maximum number of extant elements allowed

The "head" and "tail" fields define the linked elements containing the stream data that have been produced but not yet used by all consumer processes. The producer will append to the element identified by "tail" but each consumer maintains its own pointer to its current "first" element. The "head" pointer coincides with the "first" pointer of the slowest consumer, and is updated when that consumer discards the element. Compile time analysis determines the number of consumers, "nr_cons," which initializes the reference count with each produced element. The producer process is identified by "pd_proc." The end of stream signal, "eos," is **false** until the producer process sets it **true**. Other fields will be explained in later sections.

3.3.2.2. Implementation of Operations

The activities surrounding instances of the stream data type can be efficiently implemented with the data structures above.

1. Start a stream-producing process. The space for a stream descriptor is dynamically allocated, and fields initialized.

2. stream_first(S): read the first extant value. The consumer's "first" pointer identifies the stream element whose value is read. If there is no value available, this consumer must wait (see 3.3.3.2).

3. S := stream_rest(**old** S): discard the first extant value of S. Decrement the reference count in the stream element identified by "first" and update "first" to point to the successor element. If the decremented reference count is zero, then (in the stream descriptor) set "head", decrement "cur_size" and reactivate the producer if it is blocked (see 3.3.3.3); finally, recycle the element to the stream element pool.

4. **for . . . returns stream of**: append new stream values. If (in the stream descriptor) "cur_size" equals "max_size" then wait to be reactivated (see 3.3.3.3). Otherwise, obtain a stream element from the pool, store the produced value there and set its reference count to equal the number of consumers. Append the stream element and update "tail" and "cur_size." If there are waiting consumers, reactivate them (see 3.3.3.2). As a special case, if all consumers have terminated (nr_cons is zero) then return the stream descriptor to free storage and cease element production.

5. **end for**: indicate end of stream. Set "eos" in the stream descriptor. If there are waiting consumers, reactivate them (3.3.3.2). If there are no consumers left

(nr_cons is zero), return the stream descriptor to dynamic storage.

6. stream_empty(S): test for end of stream. If elements exist for this consumer, return **false**. If not and "eos" is set, return **true**. Otherwise, wait for the producer to append a value or set "eos" and then return the appropriate response.

7. Terminate a consumer. Decrement "nr_cons" and the reference counts in extant unconsumed stream elements. Recycle elements with zero reference counts. If "nr_cons" is also zero, return the stream descriptor to dynamic storage if the producer process has terminated.

3.3.3. STREAM PRODUCING AND CONSUMING PROCESSES

As mentioned above, the simple process management scheme in which every process is running or waiting for values from children is insufficient to handle stream producer and consumer processes. In this section we augment the process management algorithms to account for them.

3.3.3.1. Ready Processes

A new process that produces or consumes streams must come into existence even if there is no hardware subprocess to support its immediate execution. We introduce the process state READY for processes that are not RUNNING but are lacking only an available hardware subprocess to do so. All READY processes reside in a doubly linked "ready list" RL for future execution. To simplify process management, we impose two principles. First, a process that is changing its state *from* RUNNING to a blocked state (VBLOCKED, or one introduced below) invokes the operation "SCHEDULE" in an attempt to replace itself on the hardware subprocess being vacated. SCHEDULE compares the number of

RUNNING processes with the number of hardware subprocesses available and converts as many READY processes found in RL as possible to RUNNING. Second, if a process changes the state of another process *from* a blocked state, the new process state is READY, it is moved to RL, and the state-altering process invokes SCHEDULE. Thus the decision about which processes are to run is isolated in just one routine. Figure 3.3-A gives the complete process state transition diagram whose components we will develop in sections below.

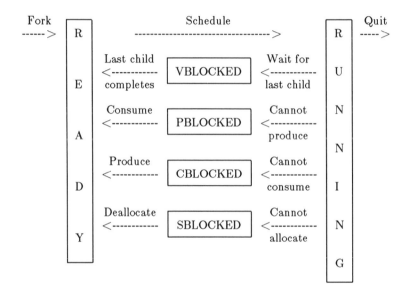

Figure 3.3-A. HEP SISAL Process State Transition Diagram.

3.3.3.2. Blocked Stream Consumers

A function with a stream argument may execute faster than the producer of the stream, and may soon have no stream element to obtain. The process states discussed so far are inappropriate, so we introduce CBLOCKED for a stream consumer that cannot proceed. The fields "cb_head" and "cb_tail" in the stream descriptor define a doubly linked list of CBLOCKED processes for this stream. When a consumer cannot proceed, it joins this list and relinquishes its hardware subprocess, calling SCHEDULE as its last act. Later, the producer will move this list to RL and will call SCHEDULE.

A consumer process inquiring whether the stream is completely consumed via the function stream_empty may receive a positive or negative response. However, if there are no extant elements for this consumer, but the producer has not set "eos," the answer cannot be obtained immediately. This consumer also joins the CBLOCKED list associated with the stream so that it will be runnable when a value can be returned.

3.3.3.3. Blocked Stream Producers

If a stream producer is faster than the (slowest) consumer, it may be able to produce many values, using large amounts of stream value storage. Inefficient execution or even unnecessary storage deadlock may result. So, we wish to restrain fast stream producers. A producer that wishes to append a new value but finds that "cur_size" equals "max_size" will become PBLOCKED and relinquish its hardware subprocess. When a consumer recycles a stream element, it will change the producer to READY and invoke SCHEDULE.

160

For both blocked consumers and producers, one may wish to delay the transitions to READY until a reasonable number of extant elements have been produced or until there is an adequate difference between "max_size" and "cur_size." Some threshold value greater than one can reduce the number of process state transitions when the producer or consumer is consistently faster or slower than its counterpart (a common occurrence).

3.3.4. DYNAMIC STORAGE ALLOCATION

HEP SISAL run time support relies on dynamic storage allocation for process descriptors, streams, and arrays. One may adapt any sequential method for concurrent execution among multiple processes. The best choice is one that uses storage efficiently, works quickly, and maximizes the possibility for concurrent access. In this section we describe an adapted boundary tag method that allows multiple concurrent allocations and deallocations, a "front end" caching scheme that can greatly speed up dynamic storage management under the conditions that obtain during HEP SISAL execution, and the relationship between dynamic storage management and process management.

3.3.4.1. Sequential Boundary Tag Method

This technique [Knuth, 1973] supports allocating and deallocating storage blocks of differing sizes. Each block has a top tag above its usable space containing block status (in use or free) and the size of usable space. After the usable space the bottom tag repeats the block status and gives a pointer to the top tag. A doubly linked circular list joins free blocks (links reside in usable space) with a free block of size zero to avoid empty list special cases.

The allocation routine searches linearly (beginning at a block identified by an external list_entry_pointer) until a block large enough to satisfy the request is found. The lower portion of the block is restructured to be an allocated block of the requested size, and a pointer to its usable space satisfies the request. Just above it, a new bottom tag defines the end of the smaller remaining free block. When an exact fit occurs, the free block becomes entirely allocated and is unlinked from the list.

Two details improve boundary tag performance. First, nearly exact fits result in the allocation of entire free blocks to avoid cluttering the list with tiny, unusable blocks. Second, the list_entry_pointer changes to point to the list-successor of the allocation site after each allocation. This "randomizes" the allocation starting point and prevents small blocks from clustering near some fixed starting point.

The deallocation routine uses the boundary tags of store-adjacent (physically neighboring) blocks to learn their states and coalesces the block being freed with one or both neighbors if possible to yield fewer but larger free blocks. If coalescing is impossible, the new free block is inserted into the free list.

3.3.4.2. Concurrent Boundary Tag Method

Our goal is to allow maximum concurrency among processes executing the allocation and deallocation routines while guaranteeing that both interference and deadlock will not occur. However, deadlock may still occur among processes because of inadequate total data memory space; its detection is discussed later. First, consider how interactions among allocators must be constrained.

1. We must prevent simultaneous consideration of a free block by two allocators. Similarly, allocators on list-adjacent blocks may both succeed with an exact fit, attempt to unlink blocks, and destroy the list structure. So an allocator must first "capture" (using the hardware empty-full state of a word in the top tag) the block under consideration as well as holding possession of its list-predecessor. This separates simultaneous allocators sufficiently. If there are N free blocks, then up to N-1 concurrent allocators may successfully consider free blocks in sequence (see the search loop in Figure 3.3-B), but if N attempt it deadlock may occur. A new allocator must wait at its entry until it may safely join others in free list access.

2. A new allocator begins its search by capturing the free block identified by the list_entry_pointer and then its list-successor. However, since obtaining the value of the list_entry_pointer and capturing the block it points to are separate actions, the block may become allocated via an exact fit allocation by another process. Once the initial block is captured, a new allocator must insure that it is in fact a free block or retry to capture its first block. This loop is necessary only when a new allocator initializes to join the free list and during coalescing by a deallocator (discussed below).

3. As a special case, the free list must retain at least two entries for safe processing, even if all space is allocated. We include two blocks with size zero instead of one. By placing these special free blocks physically apart from the storage pool in which allocating and deallocating take place, no deallocator will consider them for coalescing.

Second, consider how deallocators must behave with each other and with allocators to avoid interference and deadlock. A deallocator will attempt coalescing in two phases, with its store-adjacent neighbor with a smaller address called the "block_above" and with its store-adjacent neighbor with a larger address that we refer to as the "block_below."

1. If the block_below is free we remove it from the free list and merge it with the block being freed. This action is similar to an exact fit by an allocator and, for the same reasons, a deallocator first captures the list-predecessor of the block_below and then captures the block_below.

2. Just as in point 2 on the previous page, by the time the list-predecessor of a free block_below is acquired, some other allocator may have succeeded exactly with it and made it an allocated block. As long as this occurs, the list-predecessor pointer is re-obtained and the capture is retried.

3. In block_above coalescing, the block_above must be captured so that its size can be safely increased to subsume the block currently being freed. Since no list manipulation occurs, the list-predecessor of the block_above need not be captured. Block-above coalescing has the same potential for deadlock as an allocation because, if coalescing is impossible, a list pair must be captured to insert the new free block. It may run with allocations and with other deallocations.

4. It is simpler to do block_below coalescing before the block_above phase. However, if block_below coalescing succeeds, one fewer free block will result. So the check for safe concurrent execution must be repeated before block_above coalescing.

Figures 3.3-B and 3.3-D show pseudo-code for allocation and deallocation respectively.

```
procedure allocate( in rsize, out address );
  await nr_allocs + nr_deallocs < nr_fb - 1
  then nr_allocs := nr_allocs + 1 endawait;
  pr := list_entry_pointer; capture(pr);
  while pr is allocated do
    release(pr); pr := list_entry_pointer; capture(pr)
  endwhile;
  cu := pr^.next; capture(cu);
  while block cu is too small do
    release(pr); pr := cu; cu := pr^.next; capture(cu)
  endwhile;
  if block cu is close enough to an exact fit then
    await true then nr_fb := nr_fb - 1 endawait;
    Unlink this block; Set its status to in use;
    Set address to usable space
  else
    Form new block in lower part of this block;
    Set address to its usable space;
    Reduce cu^.size and establish new bottom tag;
  endif;
  list_entry_pointer := pr; release(pr); release(cu);
  await true then nr_allocs := nr_allocs - 1 endawait
endprocedure;
```

Figure 3.3-B. Concurrent Boundary Tag Storage Allocation.

The entry conditions that guarantee noninterference and freedom from deadlock appear as "conditional critical regions" (cf. [Hoare, 1972]) in the **await** statements in the procedures. The syntax of an **await** block is:

await <bool-expr> **then** <statements> **endawait**

Concurrent processes execute one at a time among all **await** blocks. If the boolean expression is **false,** the executing process releases exclusive execution rights and waits for the boolean expression to become **true.** If the boolean expression is **true**, the process executes statements in the block, awakens all delayed processes to re-evaluate their boolean expressions, and allows another process to attempt to execute some **await** block. Figure 3.3-C shows how **await** blocks can be implemented efficiently using binary semaphores. The semaphore "mutex" assures mutual exclusion for execution, and "delay" prevents retry after failure until another process has succeeded and altered at least one shared variable. Since the HEP architecture supports semaphore construction well, **await** blocks are also efficient.

await <bool-expr> **then** <statements> **endawait**

becomes

```
loop
  P(mutex);
  if <bool-expr> then
    <statements>;
    for delayed processes do V(delay) endfor;
    V(mutex); exitloop
  else V(mutex); P(delay)
  endif
endloop
```

with mutex = 1, delay = 0, initially.

Figure 3.3-C. Implementing **await** Blocks

```
procedure deallocate( in address );
  await nr_allocs + nr_deallocs < nr_fb - 1
  then nr_deallocs := nr_deallocs + 1 endawait;
  coalesce_below( address );
  await true then nr_deallocs := nr_deallocs - 1 endawait;
  await nr_allocs + nr_deallocs < nr_fb - 1
  then nr_deallocs := nr_deallocs + 1 endawait;
  coalesce_above( address );
  await true then nr_deallocs := nr_deallocs - 1 endawait
endprocedure;

procedure coalesce_below( in new_free );
  Compute bl_below from new_free;
  loop
    capture(bl_below);
    if bl_below is allocated then
      release(bl_below); return
    else
      pr := bl_below^.last; release(bl_below); capture(pr);
      if pr is a free block then
        if pr^.next = bl_below then exitloop endif
      endif;
      release(pr)
    endif
  endloop;
  capture(bl_below); Unlink bl_below; release(pr);
  await true then nr_fb := nr_fb - 1 endawait;
  Merge bl_below into block at new_free; release(bl_below);
endprocedure;

procedure coalesce_above( in new_free );
  Compute bl_above from new_free; capture(bl_above);
  if bl_above is free then
    Merge block at new_free into bl_above; release(bl_above)
  else
    release(bl_above); pr := list_entry_pointer; capture(pr);
    while pr is an allocated block do
      release(pr); pr := list_entry_pointer; capture(pr)
    endwhile;
    cu := pr^.next; capture(cu);
    Insert block at new_free between pr and cu;
    await true then nr_fb := nr_fb + 1 endawait;
    release(pr); release(cu)
  endif
endprocedure;
```

Figure 3.3-D. Concurrent Storage Deallocation.

3.3.4.3. Exact Fit Caching

The distribution of dynamic storage request sizes can be uneven and "spiky" [Margolin, 1971]. In addition, the size distribution may change as execution proceeds. Performance improvements have been demonstrated by statically establishing separate lists for equal-size free blocks that are searched before the storage pool is accessed [Margolin, 1971], by dynamically establishing these lists when a free block of a new size appears [Leverett, 1982], and by caching recently freed blocks in a FIFO buffer until reallocated or overwritten [Bozman, 1984]. All methods are independent of the "normal" dynamic storage algorithms used when an exact fit is not found.

Extend the idea of dynamically building exact fit lists to take advantage of nonstationary size distributions. Define an integer "clock" with value T that "ticks" at each allocation. With each size list associate the value of T that prevailed when a free block from that list last exactly satisfied a request, or failing that, the value when the first free block of this size was deallocated. An allocator searches the sizes for an exact match. On success, an element (free block) from that list satisfies the request and, if the list remains nonempty, the current T value associates with this size. For each size match failure, if the current T value minus the T value with this size exceeds a threshold W, then all the blocks in this list are deemed obsolete and recycled into the storage pool. When a deallocation occurs, the newly freed block joins a list of free blocks of this size, or a new list with one element and the current T value is established.

The set of sizes is a working set WS(T,W) so that at time T, WS(T,W) consists of:

{sizes allocated from cache during last W allocations} ∪
{new block sizes freed during the last W allocations} -
{sizes whose free blocks have all been allocated}

The working set shrinks when a size has not been re-accessed in W allocations and when allocations exhaust the list associated with a size. The set grows when a block with a size not in the working set is deallocated.

We compared the performance of this caching method via simulation with the FIFO buffer method by comparing the hit ratio (percent of exact fit allocation success) for a fixed FIFO buffer size with the hit ratio obtained when a mean working set size nearly equal to the FIFO buffer size was observed. See [Oldehoeft, 1984] for details. All results favored the working set approach. The largest difference resulted from a spiky, nonstationary distribution. Even uniformly random size distributions showed a working set hit ratio equal to the mean working set size divided by the number of possible sizes: the method is doing as well as can be expected in this worst case.

This caching technique operates with the general purpose concurrent boundary tag method described above. The parameter W is determined empirically via benchmarks, but a command execution parameter, if supplied, will override it.

3.3.4.4. Relation to Process Management

The allocation procedure above does not include the possibility for failure, viz., no extant free block satisfies the request. Future deallocations by other processes may create free blocks large enough to satisfy currently failed requests. It is not satisfactory to allow circular searching to continue without suspension because the allocating processes can prevent a deallocating process from entering the list structure. But suspending search after examining free blocks in number equal to the list size on entry, or equal to the largest number of free blocks observed during the search, or other variations, cannot guarantee that when an allocator elects suspension there is no free block that could satisfy the request. Without using an expensive algorithm, a suitable heuristic suffices.

We introduce state SBLOCKED for a process whose allocation attempt has suspended. A doubly linked list of SBLOCKED processes grows when an allocator decides to enter the SBLOCKED state. The list may shrink when a deallocation occurs. After coalescing, the list is examined for a sequence of processes all of whose requests are satisfiable by the result of the deallocation. The sequence is discovered by scanning the SBLOCKED list; processes in the sequence can each allocate from the new free block and reduce its size. Each process in the sequence is moved to the global READY list for immediate or later execution.

3.3.4.5. Storage Deadlock

The only reason that a HEP SISAL program will deadlock is for lack of data memory. The deadlock state is discovered as part of the SCHEDULE operation that occurs when a running process attempts to replace itself from among READY processes in RL. Figure 3.3-E shows a pseudo-code function that returns a decision about whether deadlock has occurred. When no READY process is available, the exact fit cache is emptied, blocks coalesced, and all SBLOCKED processes that might have requests fulfilled are made READY for another attempt at storage allocation.

```
function deadlocked: boolean;
    if the number of READY processes > 0 or
       the number of RUNNING processes > 1
    then deadlocked := false
    else
       Recycle all cached free blocks to the storage pool;
       Move all possible SBLOCKED processes to RL;
       deadlocked := the number of READY processes = 0
    endif
endfunction;
```

Figure 3.3-E. Storage Deadlock Detection.

3.3.5. ARRAYS

In section 3.2.3.1 we saw the power of the intrinsic array operations in SISAL and how arrays could be manipulated within the requirements of single assignment execution. In this section we discuss the representation of array objects in HEP SISAL and how we implement the required operations efficiently. See [Cobb, 1984] for additional details.

3.3.5.1. Data Structures

Key considerations for array manipulation are the minimization of copying overhead when new arrays are derived from extant arrays, and the minimization of dynamic storage allocation as an array grows. So, we want derived arrays to access the same elements when possible and we are willing to pre-allocate some space for array growth when it is probable that the space will be needed. To separate the information common to all array derivations from the information that may be unique to each, we introduce logical and physical arrays. A logical array corresponds to a particular array name through which access to elements is possible. The fields of a logical array are:

171

```
pa_addr:   the address of the associated physical array
lb:        lower bound
ub:        upper bound
offset:    number of bytes from pa_addr to the lb-th array element
```

A physical array contains element values along with fields that enable shared access through different logical arrays. The fields of a physical array are:

```
Prefix:
    ref_ct:   the number of logical arrays pointing here
    offset:   number of bytes to the position of the first physical array element
    last:     number of bytes to the position of the last physical array element
    space:    total allocated size of the physical array
    l_xpand:  number of times that the physical array has grown via array_addl to
              accommodate new elements
    u_xpand:  corresponding count for array_addh growth
    next_la:  utility cell for iterative traversal of array structures
Unused space for expansion via array_addl
Array elements
Unused space for expansion via array_addh
```

In the physical array prefix, "offset" corresponds to the minimum "offset" field in all logical arrays using this physical array. The "l_xpand" and "u_xpand" fields, initially zero, count the number of times that this physical array has had to be reallocated and copied because of addition of elements through the array_addl and array_addh functions respectively. Each successive expansion allocates more space than the preceding one in anticipation of future growth in the same direction. The unused spaces surrounding the extant array elements initially have size zero to minimize space usage for those arrays whose size does not change.

The array elements in the physical array are elements of the base type or are logical arrays themselves if the array consists of arrays. We avoid using the notion of "multidimensional" arrays since SISAL does not include them. Instead, a "constituent array" is an element of a "higher order" array.

3.3.5.2. Implementation of Operations

Whenever possible, an array operation that yields a new logical array shares the physical array(s) from which it was derived. Array sharing comes in two varieties. First, it is possible to re-use a physical array by adding a new end element in pre-allocated unused space or by using only a subarray of the original physical array. If the array A already exists and X and Y are values of the base type, the code fragment

B := array_addh(A, X); C := array_addh(A, Y)

shows that simple array sharing may or may not be possible. If there is room for X in the physical array used by A, the logical array B can share the physical array with A. B has a larger upper bound than A, and the physical array has a reference count of two. After the first statement, C cannot share that physical array because the existence of X (= B[ub]) after the last A element prevents Y from residing there. C must point to a new physical array containing the concatenation of A and Y in which the reference count is one.

The second kind of array sharing involves constituent arrays. Suppose above that A has elements that are themselves arrays, and that X and Y are each arrays of the same constituent structure as an element of A. Then the first assignment results in a logical array B whose last element resides in the physical array being shared with A. B[ub] is an element with a structure copied from the logical array X; the physical array used by X now has a reference count of two. To define C we must build a new physical array containing the logical arrays of A followed by that of Y. The constituent arrays (elements of A and Y) must have all their reference counts incremented, but no copying is required beyond the construction of the new physical array identified by the logical array C.

Now we briefly outline how the array operations of HEP SISAL are implemented with these array structures.

1. **array** type[], **array** type[J: V1,V2, . . .,Vm], array_fill(L, H, V): create an array. A new physical array always results from these operations. In the first form, the empty array (lower bound one, upper bound zero) results. The second form produces an array with lower bound J and elements V1, V2, . . ., Vm. The third version yields an array with lower bound L, upper bound H, and repeated elements V. If consitituent elements are logical arrays, their physical array reference counts are incremented.

2. array_liml(A), array_limh(A), array_size(A): obtain bounds or size. Only fields in the logical array A need to be accessed for these functions.

3. A[I1][I2] . . . [Ik]: select an array element. Collect the indices I1, I2, . . ., Ik and use them to descend through k-1 logical arrays of the tree structure of physical arrays identified by A and obtain an element on the k-th level. This element may be a logical array (the reference count in the associated physical array must be incremented) or a simpler value.

4. A[I1][I2] . . . [Ik: V]: replace an element. The result is an array identical to A with the selected element replaced by V. The element replacement may be done in situ if two conditions prevail. First, this must be the last reference to A in its scope of definition (a loop, for example), a condition learned by compiler analysis. Second, all the physical array reference counts encountered during selection to arrive at level k must be one (trivially satisfied for arrays of non-array elements). Otherwise, a copy must be made of all arrays traversed from the topmost level

through the array being modified (all other arrays remain shared).

5. array_reml(A), array_remh(A): remove an array element. A new physical array is never needed here. Increment the physical array reference count, set the new logical array bounds to differ from A by one in the lower or upper position, and, in the first version, the logical array "offset" field gives a new starting position in the physical array.

6. array_setl(A, L), array_adjust(A, L, H): set lower bound, adjust bounds. No new physical array results from these operations. The first function returns a logical array with its lower bound L and its upper bound modified from that of A. The second function returns a subarray in the physical array shared with A.

7. A || B || . . . || Z: concatenate arrays. The result is a new physical array whose elements are copied from the operand physical arrays. If operands are arrays with the same number of levels and base type, then the constituent arrays are shared by incrementing their reference counts.

8. array_addl(A, V), array_addh(A, V): extend an array. If the physical array identified by A has element space for the needed expansion, V is inserted into it and it is shared with the logical array returned by these functions. Otherwise, a new physical array is established. Consider the first function. A physical array is allocated with extra space before the copied array elements and V is placed there. Compute the extent of this space by (l_expand+1)*expansion_constant where l_expand comes from the original physical array, and expansion_constant is a run time default value that can be overridden. The "l_expand" field in the new physical array is one larger than before in anticipation that expansion will be necessary in the future. For arrays that do not expand at all, no overhead space is

wasted. The first time an array expands, the cost of physical array copying and reservation of additional expansion space is incurred. If expansion occurs repeatedly, this cost is incurred less frequently.

9. Array deallocation. When the syntactic scope of a logical array is exited, it is deallocated. In the general case, traverse the tree rooted by the logical array in a depth-first fashion decrementing reference counts in physical arrays until a nonzero reference count is obtained (other logical arrays point here and deeper traversal is unnecessary) or until the base level is reached. Space for physical arrays with zero reference counts whose constituents have been processed is returned to dynamic storage. The traversal algorithm is a non-recursive method using link inversion [Standish, 1980]. The "next_la" field in each physical array exists only for this traversal. It is important to avoid recursion in run time software because the C execution stack used by the routines resides in some HEP SISAL process data space. Without recursion this space can be limited to a smaller size.

3.3.6. INTERFACE WITH HEP/UPX

The HEP SISAL run time software does not rely heavily on the facilities of the HEP/UPX operating system for three reasons. First, much of it was designed before the announcement that UNIX‡ would be implemented on the HEP. Second, parallelism is available within a HEP/UPX process without operating system intervention. Finally, we can recognize cases special to HEP SISAL and devise solutions that are more efficient than possible from a general purpose

---

‡ UNIX is a trademark of ATT Bell Laboratories.

operating system utility. Nevertheless, implementing input/output and supplying the run time system with optional parameters requires use of HEP/UPX facilities.

3.3.6.1. Input-Output and Main Function Arguments-Values

A HEP SISAL program may read or write text values from the standard input and output files. At program initialization, each non-stream argument of the main function is set by reading values from standard input. At program termination the main function return values that are not streams are written in text format to standard output.

The standard diagnostics file is used extensively by many routines to report on erroneous or unusual conditions and to summarize performance measures.

Efficient voluminous input-output was a reason for introducing the stream type into SISAL. A SISAL main function may have arguments and results that are streams of some simpler type. Each of these is associated with a HEP/UPX file whose name is listed in the command that initiates program execution. Before the main HEP SISAL function executes, each of these files is opened and a daemon process is started that reads values and produces them into a stream structure (for arguments) or obtains values from a stream and writes to an output file. These files are merely byte strings read into or written from the internal representations--no conversion to or from text is performed.

3.3.6.2. Command Line Options for Run Time Control

In addition to a list of stream input and output files, a command line that starts a HEP SISAL program into execution may contain options. These override default values that affect aspects of run time support execution. All the options defined currently are concerned with how data memory is used. We briefly summarize them here.

1. Size of initial dynamic storage allocation pool. This space is obtained via **malloc** from HEP/UPX at program initiation.

2. Exact fit threshold for the concurrent boundary tag method.

3. Initial space reserved for stream elements. This is allocated from the dynamic pool at program initiation and, if more space is needed, this amount is added.

4. The value for allocating space for physical arrays when they expand.

5. The maximum number of elements that a stream producer can execute ahead of the slowest stream consumer ("max_size" in a stream descriptor). A fraction of this value is the threshold for re-enabling blocked producers and consumers.

6. The window size (W) for the working set exact fit caching method used in dynamic storage allocation.

Except for perhaps the first option (when storage deadlock was reported on a previous run), a HEP SISAL programmer may have no insight into how these values, defaulted or supplied, affect the speed or efficiency of execution. We hope that the information on performance written to the standard diagnostics file will be useful to help in tuning run time performance to the needs of a particular SISAL program.

3.3.7. REFERENCES

[Booker, 1984] L. Booker, S. Allan and R. Oldehoeft. Process management for HEP SISAL. Colorado State University Technical Report CS-84-05, June, 1984.

[Bozman, 1984] G. Bozman. The software lookaside buffer reduces search overhead with linked lists. *CACM* 27, 3, pp. 222-227.

[Cobb, 1984] S. Cobb, S. Allan and R. Oldehoeft. Arrays in SISAL. Colorado State University Technical Report CS-84-04, July, 1984.

[Hoare, 1972] C. Hoare. Towards a theory of parallel programming. In: C. Hoare, R. Perrot (eds), *Operating System Techniques*, Academic Press, New York, pp. 61-71.

[Knuth, 1973] D. Knuth. *The Art of Computer Programming.* Vol. 1, *Fundamental Algorithms.* Addison-Wesley, Reading, MA, pp. 435ff.

[Leverett, 1982] B. Leverett and P. Hibbard. An adaptive system for dynamic storage allocation. *Software--Practice and Experience* 12, 3, pp. 543-555.

[Margolin, 1971] B. Margolin, R. Parmelee, and M. Schatzoff. Analysis of free storage algorithms. *IBM Syst. J.* 10, 4, pp. 283-304.

[Oldehoeft, 1984] R. Oldehoeft and S. Allan. Adaptive exact fit storage management using working sets. Colorado State University Technical Report CS-84-03, June, 1984.

[Saponas, 1981] T. Saponas. Distributed and decentralized control in fully distributed processing systems. Georgia Institute of Technology Ph.D. dissertation.

[Standish, 1980] T. Standish. *Data structure techniques.* Addison-Wesley, Reading, MA, pp. 277ff.

3.4 Logic Programming on the HEP

John Gabriel

Tim Lindholm

E. L. Lusk

R. A. Overbeek

Argonne National Laboratory
Argonne, Illinois 60439

1. Introduction

In some areas of computing in which execution speeds are critical, it now seems reasonable to project an increase in performance of 3 to 5 orders of magnitude before the end of the decade. The factors contributing to such optimistic projections are as follows:

a) Based on experiences during the last fifteen years, an order of magnitude improvement due to advances in the basic computational algorithms is a distinct possibility.

b). The power of available processors will increase by about an order of magnitude.

c) Finally, increases in performance due to parallelism will range from about 1 to 3 orders of magnitude.

While these projections must obviously be modified to fit specific categories of computation, they are essentially reasonable projections for areas such as real-time graphics, speech analysis, and inference engines. It is this last application, inference engines, that will be the topic of this paper.

With the creation of the Fifth Generation computing project in Japan, a great deal of interest has been focused on how to construct high

*This work was supported in part by National Science Foundation grant MCS82-07496 and in part by the Applied Mathematical Sciences subprogram of the Office of Energy Research, U.S. Department of Energy, under contract nr. W-31-109-Eng-38.

performance inference engines. One central tenet of the Japanese project is that the existence of inference engines with radically improved performance will lead to advances in a number of key areas of artificial intelligence. While this position is certainly not universally held, it has generated a lively, stimulating discussion. In particular, it has caused a number of research teams to explicitly consider the question of exactly how such performance rates can be reached.

To understand the performance objectives that we will discuss, it is necessary to understand the basic unit of performance used when discussing logic programming systems. We will offer a crude description of what is meant by "logical inferences per second" (i.e., lips) here and give a somewhat different and more precise description in the next section. Consider the following widely used example of a logical inference:

From

> If man(X) then mortal(X).

and

> man(socrates).

infer

> mortal(socrates).

The inference is achieved by *unifying* man(X) with man(socrates), instantiating X to socrates. The execution of one such inference per second would constitute an execution rate of 1 lip.

Researchers in the construction of high-performance inference engines to support logic programming languages are attempting to attain execution rates of 10 megalips to 1 gigalip (i.e., one billion logical inferences per second). Currently, the best implementations of Prolog, the most widely used logic programming language, require the execution of between 50 and 100 machine instructions per logical inference on conventional computers. Three points seem clear:

1. An increase of an order of magnitude due to improved algorithms is unlikely. (The rate of 50 to 100 instructions per inference is very low. It has been achieved by carefully tuned assembler language.)

2. To achieve even the lower goal of 10 megalips will require the execution of between 500 and 1000 mips (million instructions per second).

3. To attain the rates that are desired, substantial exploitation of parallelism will be required.

It is far from clear that enough parallelism can be exploited to achieve even the lower goal. This is particularly true in the common dialects of Prolog. Other dialects of logic programming, such as Concurrent Prolog[13] and Parlog[3], may well offer substantially better opportunities for achieving significant speedups. The group at Argonne National Laboratory is focusing on the task of exploring the degree of exploitable parallelism in different dialects of logic programming in order to gain some insight into exactly what performances will be attainable. One of the primary research tools for investigating this question will be the Denelcor HEP. Because of its shared-memory architecture and low-overhead synchronization primitives, it provides a model of computation both appropriate to this research and typical of supercomputer architectures of the near future. At the same time, the work described here is implemented in such a away as to be portable among both uniprocessors and a variety of multiprocessor architectures. In some ways this is a progress report on the project initially outlined in [12].

2. What Is a Logic Program?

Since many readers of this volume will not be familiar with any of the existing dialects of logic programming, we will offer a brief introduction to the central ideas. To illustrate these concepts, we will consider a Prolog program to compute paths in a directed graph. To be concrete, suppose that we have such a graph, with the nodes labeled $n_1, n_2, \ldots n_i$. Consider the problem of computing a path from n_1 to n_i, with the restriction that the path must go through n_j. Such a problem might naturally arise in any number of applications (for example in determining whether a signal between two components in a nuclear reactor control system might have gone through a component that is known to have failed).

The graph itself is represented as a set of facts that describe the connections between the nodes. In Prolog, these would be given as follows:

connected(n_1,n_2).
connected(n_1,n_4).

.

.

.

connected(n_6,n_i).

That is, each of these lines asserts a single fact that two nodes are connected. In order to understand Prolog programs that draw conclusions from these facts, the reader will have to understand a bit more about the concept of *logical formula*. The data items manipulated by a Prolog program are all logical formulas, a concept which can be defined as follows:

1. A *variable* is a logical formula. It may be thought of as representing an arbitrary logical formula, and it can be *instantiated* during a computation to any particular logical formula. Instantiating a logical variable is sometimes referred to as *binding* the variable to a specific value. Variables are represented as words that begin with upper-case letters.

2. A *constant* is a logical formula. Most versions of Prolog support at least three types of constants -- *integers*, *reals*, and *atoms*. Atoms are represented as words that begin with lower-case letters.

3. A *structure* is a formula of the form $f(t_1,t_2,...)$, where each of the arguments must itself be a formula.

4. A *list* is a formula which is either an empty list or an ordered pair of the form [*head*|*tail*], where *head* is a logical formula and *tail* is itself a list. A list of the form [t_1|[t_2|[]]], where [] is the empty list, can be abbreviated to [t_1,t_2].

The basic algorithm that we will describe is given by the following

Prolog statement (or rule):

path_through(START,MID,END,PATH) :-   path(START,MID,P1),
                                      path(MID,END,[MID|P2]),
                                      append(P1,P2,PATH).

The corresponding statement in English would read as follows:

> In order to compute a PATH from START to END going through MID, three steps are necessary. First, we need to find a path P1 from START to MID. Then, we must find a path from MID to END. This path will begin with MID (which will also be the last point in P1), so we will be interested in only the tail of the second list (which we will call P2). Having computed the two sections of the path, the third step is to append the two paths to attain the desired answer.

That is, the main goal (or *head* goal) to the left of the ":-" operator can be solved by solving the three subgoals that follow. Another way to think of this Prolog statement is to say that the main goal can be *reduced* to a sequence of three subgoals. The process of doing so is called a *reduction*. Thus, a specific goal such as

path_through(n_1,n_j,n_i,PATH)

could be thought of as a request to compute a value for the variable PATH. That is, the variables START, MID, and END are input parameters to the procedure, and PATH is an output parameter. The computation would begin by reducing the goal to three subgoals:

path(n_1,n_j,P1)
path(n_j,n_i,[n_j|P2])
append(P1,P2,PATH)

This reduction is achieved by *unifying* the original goal with the head (i.e., the part of the rule to the left of the ":-") of the rule, and replacing the goal with the *instantiated* subgoals. This single act of reduction constitutes a *logical inference*, and the execution of one such reduction per second constitues a *lip*.

While we will not cover in detail the entire program to perform the desired computation, the reader might find it interesting to examine the Prolog code:

```
path(START,END,PATH) :- path_recurs(START,END,PATH,[START]).

path_recurs(START,END,[START,END],EXCLUDE_LIST) :-
        connected(START,END).
path_recurs(START,END,[START|REST],EXCLUDE_LIST) :-
        connected(START,NEXT),
        not_in(NEXT,EXCLUDE_LIST),
        path_recurs(NEXT,END,REST,[START|EXCLUDE_LIST]).

not_in(X,[]).
not_in(X,[H|T]) :-  not X=H,
                    not_in(X,T).
```

There are three distinct Prolog procedures in the above algorithm—*path*, *path_recurs*, and *not_in*. We examine these procedures one by one. First,

```
path(START,END,PATH) :- path_recurs(START,END,PATH,[START]).
```

states that the goal of finding a PATH from START to END can be reduced to satisfying the goal

```
path_recurs(START,END,PATH,[START]).
```

which might be thought of as a request to compute a path from START to END which does not include as intermediate nodes any node included in the list which is specified as the fourth argument. The addition of this fourth argument of "excluded nodes" is used as a technique to handle cycles in the graph.

The entire *path_recurs* routine is given as

```
path_recurs(START,END,[START,END],EXCLUDE_LIST) :-
        connected(START,END).
path_recurs(START,END,[START|REST],EXCLUDE_LIST) :-
        connected(START,NEXT),
        not_in(NEXT,EXCLUDE_LIST),
        path_recurs(NEXT,END,REST,[START|EXCLUDE_LIST]).
```

This procedure is composed of two distinct rules. This means that a solution will be attempted using the first rule. Should that attempt fail, a solution will be attempted using the second rule. That is, a procedure specifies an ordered set of alternative approaches to computing a desired value.

The first approach will cause a goal to be reduced to finding a direct connection between the two nodes. Once that approach is initiated, it will cause a scan through the set of facts specifying connections. The set of *connection* statements might itself be viewed as an ordered set of ways to solve a request. If there is a connection, then the first approach will lead to success, returning the answer [START,END]. If not, the second alternative must be examined.

The second approach specifies a more complex attack on the problem. That is, it can be used to reduce the original goal to the three subgoals:

1. Find a node NEXT directly connected to START.

2. Verify that NEXT is not in the list of nodes that have already been visited (the EXCLUDED_LIST).

3. Finally, compute REST, which is a path from NEXT to END that does not visit either NEXT or any of the nodes in EXCLUDED_LIST.

If all three subgoals can be solved, [START|REST] represents the desired path.

The only remaining procedure, *not_in*, can be invoked to try to show that a given node (the first argument) does not occur in the specified list (the second argument). The procedure

```
not_in(X,[]).
```

```
not_in(X,[H|T]) :-   not X=H,
                     not_in(X,T).
```

includes two alternative approaches. The first simply states that if the
list is empty, then X is not in the list. The second reduces the original
goal to two subgoals--showing that the given element is not the head of
the list, and showing that the given element does not occur within the tail
of the list. The first subgoal

        not X=H,

is slightly different than those that we've examined before. Both *not* and
"=" are special symbols. The goal *not G* succeeds exactly when *G* cannot
be established. A goal *X=H* can be solved if *X* and *H* can be unified (i.e.,
made identical by binding variables to specific values). For our purposes,
there is no point in learning these built-in aspects of the language; all
that is important is to understand that the goal will succeed whenever *X*
cannot be matched successfully with *H*.

Our short example has been both brief and informal. It does, however, include several features that are relevant to the implementation of
a logic programming dialect on multiprocessors. First, let us consider
the rule describing how to find a path between two points going through a
specified midpoint:

```
path_through(START,MID,END,PATH) :-   path(START,MID,P1),
                                      path(MID,END,[MID|P2]),
                                      append(P1,P2,PATH).
```

Note that it would be quite possible to begin a solution to the overall
problem by starting to work on the first two goals simultaneously. This
would constitute an instance of *AND-parallelism*. Prolog normally
methodically explores all alternative solutions to every goal until one
approach can be carried through to a complete solution. When using
AND-parallelism, however, the control of the computation is dramatically
simplified if only one solution is ever considered from goals that are
solved in parallel. This is quite feasible in many cases without seriously

constricting the power of expression and is termed *determinate AND-parallelism.*

Another instance of exploitable parallelism is illustrated by the rule

path_recurs(START,END,[START|REST],EXCLUDE_LIST) :-
        connected(START,NEXT),
        not_in(NEXT,EXCLUDE_LIST),
        path_recurs(NEXT,END,REST,[START EXCLUDE_LIST]).

Here, there may be multiple ways to solve the first subgoal (corresponding to the different nodes that are directly connected to START). These solutions to the first subgoal initiate distinct attempts to solve the last two subgoals. These could be carried on in parallel. The source of the parallelism here comes from considering alternative reductions of a given goal (and the ensuing computation) in parallel. This type of parallelism is called *OR-parallelism.*

A number of papers have been written describing the different sources of parallelism within logic programs and how to exploit them[4, 2, 3, 13]. In this chapter it is not possible to treat the topic in detail. For our purposes, it will suffice if the reader understands the basic notions of determinate AND-parallelism and OR-parallelism. To attain a firm grasp of these notions, we urge the reader to verify that most of the parallelism described in the other chapters of this book is, in fact, determinate AND-parallelism. Finally, note that OR-parallelism amounts to exploring alternative solutions in parallel. For example, such parallelism could be exploited in an algorithm based on a "generate-and-test" computational paradigm.

3. An Overview of the Projected Research

The research effort that we have initiated to investigate attainable levels of parallelism in logic programs will proceed through several fairly well specified stages:

1. First, we developed a high-performance implementation of an abstract machine designed to support logic programming languages. The work was done in C and resulted in execution rates well above other existing systems done in portable languages.

2. The data structures in the uniprocessing implementation were designed to support an extension to multiprocessors. The initial exploration of parallelism has focused on the construction of a system capable of supporting OR-parallelism.

3. Once we have completed our implementation of OR-parallelism, we intend to extend the abstract machine to support determinate AND-parallelism.

The reader should note that our effort has been based on the belief that we can implement portable software that can be moved to a number of machines. The Denelcor HEP was selected as an ideal machine for investigating achievable parallelism and for software development. It has a number of characteristics--such as low-overhead synchronization, minimal cost for spin locks, and global memory—that make it attractive for such uses. However, we certainly did not plan on developing software that was limited to use on the HEP.

We began our implementation effort by developing a set of macros that implement *monitors*. Monitors have been used for many years as a basis for process synchronization[1, 6, 7, 8, 9, 15]. After some experimentation, we have found that portable programs for use on multiprocessors can be written using monitors implemented by means of macros. Furthermore, once a programmer is familiar with the use of the macros, they offer him a relatively convenient mechanism for writing programs that require the synchronization of multiple processes, without his having to use the low-level synchronization primitives offered on a specific machine (such as HEP asynchronous variables).

Two earlier publications[10, 11] discussed the basic concept of macros and briefly described their use. The appendix in this volume describes a version of our macros that was created to support portable FORTRAN programs on multiprocessors. The version used in this project, of course, supports the coding of portable C for multiprocessors, but the essential synchronization questions and implementation techniques are identical.

4. Implementation of the Warren Machine

Our first stage involved the creation of a high-performance implementation of sequential Prolog, using data structures that would allow a generalization to the multiprocessing environment. Most of the better Prolog implementations compile Prolog to an abstract instruction set, much the way UCSD Pascal compiles to an abstract p-code. Our survey of implementation approaches resulted in the belief that high-performance Prolog implementations of the future would be based on David H. D. Warren's abstract Prolog machine[14]. Hence, we implemented an interpreter for a modified version of Warren's abstract machine.

Our implementation of the abstract machine was done in C on a VAX 11/780 long before C was actually available on the Denelcor HEP. We made extensive use of macro capabilities to hide machine peculiarities and optimized frequently executed sections of code. We used data structures that introduce some minimal overhead when the program is run with only one process, but will generalize to and be optimal for the multiprocessor environments for which the interpreter is ultimately intended. The result is a version of the Warren machine that executes at about 5K to 6K lips on our VAX 11/780. This execution rate is considerably better than most Prolog systems available for the VAX (such systems at this time execute at about 1K to 2K lips). It is perhaps worth noting, however, that a highly tuned version of the machine developed by Warren himself in assembler language will be available by the time this article is in print; that implementation will almost certainly offer speeds somewhat in excess of what we attained in our C version.

The Warren machine cannot be described in detail within the space limits of this paper, but we will attempt to present the essential aspects that are relevant to an understanding of the synchronization issues that are present in the multiprocessor implementation. The reader interested in the details should consult Warren's original report or our tutorial discussion of the machine[5].

The Warren machine makes extensive use of two stacks, which we will refer to as *the local stack* and *the global stack*. The local stack is used for two main purposes:

1. When alternative rules within a Prolog procedure all might be used to reduce a goal, a record must be maintained in the local stack that will allow "restarting" the computation on the next alternative (if that becomes necessary). This position within a set of alternatives is frequently called a *choice point*.

2. A Prolog procedure that reduces to a set of subgoals frequently requires "scratch areas" to maintain the results of subcomputations that must be passed as arguments to successive subgoals. These scratch areas are actually *valuecells* maintained in the local stack. A valuecell represents a logical variable (such as *NEXT* in the *path_recurs* procedure) that may get bound to a value during a computation.

The global stack is used to contain logical formulas that must be retained after the procedure exits. For example, when the routine *path_recurs* is invoked to construct a list of nodes in a subpath, that subpath must be retained as an answer after the procedure that computed it has completed all of its computations. The formulas constructed in the global stack may also contain valuecells (which can be later bound to other logical formulas).

For our purposes, it is important that the reader grasp that the two stacks contain most of the information that determine the "state of a computation", and that they may contain valuecells which can get bound to new formulas at some later point in a computation. Furthermore, there is one added feature of the stacks that is worth mentioning: if we think of the stacks as growing from low addresses to higher memory addresses, then it is important that all of the global stack occurs before (i.e., at lower memory addresses) than the local stack. This constraint is used to define an ordering on the valuecells that occur within the stacks such that

a) all valuecells within the global stack precede all valuecells within the local stack, and

b) if two valuecells occur in the same stack, then the valuecell that was allocated at an earlier point in the computation occurs before the valuecell that was allocated at a later point.

There is not room in this document to explain why such an ordering is necessary; the reader should consult the previous references on the War-ren machine for a detailed discussion. There are, of course, other ways to maintain such an ordering, but it is very important that the computa-tion required to compare the "positions" of two valuecells be rapid. We experimented with a somewhat more costly method, but abandoned it because of the overhead involved.

Finally, some mention should be made of the use of choice points. A choice point in the local stack retains the information required to "reset" the machine back to the state that it was in when the last choice between alternatives occurred. This allows the machine to rapidly *backtrack* to a previous point in a computation and begin attempting a solution via an alternative reduction. The act of "resetting" the machine includes not only resetting the stack pointers (and machine registers, which we have not discussed), but also unbinding any valuecells that may have been bound at some point after the last alternative.

5. The Implementation of OR-Parallelism

To capitalize on OR-parallelism requires the extension of the unipro-cessor implementation in ways that allow multiple alternative reductions of a goal to be explored in parallel. This involved the development of what we term a *context*. A context may be thought of as an instance of the Warren machine. It includes the set of Warren machine registers that control execution of a Warren machine. In a multiprocessor environment, we will have multiple contexts (each being executed by a separate pro-cess) working on a set of shared data structures, which will include extended versions of the local and global stacks. These contexts are maintained in a *dispatching pool*, which keeps track of available work to be done. Processes access the dispatching pool to acquire a context that can be "extended" (i.e., for which the exploration of an alternative can be initiated). This dispatching pool is maintained via a *monitor* which con-trols operations against the shared pool. The detailed logic of this moni-tor is somewhat complex and is described elsewhere [11] (see the appendix to this volume for a description of a FORTRAN incarnation of this monitor to manage dispatchable units of work).

5.1. Maintaining Local and Global Trees

The central problems involved in coordinating multiple processes (each executing a distinct context) involve the access and updating of shared sections of what we called the local and global stacks in the previous section. Consider the case in which a single context begins execution of a logic program. At some point, the computation reaches a stage in which alternative reductions are possible. In the case of a uniprocessor implementation, a choice point would be introduced in the local stack, and the computation would simply continue (extending both stacks). However, if multiple alternatives are to be considered in parallel, a *branch point* must be introduced in the stacks. That is, the stacks will actually be trees in which distinct branches are extended simultaneously. We will continue to refer to the structures as stacks, assuming that the reader understands that what we mean by a stack is a single path from the root to the end of some particular branch.

The alternative to creating branch points is to copy the contents of the stacks that occur before the alternatives arose. This turns out to be unwise (at least, we believe that is unwise), because the amount of copying would in many cases overshadow the gains of multiprocessing. Actually, no true consensus exists on this point, and there are certainly cases in which copying is preferable. Suffice it to say that we are exploring the alternative in which copying is not performed.

In the case in which branch points are introduced, it is still imperative that a rapidly evaluatable ordering on valuecells is maintained. We have achieved this ordering as follows:

1. The stacks are implemented as linked lists of fixed-length segments. If no branch points occurred throughout an entire computation, the local stack would still be formed as a linked list of these segments. When a branch point is introduced, a pointer to a new segment (from within the current segment) is created.

2. All of the segments in any branch of the tree must occur in ascending order, based on the memory address of the segment. This is achieved by maintaining lists of available segments which are ordered based on address of the segments. Thus, when a branch must be extended, the first segment in the list of available segments which has an address greater than the current segment is attached to the current segment.

By maintaining two preallocated lists of available segments (one for the local stack and one for the global stack), the proper ordering by memory address can be maintained. Since the allocation of new segments is relatively infrequent, the cost of locating the first segment in the list with a high enough address is not overly expensive (and could be further reduced, if required, by maintaining a B-tree to access the segments using the physical address of a segment as its key). This solution allows shared access to the pool of available segments (rather than allocating a maximum length stack at each branch), while maintaining the desired ordering.

5.2. Shadow Valuecells

Consider the case in which a single context has been extending the stacks, a branch point has been created, and now two distinct contexts are progressing on separate branches. For now, we will limit our discussion to the local stack, but our comments would apply equally to the global stack. An unbound valuecell that occurs before the branch point represents a logical variable that was not instantiated before the branch point was created. Later computation on either (or both) branches may cause the logical variable to be instantiated. However, because the two contexts are working on alternative solutions, the instantiation of such a variable must be visible only to the context that caused it (and the valuecell must remain unbound to the sibling contexts).

These brief considerations should make it clear that some mechanism is required for maintaining "shadow" valuecells that are local to subtrees of each stack. Then, when a reference is made to an unbound valuecell in a shared portion of the stack, a check is required to verify that the variable does not have a "shadow" binding. The creation, maintenance, and access of such shadow bindings is a central difficulty in the successful implementation of OR-parallelism.

In this section, we will discuss the mechanism that we use to maintain shadow bindings, and in the next section we will modify our discussion to include an optimization designed to reduce the overhead that is introduced. Shadow valuecells may be thought of as data items that are accessed via a key, where the key is the memory address of the original valuecell. Hence, one approach would be to simply associate with each context a hash table of shadow valuecells referenced by their associated keys. This may not really suffice, however. When a context reaches a new branch point, the sibling contexts must inherit the shadow bindings that existed at the point when the branch occurred. This could be achieved by simply copying all of the shadow bindings of the original context (which then forms the initial hash table for any sibling contexts). Again, we have chosen to avoid the solution based on copying (and, again, our decision can be reasonably questioned). Instead, we will associate with each context a stack of associated hash tables, where introducing a new branch point causes the addition of another table on the stack. Access to locate a shadow valuecell proceeds by computing the hash value, and then accessing every table in the stack until either a shadow valuecell is located or no more tables are left to examine. In this case, sibling contexts may share a common set of hash tables (but always have a unique table at the top of the stack).

This solution will work well only if the stack of hash tables stays very, very small. Note that the hash function is computed just once, and the time required to scan any single table is quite small. However, if any sizable number of branch points are introduced in a single branch of the local stack, the overhead would become substantial. This naturally leads to the topic of "favored contexts".

5.3. Favored Contexts

One central design goal of our multiprocessor implementation is that it run on uniprocessors. This allows one to perform a significant amount of testing and debugging in a familiar environment. In addition, however, we believe that the implementation should perform "reasonably well" in the uniprocessor environment. The introduction of branch points, and the associated overhead of shadow reference hash tables, could clearly impair that goal. Hence, we will implement the following optimization:

1. Each valuecell will be tagged to indicate whether it is "unbound", "bound only for the leftmost sibling (the favored context)", or "bound for all siblings". By tagging the valuecell this way, the valuecell itself may be thought of as the shadow binding for the leftmost sibling.

2. Each context is extending a single branch of the stack. This branch is divided into 3 distinct sections: that which is "private to the context", that which is "shared, but this context is favored", and that which is "shared, and this context is not favored". Hash tables for maintaining shadow bindings are necessary only for the section of the branch that is "shared, and this context is not favored".

This technique will (we conjecture) keep the size of the stack of hash tables fairly small for an implementation in which a limited number of processes are actually extending contexts. In the case in which a only a single process is used, no shadow valuecells are ever introduced.

6. Determinate AND-Parallelism

Determinate AND-parallelism refers to the simultaneous reduction of more than one of the remaining goals, with the proviso that only one solution of each of the goals need be considered. In the Prolog example covered earlier in this paper, if only a single path from one node to another going through a specified intermediate node were required, then it would make sense to reduce the goals searching for the two distinct subpaths simultaneously. This would constitute determinate AND-parallelism.

The exact coordination of determinate AND-parallelism is a complex topic. However, let us consider the relatively straightforward case of searching for the desired path. The rule that we are interested in is

```
path_through(START,MID,END,PATH) :-   path(START,MID,P1),
                                       path(MID,END,[MID|P2]),
                                       append(P1,P2,PATH).
```

197

At the point where this rule can be applied to reduce a goal, consider what it would mean to use determinate AND-parallelism. We can view a branch point being formed in which three sibling contexts are created (one for each of the goals). Valuecells for *P1* and *P2* are created just before the branch point, so that these valuecells are shared among the three contexts. The first two contexts then proceed in parallel computing answers which are eventually bound to these shared valuecells. The third context "waits" until these bindings occur and then proceeds to complete the overall computation.

The technique used to cause the third context to "wait" is frequently referred to as the use of "read-only" occurrences of variables. Here, the third context can proceed until it attempts to use the value of either *P1* or *P2*. Then it must be queued on the valuecell, waiting for another context to bind the valuecell. This introduces a number of distinct synchronization problems which are beyond the scope of this introductory paper. The interested reader should consult the references previously cited for Concurrent Prolog and Parlog to get a detailed description of how the computation should proceed. Since we have not yet made substantial progress in the implementation of determinate AND-parallelism, we do not offer here any discussion of implementation details.

It is worth noting, however, that determinate AND-parallelism corresponds to the type of parallelism commonly found in numerical algorithms. In Prolog, such parallelism is expressed in clauses that have subgoals (the literals in the body of the clause) that can be solved in parallel, and the literals correspond to the parallel processes. As in other types of parallel programs, a variety of interprocess communication protocols have arisen. (For example, the read-only variables referred to above represent an implementation of the Send/Receive method.)

7. Synchronization Issues

Implementing a multiprocessor version of the Warren machine introduces a small number of significant process synchronization problems. It is these, together with the data structures to support multiple active contexts, that differentiate this project from more traditional high-performance Prolog implementations projects.

1. The most obvious is the dispatching mechanism for assigning tasks to active processes. This is a standard synchronization pattern that we handle with the "askfor" monitor described elsewhere[11].

2. The degree to which valuecells are shared, and therefore the level of synchronization required for accessing and updating them, is Prolog dialect-dependent. Read-only variables, for example, require a mechanism by which a process can be made to wait for an event. This is just an example of the general phenomenon of communication between two contexts that are siblings in the context tree.

3. A thornier set of problems is connected with changes in the shape of the context tree itself. For example, when a "favored" context fails, it is necessary to make one of its siblings the new favored context. The communication and synchronization required to coordinate sibling procsses represents a major source of complexity (but not necessarily of overhead).

8. Comments on Our Use of the HEP

We are now faced with the fact that multiprocessors will become widely available over the next few years. Indeed, at Argonne we have a small 8-processor system that may well be a prototype for systems that will be commercially available for less than $50,000. At the same time, machine such as the CRAY-2 will offer multiple high-performance processors with access to a globally shared memory. The central question is how to develop software to harness this potential.

In many ways, the HEP has offered a unique environment for creating software that will be usable on a broad class of machines. It features the ability to implement and evaluate multiprocessing algorithms that capitalize on its extremely low-overhead synchronization primitives, and are yet portable to whatever machines become available in the future.

Our early work on the HEP was done in an extremely primitive software environment, which seems quite typical of most currently available multiprocessors. It taught us the value of developing portable implementations that could be debugged on uniprocessors and then moved to new machines as the hardware and software environments became available. Now, with the availability of UPX on the HEP, we are rapidly acquiring access to most of the tools one associates with a good programming environment. It is allowing our work on investigating achievable parallelism to progress without an inordinate effort to learn or master the peculiarities associated with most multiprocessors.

From our earliest experiences with the HEP, we have been convinced that it should be used to develop portable software to be run on a wide class of machines. It may well be that the HEP 2 will be appropriate machine to attain megalips, but it is also tenable that any number of other projected systems would be equally suitable. The point that we wish to make is that the HEP has offered us, and is now offering us, a unique ability to start a rather long term project without waiting for special-purpose machines. We will be able to evaluate many detailed design decisions that simply could not be examined accurately without access to such a machine.

9. Summary

This paper describes an effort that is still in its initial stages. We are extremely optimistic about the potential to construct high-performance inference engines over the next 5 to 6 years. To capitalize on the projected hardware advances, however, will require solutions to numerous demanding design problems. The effort required to arrive at these solutions can begin now, and need not be deferred until the availability of special-purpose hardware at some unspecified point in the future.

Much of the early work on multiprocessors has quite properly been devoted to evaluating programming techniques and attempting to gain some insight into the proper use of such machines. However, as these machines are now clearly going to become a commercial reality, it is time to initiate efforts to construct complete systems to capitalize on their capabilities. The ambitious goals set by a number of research groups in AI may or may not be realizable--we will only know after several more years of intense work. The tools to begin now exist.

References

1. M. Ben-Ari, *Principles of Concurrent Programming*, Prentice-Hall, Inc., Englewood Cliffs, New Jersey (1982).

2. Peter Borgwardt, "Parallel Prolog using stack segments on shared-memory multiprocessors," *Proceedings of the 1984 International Symposium on Logic Programming*, pp. 2-11 (February 1984).

3. Keith Clark and Steve Gregory, "PARLOG: Parallel Programming in Logic," Research Report DOC 84/4, Department of Computing, Imperial College of Science and Technology (April 1984).

4. J. S. Conery and D. F. Kibler, "Parallel interpretation of logic programs," *Proceedings of the ACM Conference of Functional Programming Languages and Computter Architecture*, pp. 163-170 (October 1981).

5. J. Gabriel, T. Lindholm, E. Lusk, and R. A. Overbeek, "A tutorial on the Warren abstract machine," Technical Report ANL-84-84, Argonne National Laboratory, Argonne, Illinois (October, 1984).

6. Per Brinch Hansen, "The programming language Concurrent Pascal," *IEEE Transactions on Software Engineering SE-1* 2 pp. 199-207 (June 1975).

7. Per Brinch Hansen, *The Architecture of Concurrent Programs*, Prentice-Hall, Inc., Englewood Cliffs, New Jersey (1977).

8. C. A. R. Hoare, "Monitors: an operating system structuring concept," *Communications of the ACM*, pp. 549-557 (October 1974).

9. R. C. Holt, G. S. Graham, E. D. Lazowska, and M. A. Scott, *Structured Concurrent Programming with Operating Systems Applications*, Addison-Wesley Publishing Co., Menlo Park, California (1978).

10. Ewing L. Lusk and Ross A. Overbeek, "An Approach to Programming Multiprocessing Algorithms on the Denelcor HEP," Technical Report ANL-83-96, Argonne National Laboratory, Argonne, Illinois (December 1983).

11. Ewing L. Lusk and Ross A. Overbeek, "Implementation of Monitors with Macros: A Programming Aid for the HEP and Other Parallel Processors," Technical Report ANL-83-97, Argonne National Laboratory, Argonne, Illinois (December 1983).

12. Ewing L. Lusk and Ross A. Overbeek, "Stalking the Gigalip," pp. 15-24 in *New Directions in Software for Advanced Computer Architectures*, *ANL/MCS-TM-32*, Mathematics and Computer Science Division, Argonne National Laboratory (August 1984).

13. Ehud Y. Shapiro, *A Subset of Concurrent Prolog and Its Interpreter*, (preprint, Weizmann Institute of Science, January 1983)

14. D. H. D. Warren, "An Abstract Prolog Instruction Set," SRI Technical Note 309, SRI International (October 1983).

15. N. Wirth, "MODULA: a language for modular programming," *Software Practice and Experience* 7 pp. 3-35 (January-February 1977).

3.5 PROGRAMMING THE HEP WITH LARGE-GRAIN DATA FLOW TECHNIQUES†

R. G. BABB II
Department of Computer Science and Engineering
Oregon Graduate Center
Beaverton, Oregon

1. INTRODUCTION

Programming parallel processors can be very frustrating. In addition to the usual software engineering problems common to all forms of program development, an additional set of problems must be avoided and additional criteria must be met for a parallel program to be judged successful. Software engineering problems directly related to the introduction of parallelism include:

- Deadlock and livelock avoidance
- Preventing race conditions
- Avoiding creation of too many parallel processes
- Detecting program termination

New evaluation criteria for parallel programs include:

- Program speedup versus number of processors
- Size of synchronization overhead
- Effect of problem size on speedup
- Max. number of processors that can be kept busy
- Is the program deterministic?

In addition, new software design issues arise, such as:

- What size program "chunks" should be used?
- How many parallel processes should be created?
- What form of process synchronization should be adopted?
- How should access to shared data be managed?
- How can deterministic program execution be guaranteed?

† This work was supported in part by Denelcor, Inc., Aurora, Colorado, under Contract 84-S-010, and Los Alamos National Laboratory under Contract 9-Z-34-P-3915-1.

- How should be processing tasks be sub-divided to make the most effective use of available parallel hardware?

Debugging parallel programs is notoriously difficult. Race conditions can masquerade as program logic errors. When deadlock occurs on the HEP, for example, the addresses where the various parallel processes are "hung" can be determined. However, figuring out how the program got *into* the deadlock situation is usually much more difficult. Debug tracing can affect the parallel behavior of the program being debugged. Non-deterministic programs sometimes "fix themselves" when debug tracing is added, since the tracing serializes a portion of the execution.

The Large-Grain Data Flow (LGDF) methods described in this chapter represent an attempt to provide an abstract computational model for parallel processing that is easy to understand, yet powerful enough to address the questions and issues listed above. Another goal of the methods is to provide a model that can be implemented on a wide variety of *both* parallel and sequential architectures. In this paper the discussion and all of the examples refer to HEP-OS Fortran77[1] for the Denelcor HEP-1 parallel processor[2].

The next section presents an introduction to the LGDF computational model, notation, and semantics. Section 3 presents an overview of the steps involved in using the LGDF Macro Toolset to implement parallel programs. In Section 4 the solution to a small numerical programming example is presented—the parallel solution of a triangular system. Conclusions and references to related work can be found in Section 5.

2. LARGE-GRAIN DATA FLOW

Considerable research effort during the past 15 years has been devoted to the study of dataflow machine architectures and languages as a means to achieve highly parallel computation[3]. The source of parallelism in the data flow approach arises from the possibility of simultaneous execution of a large number of independent operations whose operands have been previously computed. Operations are conceptually linked in a network so that the result of each local computation is fed automatically into the appropriate inputs of other operations. Although traditional dataflow approaches provide an attractive basis for parallel processing, only a few experimental dataflow machines have actually been built[4] [5] and data flow languages such as ID[6], VAL[7], SISAL[8] and LAU[9] have not been widely accepted.

A major parameter in parallel processing is the size of the "granule" of computation that is executed in parallel. In traditional programs for Von Neumann computers, a granule corresponds to an entire application program, and little parallelism within an application program can be exploited. On the other hand, in most dataflow work to date, the grain size chosen for parallel scheduling has been at the level of a single arithmetic or logical operator. Large-Grain Data Flow combines features of both approaches. The large grain structure of application programs is represented explicitly.

The LGDF computation model resembles traditional data flow in that LGDF processes are activated and controlled by the arrival of and consumption of data values. An *LGDF process* can be in one of three process-states: *executing*, *suspended*, or *terminated*. While executing, in addition to arithmetic and logical computation on input data values it can also perform data flow control actions corresponding to:

- the consumption of data values
- the production of data values
- changing the case-state of process
- reiteration of a process
- suspension of a process

All processes are initially suspended. Processes are represented diagrammatically by circles as shown in Fig. 1. Each process is given an associated descriptive name, and a unique p# tag. An *LGDF data path* is a data memory shared among a number of LGDF processes. Data paths are represented by several types of directed arcs, as shown in Fig. 2. Each data path is also given a descriptive name, and has associated a unique d#. In addition to data values, each data path has a data-state: *empty* or *full*. All data paths are initially empty. Processes and data paths are linked together into acyclic networks of producers and consumers of data as shown in Fig. 3. LGDF networks can achieve parallel operation based on simple producer/consumer data flow interactions. Processes are activated asynchronously depending only upon the empty/full data-states of their associated input and output data paths. All LGDF processes must obey the following two rules:

Fig. 1. Graphic representation of an LGDF process.

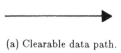

(a) Clearable data path.

(b) Non-clearable data path.

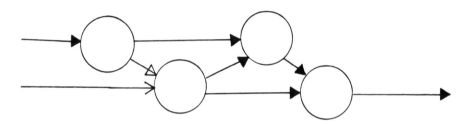

(c) Side-effect (non-controlling) data path.

Fig. 2. Graphic representation of LGDF data paths.

Fig. 3. Graphic representation of an LGDF process network.

Execution Rule. An LGDF process may change its process-state from suspended to executing only after all of its associated input data paths are full, and all of its output data paths are empty.

Data Flow Progress Rule. Upon suspension of an execution cycle, an LGDF process is required to have made data flow progress. This means that it has cleared (consumed) at least one input, or it has set (produced) at least one output during the current execution cycle. Otherwise, the process is terminated.

Setting an output data path has the effect of making the data path available to activate downstream processes. In a similar fashion, processes that clear their input data paths can indirectly activate upstream processes by making a data path available for writing. During any one execution cycle for a process, each of its input data paths can be cleared at most once. Similarly, each of its output data path can be set at most once. Processes are allowed to read data values only from full input data paths and write data values only on empty output data paths.

Processes can have two types of access to values on input data paths:

- *Read-only*—associated data values may be referenced, but not changed.
- *Update*—associated data values may be both read and changed.

Input data paths that are of type update correspond to variables in ordinary programming languages. Read-only data paths correspond, for example, to constants or call-by-value function arguments. Graphic notations for read-only and update data paths are shown in Fig. 4. LGDF processes are restricted to write access to their output data paths.

Access to data values, for example, arrays, can be shared among a set of LGDF processes in two different ways:

- sequential shared access
- parallel shared access

A sequentially shared data path represents a data memory which is controlled so that at most one process has access to the shared data values at a time. This corresponds to forcing serialization of that portion of the computation. A parallel shared data path represents a data memory in which asynchronous access is possible by a set of processes. Processes that access a parallel shared data path can also compete non-deterministically for exclusive access to the shared input or output. Notations for sequential and parallel shared data paths, for both read-only and update access, are shown in Fig. 5.

LGDF process networks can also be defined hierarchically. This means that any node in a network may be specified either by an LGDF process (as discussed above) or by another network. The semantics of this are the same as if all references to lower level networks were replaced by their defining networks. This

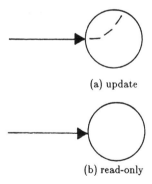

(a) update

(b) read-only

Fig. 4. Graphic representations for update and read-only data paths.

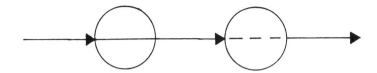

(a) Sequential shared read-only and update data paths.

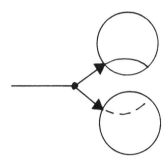

(b) Parallel (asynchronously) shared read-only and update data paths.

Fig. 5. Graphic notations for shared data paths.

grouping mechanism is used to cluster processes that execute with approximately the same frequency[1].

LGDF application designs tend to deal with data-activated chunks that correspond typically to 5 to 50 lines of executable higher-level language statements. This has the effect of providing a relatively familiar subroutine-like interface for programmers, as shown in Fig. 6.

LGDF network diagrams specify unambiguously which SUBROUTINE parameters are inputs (X), which are outputs (Y,J) , and which are both (I). Another difference is that a programmer does not CALL a SUBROUTINE for execution, but activates it indirectly by sending data to it.

---

[1]On a single PEM HEP, the process grouping information is not used directly, since all processes are effectively at the same scheduling level (a 128-way single-level parallel process scheduler is built in to the hardware). However, when emulating LGDF parallel operation on a sequential computer, the round-robin scheduling mechanism can be made more efficient, because processes that execute infrequently are checked less often for executability.

SUBROUTINE A(X,I,Y,J)

.

.

.

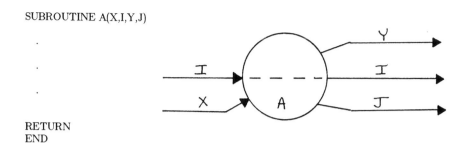

RETURN
END

Fig. 6. Comparison between a SUBROUTINE and an LGDF process.

3. USING LGDF MACROS FOR PARALLEL PROGRAMMING

In this section, we give an overview of the steps involved in implementing a parallel Fortran program on the HEP using the Large-Grain Data Flow Macro Toolset. The steps involved in using the LGDF macro tools are:

1) *Draw LGDF Network Diagrams*—The goal in designing an LGDF process network to solve a problem is to produce a hierarchical, consistent[2] set of network data flow graphs that embody the large grain logical data dependencies inherent in the problem.

Parallelism can be achieved in several ways. The simplest kind of parallelism in the LGDF computation model is *data-independent* parallel processing. Any two executable LGDF processes that share no data paths can safely execute simultaneously since they cannot interfere with each other.

The next simplest method is *data-sequential* or *pipelined* parallelism. In a pipeline, a series of processes can be active simultaneously on different phases of the production of a final result. This is the same idea exploited in the floating point units of vector processor supercomputers and in UNIX[3] pipes[10].

The third method is *asynchronous-parallel-update*. This is "risky" parallel processing, where multiple processes have asynchronous read and/or update access to a shared data structure (usually an array). It is the LGDF programmer's responsibility to ensure that the updates are performed safely and correctly. A common way to ensure this safety is to prevent two processes from trying to update the same array element at the

---

[2]A set of data flow graphs is consistent if the inputs and outputs of each LGDF system process match the input and output data paths shown on the corresponding lower level defining network.

[3]UNIX is a trademark of Bell Laboratories.

same time.

The Triangular Solver example contains examples of all three types of parallelism.

2) *Create Wirelist File*—The Wirelist file uses macros to declare names and internal tags for processes and data paths. The data flow dependencies of the set of data flow diagrams from step 1) are also encoded using macro calls[4]. The macros indicate which data paths are inputs and which are outputs for each process and process network. Also encoded are the type of access each process has to its input data paths: clearable (CL) or non-clearable (NC), and read-only (RO) or update (UP).

3) *Package Data Declarations*—Fortran data declarations corresponding to each data path in the data flow diagrams are put into separate files whose names correspond to their data path tags. (These become labeled COMMON declarations in the generated programs).

4) *Write LGDF Programs*—Combine LGDF macro calls with appropriate Fortran code to implement each program. The LGDF programmer writes macros for execution barriers and actions. Data flow control macros are used to signal consumption of inputs and production of output values. Other macros are used to change the case-state of a process, and to reiterate, or suspend execution.

5) *Macro Expand LGDF Programs*—The wirelist and data declaration files are used to control the macro-expansion of the LGDF program files to produce compilable Fortran for a particular machine. The expansion is based on the data path connectivity information encoded in the Wirelist File. SUBROUTINE headers and labeled COMMON statements corresponding to a program's input and output data paths are inserted automatically.

6) *Compile and Execute*—The resulting source code is then compiled including, if desired, pre- and/or post-compilation optimization steps available for the particular target environment.

See [11] and [12] for further details on LGDF methods for software engineering and parallel processing.

---

[4]This step is currently done manually, but will eventually be an automatic result of a graphics-based tool used to draw LGDF network diagrams.

4. SOLVING A TRIANGULAR SYSTEM

Presented below is a detailed example of LGDF programming for the HEP. The development of the example assumes familiarity with the terms and notation defined in Section 2. All user-coded inputs to the macro expansion process are shown, as well as samples of the expanded Fortran code.

The problem is to solve a lower triangular matrix T (of dimension N by N) to yield a result vector Y (of dimension N). The parallel solution strategy employed is to break T up into sub-matrices of dimension (usually) K by K. Since K may not evenly divide N, we will in general have a column block of submatrices left over that will be less than K columns wide. We choose to put this narrow column of submatrices at the left edge of T, as shown in Fig. 7 for the case N=8, K=3.

Again, referring to Fig. 7., the basic approach is employ a triangle solver (TS) to update Y for the first triangular group of T values labeled TS_1. After this TS process has finished updating the result vector Y, a series of matrix multiply (MM) processes can begin execution in parallel for the column block below. Each of the matrix multiply steps is independent. However, care must be taken that parallel updates to the result vector Y by the various MM's are performed safely.

The next triangle solver step on the diagonal (TS_2) must wait until all of the matrix multiply steps in the same row block to its left have completed their updates of Y. Then a series of matrix multiply processes can be started in the column block below, and the pattern repeats. The LGDF solution to this problem employs an "interlock" data path to block the next triangle solver step until

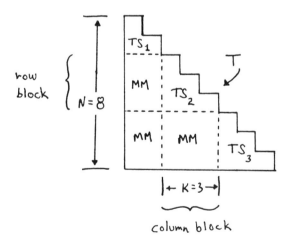

Fig. 7. Solution strategy for the parallel triangular solver.

the appropriate matrix multiply steps have completed. The interlock is cleared by use of a matrix multiply "check-in" process (MMCKIN) that counts the number of matrix multiplies that have completed in each row block. When the row block of MM's has finished, a row block completion signal is produced that causes the triangle solver interlock data path to be cleared.

In the discussion of the LGDF solution below, p and d numbers are used to cross-reference the various networks, processes, and data paths with program texts.

4.1. *Draw LGDF Network Diagrams*

The LGDF solution to the parallel triangular matrix solver is shown on three process network diagrams, in Figs. 8-10. The top level network (p00), shown in Fig. 8, consists of a process TSINIT (p10) that sets up a problem to be solved (d01), initializes the result vector Y (d02) to zeros, and initializes various counters and index values (d03, d04). TSINIT can execute immediately because all internal data paths in a network hierarchy are initially empty. The system[5] TMWORK (p01) then updates the result vector Y in place to produce the final result vector (d02a)[6]. The dashed lines inside the circle for p01 for data paths d03 and d04 indicate that their contents can be updated by processes running inside p01. Note that data path d01 can be cleared by processes internal to p01, but the associated TS problem values can not be changed.

An LGDF process network definition of TMWORK (p01) is shown in Fig. 9. The notation in square brackets "[p00]" below p01 on Fig. 9 indicates the parent (context) network process for a network. The program TSWORK (p11) controls all of the remaining processes in the solution, either directly or indirectly. Since it "knows" the global state of computational progress, it can produce the answer by setting the result vector Y (d02a) after all final Y values have been computed. TSWORK causes a triangle to be solved by TS (p12) by setting appropriate TS control values on d04a. It then blocks itself from further execution until the appropriate matrix multiplies have completed inside MMWORK (p02) by setting the next row block interlock NRBI (d05). NRBI is cleared by WAITRB (p13) after the next row block complete signal NRBC (d07) is produced inside p02. After TS has updated Y (d02), it starts the matrix multiplies below it by setting appropriate MM control parameters (d06). Note that both p12 and the processes inside p02 have asynchronous update access to Y (d02), a potentially unsafe situation.

---

[5]We use the term "system" for processes that are defined by a network, rather than by an LGDF program.

[6]Note that even though d02 and d02a represent the same array, they are assigned different data path tags, and can be independently set and cleared. The open arrowhead on data path d02 indicates that no process inside p01 is allowed to explicitly clear the result vector. (It is said to be *non-clearable*). However, a mechanism is provided in the generated Fortran code to automatically propagate a "clear" backwards for shared data paths when the corresponding shared output is cleared, which in this case would have to be done by a process external to this network.

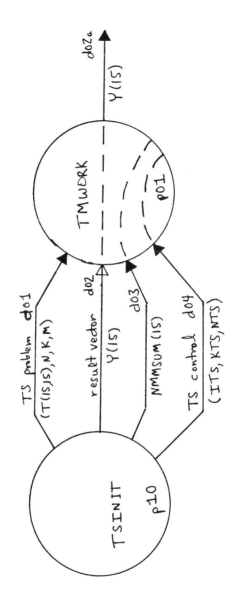

Fig. 8. LGDF process network for TSOLVE (p00).

213

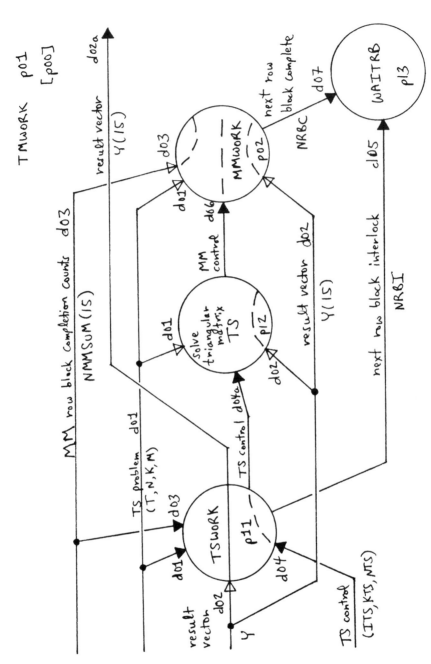

Fig. 9. LGDF process network for TMWORK (p01).

The lowest level LGDF process network for this example is for MMWORK (p02), shown in Fig. 10. MMWORK (p14) generates the next MM sub-problem (d06a). A collection of MM processes (p15) compete asynchronously for work on d06a. After an MM process gets exclusive read access to d06a, it makes local copies of the MM control values and clears d06a, allowing p14 to generate the next MM sub-problem immediately. Each MM computes its contribution to the result vector Y using an array local to each copy of p15. When it has completed its computation, it competes for exclusive write access to the MM checkin data path (d08). Since only one MM process can be checking in at a time, it can also safely update Y during this time. MMCKIN (p16) counts the number of MM processes that have completed by row, and when all have checked in, sets the next row block completion signal NRBC (d07).

4.2. Create Wirelist File

A *Wirelist File* is a set of macro calls consisting of two parts. The first part, shown in Fig. 11, defines data path and program names and tags. The tags are then used in the second part, which consists of a series of macro calls that encode the connectivity, and data path and process types of a set of LGDF process network diagrams. The wirelist corresponding to the diagrams in Figs. 8-10 are shown in Fig. 12. Error checking is incorporated in the macro expansion process. Errors diagnosed include use of an undefined d or p tag and input of a data path that is neither an external input, nor the output of another LGDF program. Data path type errors are also diagnosed, such as inconsistent usage of clearable and non-clearable data paths.

4.3. Package Data Declarations

Data declarations corresponding to data paths are retrieved from separate files. The data declaration files for this example are shown in Fig. 13.

4.4. Write LGDF Programs

The complete LGDF macro forms for programs p10 through p16 are shown in Fig. 14.

4.5. Macro Expand LGDF Programs

A sample program (p12) macro-expanded for the HEP is shown in Fig. 15. Also generated is a top-level initiation program and a set of network initiator subroutines, one for each network diagram. The top-level initiation program that contains trace aid facilities and code which prints out run statistics and the final set of data path states. It also calls the top-level network initiator subroutine (in this case p00) which creates the other LGDF processes in the network. Each process can be created only once in the current version of the tools. Network initiator subroutines for TSOLVE (p00), TMWORK (p01), and MMWORK (p02) are shown in Fig. 16.

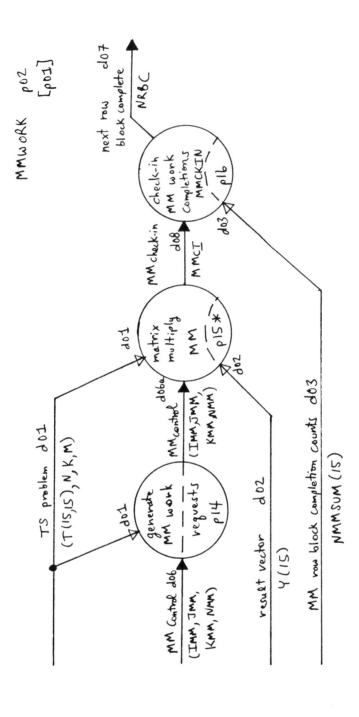

Fig. 10. LGDF process network for MMWORK (p02).

```
*** DEFINE DATA PATHS

***      tag    short name      descriptive name

_defdp(d01,  "TS problem",  "(T(15,15),N,K,M)")
_defdp(d02,  "Y",           "result vector (space)")
_defdp(d03,  "NMMSUM",      "MM row block completion counts")
_defdp(d04,  "TS control",  "(ITS,KTS,NTS)")
_defdp(d05,  "NRBI",        "next row block interlock")
_defdp(d06,  "MM control",  "(IMM,JMM,KMM,NMM)")
_defdp(d07,  "NRBC",        "next row block complete")
_defdp(d08,  "MMCI",        "MM check-in")

*** DEFINE PROGRAMS & NETWORKS

***      tag    short name      descriptive name

_defpn(p00,  "TSOLVE",   "parallel triangular matrix solver")
_defpn(p01,  "TMWORK",   "perform TS and MM work")
_defpn(p02,  "MMWORK",   "perform MM work")
_defpn(p10,  "TSINIT",   "initialize TS test problem parameters")
_defpn(p11,  "TSWORK",   "generate TS work requests")
_defpn(p12,  "TS",       "solve triangular matrix")
_defpn(p13,  "NEXTTS",   "interlock TS and MM work progress")
_defpn(p14,  "MMWORK",   "generate MM work requests")
_defpn(p15,  "MM",       "matrix multiply")
_defpn(p16,  "MMCKIN",   "checkin MM work completions")
```

Fig. 11. Data path and program definitions for the parallel triangular solver example.

217

```
*** WIRELIST

****************************
_net (top, [])
    _sys (p00, [top])
        _waitout (d02a, CL)
    _endsys (p00, [top])
_endnet (top, [])
****************************
_net (p00, [top])
    _prog (p10, [p00])
        _out (d04, CL)
        _out (d01, CL)
        _out (d02, NC)
        _out (d03, CL)
    _endprog (p10, [p00])
    _sys (p01, [p00])
        _in (d01, CL, RO)
        _in (d02, NC, UP)
        _in (d03, CL, UP)
        _in (d04, CL, UP)
            _shared (d02, d02a, NC, UP)
        _out (d02a, CL)
    _endsys (p01, [p00])
_endnet (p00, [top])
****************************
_net (p01, [p00])
    _in (d01, CL, RO)
    _in (d02, NC, UP)
    _in (d03, CL, UP)
    _in (d04, CL, UP)
    _prog (p11, [p01])

        _in (d01, CL, RO)
        _in (d02, NC, RO)
        _in (d03, CL, RO)
        _in (d04, CL, UP)
            _shared (d02, d02a, NC, RO)
            _shared (d04, d04a, CL, UP)
        _out (d04a, CL)
        _out (d02a, CL)
        _out (d05, CL)
    _endprog (p11, [p01])
```

```
    _prog (p12, [p01])
        _in (d01, NC, RO)
        _in (d02, NC, UP)
        _in (d04a, CL, RO)
        _out (d06, CL)
    _endprog (p12, [p01])
    _sys (p02, [p01])
        _in (d01, NC, RO)
        _in (d06, CL, RO)
        _in (d02, NC, UP)
        _in (d03, NC, UP)
        _out (d07, CL)
    _endsys (p02, [p01])
    _prog (p13, [p01])
        _in (d07, CL, RO)
        _in (d05, CL, RO)
    _endprog (p13, [p01])
_endnet (p01, [p00])
****************************
_net (p02, [p01])
    _in (d01, NC, RO)
    _in (d06, CL, UP)
    _in (d02, NC, UP)
    _in (d03, NC, UP)
    _prog (p14, [p02])
        _in (d01, NC, RO)
        _in (d06, CL)
            _shared (d06, d06a, CL, UP)
        _out (d06a, CL)
    _endprog (p14, [p02])
    _prog (p15, [p02], *6)
        _in (d01, NC, RO)
        _in (d06a, CL, RO)
        _in (d02, NC, UP)
        _out (d08, CL)
    _endprog (p15, [p02])
    _prog (p16, [p02])
        _in (d08, CL, RO)
        _in (d03, NC, UP)
        _out (d07, CL)
    _endprog (p16, [p02])
_endnet (p02, [p01])
****************************
```

Fig. 12. Encoded data path/program connectivity in the Wirelist File.

```
dO1:                                      dO5:

T,N,K,M                                   NRBI
      REAL T(15,15)                             INTEGER NRBI
      INTEGER N,K,M
─────────────────────────────            ─────────────────────────────

dO2:                                      dO6:

Y                                         IMM,JMM,KMM,NMM
      REAL Y(15)                                INTEGER IMM,JMM,KMM,NMM
─────────────────────────────            ─────────────────────────────

dO3:                                      dO7:

NMMSUM                                    NRBC
      INTEGER NMMSUM(15)                        INTEGER NRBC
─────────────────────────────            ─────────────────────────────

dO4:                                      dO8:

ITS,KTS,NTS                              MMCI
      INTEGER ITS,KTS,NTS                       INTEGER MMCI
```

Fig. 13. Data declaration files for the parallel triangular solver example.

```
program_(p10,[p00])
C--LOCAL VARIABLES
      REAL TEMP
      INTEGER I,J
begin_
C--SET UP TEST PROBLEM VALUES (N IS ASSUMED TO BE .GE. K)
      N=8
      K=3
      M=((N-1)/K)+1
C--INITIALIZE THE RESULT VECTOR Y AND T
      DO 5 I=1,N
         Y(I)=0.0
    5 CONTINUE
      DO 20 J=1,N
         DO 10 I=J,N
            TEMP=I*J
            T(I,J)=TEMP
            Y(I)=Y(I)+TEMP
   10    CONTINUE
   20 CONTINUE
      set_(d02)
      set_(d01)
C--INITIALIZE THE ROW BLOCK COMPLETION COUNTS
      DO 50 I=1,K
         NMMSUM(I)=0
   50 CONTINUE
      set_(d03)
C--INITIALIZE TS WORK VARIABLES
      ITS=1
      KTS=N-((M-1)*K)
      NTS=1
      set_(d04)
end_(p10)
```

Fig. 14(a). An LGDF program for TSINIT (p10).

```
program_(p11,[p01])
begin_
states_(s00,s01,s02)
state_(s00,issue first TS work request)
      set_(d04)
C--(NOTE: NO SET OF d05 ROW BLOCK INTERLOCK)
C--CHECK FOR LAST TRIANGLE
      IF(NTS.EQ.M) THEN
          next_(s02,set result vector)
      ELSE
          next_(s01,issue next TS work)
      ENDIF
      suspend_
state_(s01,issue next TS work)
      ITS=ITS+KTS
      KTS=K
      set_(d04)
C--SET ROW BLOCK INTERLOCK
      NRBI=NTS
      set_(d05)
C--CHECK FOR LAST TRIANGLE
      NTS=NTS+1
      IF(NTS.EQ.M) THEN
          next_(s02,set result vector)
      ENDIF
      suspend_
state_(s02,set result vector)
      set_(d02)
      WRITE(6,40)  (Y(I),I=1,N)
   40 FORMAT(' Y=',15F5.2)
      clear_(d01)
      clear_(d03)
      clear_(d04)
      suspend_
end_(p11)
```

Fig. 14(b). An LGDF program for TSWORK (p11).

```
program_(p12,[p01])
      INTEGER I,J,LL
begin_
      LL=KTS
      DO 20 J=ITS,ITS+LL-1
          Y(J)=Y(J)/T(J,J)
          LL=LL-1
          DO 10 I=J+1,J+LL
              Y(I)=Y(I)-T(I,J)*Y(J)
   10     CONTINUE
   20 CONTINUE
      clear_(d04)
      IF(NTS.LT.M) THEN
C -- ENABLE MMWORK
          IMM=ITS+KTS
          JMM=ITS
          KMM=KTS
          NMM=NTS+1
          set_(d06)
      ENDIF
      suspend_
end_(p12)
```

Fig. 14(c). An LGDF program for TS (p12).

220

```
        program_(p13,[pO1])
        begin_
               clear_(dO5)
               clear_(dO7)
               suspend_
        end_(p13)
```

Fig. 14(d). An LGDF program for WAITRB (p13).

```
program_(p14,[pO2])
begin_
states_(sOO,sO1)
state_(sOO,issue first MM work request)
      set_(dO6)
      next_(sO1, issue next work request)
      suspend_
state_(sO1,issue next work request)
      IMM=IMM+K
      IF(IMM.GT.N) THEN
         next_(sOO,issue first MM work request)
         clear_(dO6)
      ELSE
         NMM=NMM+1
         set_(dO6)
      ENDIF
      suspend_
end_(p14)
```

Fig. 14(e). An LGDF program for MMWORK (p14).

```
program_(p15,[pO2],*)
C--LOCAL VARIABLES
      REAL YHAT(15),TEMP
      INTEGER LI,LJ,LK,LN,I,J,II
begin_
C--WAIT FOR EXCLUSIVE READ ACCESS TO INPUT ARGS
      aread_(dO6)
C--MAKE LOCAL COPIES OF INPUT ARGS
      LI=IMM
      LJ=JMM
      LK=KMM
      LN=NMM
C--ALLOW GENERATION OF MORE MM WORK
      aclear_(dO6)
C--YHAT IS A LOCAL ARRAY USED LATER TO UPDATE Y
      DO 10 I=1,K
        YHAT(I)=0.0
   10 CONTINUE
C
      DO 20 J=LJ,LJ+LK-1
        TEMP=Y(J)
        II=LI
        DO 15 I=1,K
          YHAT(I)=YHAT(I)+T(II,J)*TEMP
          II=II+1
   15     CONTINUE
   20 CONTINUE
C--WAIT FOR EXCLUSIVE WRITE ACCESS TO OUTPUT DATA PATH dO8
C--(ALSO USED TO SERIALIZE UPDATES TO Y BY MM'S)
      awrite_(dO8)
C--UPDATE RESULT VECTOR
      DO 30 L=1,K
        Y(LI)=Y(LI)-YHAT(L)
        LI=LI+1
   30 CONTINUE
C--SIGNAL MM COMPLETION (GIVING CURRENT ROW BLOCK NO. LN)
      MMCI=LN
      aset_(dO8)
      suspend_
end_(p15)
```

Fig. 14(f). An LGDF program for TSINIT (p15).

```
program_(p16,[pO2])
C--LOCAL VARIABLE
      INTEGER LNRB
begin_
C-MAKE LOCAL COPY OF INPUT ARG
      LNRB=MMCI
      clear_(dO8)
      NMMSUM(LNRB)=NMMSUM(LNRB)+1
C -- CHECK FOR ALL MM's CHECKED IN THIS ROW BLOCK
      IF( (NMMSUM(LNRB)+1) .EQ. LNRB) THEN
        NRBC=LNRB
        set_(dO7)
      ENDIF
      suspend_
end_(p16)
```

Fig. 14(g). An LGDF program for MMCKIN (p16).

```
C---- TS -- solve triangular matrix
      SUBROUTINE P12(IPN,IPCTXT)
C--------------- (HEP FORTRAN SYSTEM TABLES) ---------------
      COMMON /SYSTAB/ $LTR,$DW,$DR,LPR(16),LPS(16),LPX(16),LNL(16)
      LOGICAL $LTR,$DW(11),$DR(11)
      LOGICAL GO,DFPROG
C-> d01: TS problem - (T(15,15),N,K,M)
      COMMON /D01/ T,N,K,M
      REAL T(15,15)
      INTEGER N,K,M
C-> d02: Y          - result vector (space)
      COMMON /D02/ Y
      REAL Y(15)
C-> d04: TS control - (ITS,KTS,NTS)
      COMMON /D04/ ITS,KTS,NTS
      INTEGER ITS,KTS,NTS
C-> d06: MM control - (IMM,JMM,KMM,NMM)
      COMMON /D06/ IMM,JMM,KMM,NMM
      INTEGER IMM,JMM,KMM,NMM
      INTEGER I,J,LL
      IF(LPR(IPN).EQ. -1) RETURN
 7799 DFPROG=.FALSE.
      $DR(3)=$DR(3)
      $DR(4)=$DR(4)
      $DR(6)=$DR(6)
      $DW(8)=GO
      GO=$DW(8)
 7798 LPX(IPN)=LPX(IPN)+1
      LPR(IPN)=1
      LPR(IPCTXT)=LPR(IPCTXT)+1
      LL=KTS
      DO 20 J=ITS,ITS+LL-1
         Y(J)=Y(J)/T(J,J)
         LL=LL-1
         DO 10 I=J+1,J+LL
            Y(I)=Y(I)-T(I,J)*Y(J)
   10    CONTINUE
   20 CONTINUE
      GO=$DR(6)
      GO=$DW(6)
      DFPROG=.TRUE.
      IF(NTS.LT.M) THEN
C -- ENABLE MMWORK
         IMM=ITS+KTS
         JMM=ITS
         KMM=KTS
         NMM=NTS+1
         $DW(8)=.FALSE.
         DFPROG=.TRUE.
         $DR(8)=.FALSE.
         DFPROG=.TRUE.
      ENDIF
      GO TO  7797
 7797 IF(.NOT.DFPROG) THEN
         GO=$LTR
         CALL PTRACE(IPN,48,0,LPX(IPN),0.0)
         $LTR=VALUE($LTR)
         LPR(IPN)= -1
         RETURN
      ENDIF
      GO TO  7799
      END
```

Fig. 15. Macro-expanded version of TS (p12) for the HEP.

223

```
C
C--- HEP FORTRAN PROCESS INITIATORS ---
C
      SUBROUTINE POO (IPN, IPCTXT)
C
C-------------- (HEP FORTRAN SYSTEM TABLES) --------------
      COMMON /SYSTAB/ $LTR, $DW, $DR, LPR (16) , LPS (16) , LPX (16) , LNL (16)
      LOGICAL $LTR, $DW (11) , $DR (11)
 7798 LPX (IPN) =LPX (IPN) +1
      CREATE P10 (3, IPN)
        CALL PO1 (4, IPN)
      RETURN
      END
C
      SUBROUTINE PO1 (IPN, IPCTXT)
C
C-------------- (HEP FORTRAN SYSTEM TABLES) --------------
      COMMON /SYSTAB/ $LTR, $DW, $DR, LPR (16) , LPS (16) , LPX (16) , LNL (16)
      LOGICAL $LTR, $DW (11) , $DR (11)
 7798 LPX (IPN) =LPX (IPN) +1
      CREATE P11 (5, IPN)
      CREATE P12 (6, IPN)
        CALL PO2 (7, IPN)
      CREATE P13 (8, IPN)
      RETURN
      END
C
      SUBROUTINE PO2 (IPN, IPCTXT)
C
C-------------- (HEP FORTRAN SYSTEM TABLES) --------------
      COMMON /SYSTAB/ $LTR, $DW, $DR, LPR (16) , LPS (16) , LPX (16) , LNL (16)
      LOGICAL $LTR, $DW (11) , $DR (11)
 7798 LPX (IPN) =LPX (IPN) +1
      CREATE P14 (9, IPN)
      CREATE P15 (10, IPN)
      CREATE P15 (11, IPN)
      CREATE P15 (12, IPN)
      CREATE P15 (13, IPN)
      CREATE P15 (14, IPN)
      CREATE P15 (15, IPN)
      CREATE P16 (16, IPN)
      RETURN
      END
```

Fig. 16. Network initiator subroutines for the parallel triangular solver example.

4.6. *Compile and Execute*

The output of the macro-expansion step is compilable Fortran for the particular target machine. The code can be further pre-processed in environments where Fortran pre-processing tools such as vectorizers are available. Of course, the object code can be further optimized automatically also.

5. CONCLUSION

The basic asynchronous variable mechanism available on the HEP appears deceptively simple. This apparent simplicity can lead even very good programmers, with a good understanding of parallel processing and of the HEP architecture, into very deep asynchronous-parallel update trouble. Several other researchers[13] [14] [15] have concluded that a good way to avoid some of the pitfalls of bare-knuckled parallel processing on the HEP is to program using a relatively simple set of macros to express barriers and other synchronization abstractions. The macros are then expanded into appropriate primitive synchronization actions. Despite the fact that the parallel abstractions supported by the various macro packages are quite different, most people who have tried any of them have found parallel programming much easier. This would appear to be a time to experiment with various abstractions, and to gain experience with software engineering methods to aid in parallel programming. Eventually, the more successful of these abstractions could be encapsulated in later versions of Fortran and other scientific programming languages.

We have come to some unexpected conclusions as a result of our work in modeling algorithms using "safe" parallel (data-independent), pipelined (data-sequenced), and "risky" parallel (asynchronous shared update) LGDF network data flow patterns. The most surprising is that "sequential" programs are often easier to design and implement reliably when based on a parallel (asynchronous) model of computation. The extra difficulty of the traditional implementation approach arises because of the artificial sequencing imposed by conventional programming.

Using the prototype toolset based on macro expansion techniques, we have demonstrated that the the same "macro" program can be run efficiently (unchanged) on a sequential and a parallel processor. The program ran with simulated parallelism on the sequential processor (a VAX) and with real parallelism on the parallel processor (a HEP-1). It is hoped that the software engineering methods described in this section will form the basis for programming a wide variety of parallel architectures.

6. Acknowledgment

The ideas in this paper have been developed over a period of several years, and many people have contributed to their current form. The author would like to acknowledge especially the contributions of James Hardy, Robert Hiromoto, Richard Kieburtz, Richard Hamlet and Danny Sorensen. Dr. Sorensen suggested the Parallel Triangle Solver problem and solution approach, and helped develop both the LGDF process network diagrams and the LGDF programs.

7. REFERENCES

[1]   *HEP FORTRAN 77 User's Guide.* Aurora, CO: Denelcor, Inc., 1982

[2]   M.C. Gilliland, B. J. Smith, and W. Calvert, "HEP--A semaphore-synchronized multiprocessor with central control," in *Proc. 1976 Summer Computer Simulation Conf.,* Washington, D.C, July 1976, pp. 57-62.

[3]   T. Agerwala and Arvind, (eds.), Special Issue of *Computer* on Data Flow Systems, Vol. 15, No. 2, Feb. 1982.

[4]   M. Amamiya, et al., "Data Flow Machine Architecture". Internal Notes 1 and 2, Musashino Electrical Communications Laboratories, Nippon Telephone and Telegraph Corporation, Tokyo, Japan, May 1980.

[5]   I. Watson and J. Gurd, "A practical data flow computer," *Computer*, Vol. 15, No. 2, Feb. 1982, pp. 51-57.

[6]   Arvind, K. P. Gostelow, and W. E. Plouffe, "An Asynchronous Programming Language and Computing Machine," Dept. of Information and Computer Science Report TR114a, University of California, Irvine, CA, Dec. 1978.

[7]   J. B. Dennis, "First Version of a Data Flow Procedure Language," in *Lecture Notes in Computer Science*, Vol. 19, Springer-Verlag, 1974, pp. 362-376.

[8]   J. R. McGraw, et al., "SISAL: Streams and Iterations in a Single-Assignment Language, Language Reference Manual, Version 1.1", U. of California, Livermore Livermore National Laboratory, Technical Report M-146, July 1983.

[9]   D. Conte, N. Hifdi, and J. C. Syre, "The Data Driven LAU Multiprocessor System: Results and Perspectives," in *Proc. IFIP Congress*, 1980.

[10]   B. W. Kernighan and R. Pike, *The UNIX Programming Environment.* Englewood Cliffs, NJ: Prentice-Hall, Inc., 1984.

[11]   R. G. Babb II, "Data-driven implementation of data flow diagrams," in *Proc. 6th Int. Conf. on Software Engineering*, Tokyo, Japan, Sept. 1982, pp. 309-318.

[12]   R. G. Babb II, "Parallel Processing with Large-Grain Data Flow Techniques," *Computer*, Vol. 17, No. 7, July 1984, pp. 55-61.

[13]   H. F. Jordan, "Structuring Parallel Algorithms in an MIMD, Shared Memory Environment," to appear in *Proc. 18th Hawaii Int. Conf. on System Sciences,* Jan. 1985.

[14]   E. L. Lusk and R. A. Overbeek, "An Approach to Programming Multiprocessing Algorithms on the Denelcor HEP," Argonne National Laboratory, Mathematics and Computer Science Division, Technical Report No. ANL-83-96, Dec. 1983.

[15]   E. L. Lusk and R. A. Overbeek, "Implementation of Monitors with Macros: A Programming Aid for the HEP and other Parallel Processors," Argonne National Laboratory, Mathematics and Computer Science Division, Technical Report No. ANL-83-97, Dec. 1983.

PART 4

APPLICATIONS

4.1 Solving Ordinary Differential Equations on the HEP Computer

Swarn P. Kumar
Department of Computer Science
Colorado State University
Fort Collins, CO 80523

Robert E. Lord
Department of Computer Science
Washington State University
Pullman, WA 99164

1. Introduction

Ordinary differential equations (ODE) present a natural opportunity for investigating parallel methods for their solution. Parallel electronic analog computers have been commercially available for more than 35 years and are used almost exclusively for the solution of ODE's. Indeed, a very early digital computer (ENIAC) was of parallel design and intended for the solution of ODE's. In addition to this early hardware, considerable attention has been given by researchers to inherently parallel methods of solving ODE's. Nievergelt [1] proposed a method in which parallelism is introduced at the expense of redundancy of computation. Other parallel methods are given by Miranker and Liniger [2], and Worland [3].

Our interest in using the HEP parallel computer to solve ODE's can be expressed in terms of the following questions:

a.   Given some measure of the size (e.q., the number of independent variables) of a particular set of ODE's, how many parallel processes can be efficiently employed in their solution?

b.   What are the benefits of some specific techniques (parallel methods of updating the independent variables and scheduling methods) to increase the parallelism of the solution of ODE's?

c.   To what extent do the methods employed lend themselves to the specification of the design of a translator which would process the specification of a set of ODE's into efficient parallel codes?

231

We chose to investigate two specific instances of ODE's. The first problem was a set of ten nonlinear first order equations which describe flight characteristics of a ground launched guided missile. More details on this particular problem together with preliminary results are given in [4]. The second problem was a set of six equations describing a reaction wheel stabilization device. The problem is described by Grierson, et al., in [5].

For both the problems, our initial effort was devoted to segmenting the code for evaluation of derivatives and integration of state variables into several distinct tasks. We chose to segment the code at the source level rather than at the machine instruction level in order to be somewhat machine independent and to keep the bookkeeping aspects of producing parallel code at a manageable size.

The determination of how much code constituted a task was based only on judgement but was bounded by consideration that a task consists of at least one source statement and that if the code consisted of any data dependent branches then all of the targets of the branches must also be part of the task. This latter consideration was required since we wished to view the selected tasks as a task system complete with precedence constraints. Once a complete task system was defined, the next step was to obtain an equivalent maximally parallel task system followed by the process of scheduling its execution on p processors of the MIMD multiprocessor system.

The rest of this presentation is divided into four sections. A model of HEP Fortran extensions which were used in our test programs is shown in section 2. In section 3, we discuss some of the integration techniques for which parallel versions have been developed, and also the methods and methodology used in our implementation. Section 4 contains the actual performance achieved by the test programs on HEP. The concluding section 5 attempts to answer the questions raised above.

2. HEP Fortran Extensions Model

HEP Fortran is extended to allow the programmer access to some of the unique features of an MIMD machine. Some of these extensions which we used for our purposes are the following:

(i)   CREATE Instruction

Upon commencing execution of a Fortran program, the HEP computer behaves exactly like an SISD computer. That is, a single instruction stream is sequentially executed by one of the processors. The method of achieving parallel execution is to write a subroutine which can be executed in parallel with the calling program and then to CREATE that subroutine rather than calling it. At that point the instruction stream of the CREATEd subroutine is executing on another processor in parallel with the program segment which invoked it. In HEP Fortran, CREATE may be used at any point where a call statement could have been used.

(ii)   Synchronization

Another extension of the HEP Fortran language is in the area of synchronization. Since subroutines may be executing in parallel, they may produce or consume data elements in conjunction with one another. To facilitate this, HEP Fortran allows an extension for what is termed asynchronous variables. These variables are distinguished by a naming convention in which the first character of the name is '$'. An integral part of each asynchronous variable, in addition to its data value, is a full-empty semaphore. The appearance of an asynchronous variable on the left-hand side of an assignment statement causes that assignment to be executed only when the associated semaphore is in the empty state, and when the assignment is made the semaphore is set full. Similarly, the appearance of an asynchronous variable within an expression on the right-hand side of an assignment statement causes the expression evaluation to continue only if the associated semaphore is full, and when the expression evaluation continues the semaphore is set empty. Since these semaphores are supported in hardware, if the required conditions are met, no additional execution time penalties are imposed.

With each asynchronous variable, reading (using in a right-hand side expression or as a subscript) may take place only when the state is FULL. Conversely, writing (assignment) may take place only when the state is EMPTY. Writing an asynchronous variable always sets the state to FULL; reading an asynchronous variable always sets the state to EMPTY.

The PURGE statement is used to set the state of one or more asynchronous variables to EMPTY regardless of the previous state. These elementary producer/consumer synchronizations can be seen as "wait until empty, then write" and "wait until full, then read."

(iii)   VALUE Function

The VALUE function returns the value of an asynchronous variable, regardless of the state of the variable, and does not alter the access state of the variable. In the example

A=VALUE($Q)

A becomes defined with the current value of $Q, without waiting for $Q to be full, and does not set $Q to empty afterwards.

(iv)   SETE Function

The SETE function returns the value of an asynchronous variable, regardless of the state of the variable, and sets the access state of the variable to empty. In the example

A=SETE($Q)

A becomes defined with the current value of $Q, without waiting for $Q to be full, and the access state of $Q is set to empty.

(v)   WAITF Function

The WAITF function waits for the access state of an asynchronous variable to become full, before returning its value, but does not set the variable to empty. In the example

A=WAITF($Q)

A waits for $Q to become full and returns its value, and does not set the access state of $Q to empty.

(vi)   FULL Function

The FULL function tests the access state of an asynchronous variable, and yields the logical results .TRUE. or .FALSE. according to the access state of the variable. The access state is not altered as a result of the function. In the example

A=FULL($Q)

A is a logical variable. A is .TRUE. if $Q is FULL; A is .FALSE. if $Q is not FULL.

(vii)   EMPTY Function

The EMPTY function tests the access state of an asynchronous variable, and yields the logical results .TRUE. or .FALSE. according to the access state of the variable. The access state is not altered as a result of the function. In the example

A=EMPTY($Q)

A is a logical variable. A is .TRUE. if $Q is EMPTY; A is .FALSE. if $Q is not EMPTY.

Remember, the passive logical intrinsic functions FULL and EMPTY test, but do not alter, the state of asynchronous variables.

3. Methodology

For the development of parallel codes, to solve ODE's on the HEP computer, two integration techniques were considered and compared, (i) a fourth-order Runge-Kutta (RK4) formula, and (ii) parallel predictor-corrector (PPC) method described in [2]. A brief description of these methods and an overview of some other parallel integration methods are given in the subsection (a) of this section. This presents the idea of algorithm decomposition in parallel computing. The methodology employed in these codes for both of our test problems can be divided in to several categories. These include equation segmentation, scheduling, and synchronization. These three techniques are described in the following subsections (b), (c), and (e). The segmentation technique presents the idea of problem decomposition in parallel processing.

a. Integration Techniques

This section deals with the parallel methods for the solution of a set of n ODE's denoted by

$$y'(t) = f(t,y(t)), \quad y(t_0) = y_0 \tag{1}$$

where

$$t_0, \; t \in R, \; y_0 \in R^n, \; y : R \to R^n, \; f : R \times R^n \to R^n$$

Most of the methods to solve (1) generate approximations y_n to $y(t_n)$ on a mesh $a = t_0 < t_1 < \ldots < t_N = b$. These are called step-by-step difference methods. An r-step difference method is one which computes y_{n+1} using r earlier values y_n, y_{n-1}, ... , y_{n-r+1}. This numerical integration of (1) by finite differences is a sequential calculation. Lately, the question of using some of these formulas simultaneously on a set of arithmetic processors to increase the integration speed has been addressed by many authors.

(i)   Interpolation Method

Nievergelt [1] proposed a parallel form of a serial integration method to solve a differential equation in which the algorithm is divided into several subtasks which can be computed independently. The idea is to divide the integration interval [a,b] into N equal subintervals $[t_{i-1}, t_i]$, $t_0 = a$, $t_N = b$, $i = 1,2,3,...,N$, to make a rough prediction y_i^0 of the solution $y(t_i)$, to select a certain number M_i of values y_{ij}, $j = 1,...,M_i$ in the vicinity of y_i^0 and then to integrate simultaneously with an accurate integration method M all the systems

$$y' = f(t,y), \ y(t_0) = y_0, \ t_0 \leq t \leq t_1$$

$$y' = f(t,y), \ y(t_i) = y_{ij}, \ t_i \leq t \leq t_{i+1}$$

$$j = 1,...,M_i, \ i = 1,...,N-1$$

The integration interval [a,b] will be covered with lines of length (b-a)/N, which are solutions of (1) but do not join at their ends. The connection between these branches is brought by interpolating at $t_1,t_2,...,t_{N-1}$, the previously found solution over the next interval to the right. The time of this computation can be represented by

$$T_{pI} = 1/N \ (\text{time for serial integration})$$

+ time to predict y_i^0

+ interpolation time + bookkeeping time

Interpolation can be done in parallel. If we assume that the time consuming part is really the evaluation of $f(t,y)$, the other contributions to the total time of computation become negligible, so that the speed-up is roughly $1/N$. But to compare this method with serial integration from a to b using method M, the error introduced by interpolation is important. This error depends on the problem, not on the method. For linear problems the error is proved to be bounded but for nonlinear problems it may not be. Thus, the usefulness of this method is restricted to a specific class of problems, and depends on the choice of many parameters like y_i^0, M_i, and the method M.

(ii)   Runge-Kutta (RK) Methods

In the general form of an r-step RK method, the integration step leading from y_n to y_{n+1} consists of computing

$$K_1 = h_n f(t_n, y_n)$$
$$K_i = h_n f(t_n + a_i h_n, y_n + \sum_{j=1}^{i-1} b_{ij} K_j)$$

$$y_{n+1} = y_n + \sum_{i=1}^{r} R_i K_i$$

with appropriate values of a's, b's, and R's. A classical 4-step serial RK method is

$$K_1 = h_n f(f_n, y_n)$$

$$K_2 = h_n f(t_n + h_n/2, y_n + (1/2)K_1)$$

$$K_3 = h_n f(t_n + h_n/2, y_n + (1/2)K_2) \qquad \text{(RK4)}$$

$$K_4 = h_n f(t_n + h_n, y_n + K_3)$$

$$y_{n+1} = y_n + 1/6(K_1 + 2K_2 + 2K_3 + K_4)$$

Miranker and Liniger [2] considered Runge-Kutta formulas which can be used in a parallel mode. They introduced the concept of computational front for allowing parallelism. Their parallel second and third order RK formulas are derived by a modification of Kopal's [6] results, and the parallel schemes have the structure:

first order: $\quad K_1 = h_n f(t_n, y_n^1)$ $\qquad\qquad$ (RK1)

$$y_{n+1}^1 = y_n^1 + K_1$$

second order: $\quad K_1^2 = K_1 = h_n f(t_n, y_n^1)$

$$K_2 = h_n f(t_n + \alpha h_n, y_n^1 + \beta K_1^2) \qquad \text{(RK2)}$$

$$y_{n+1}^2 = R_1^2 K_1^2 + R_2^2 K_2$$

third order: $\quad K_1^3 = K_1$

$$K_2^3 = K_2$$

$$K_3 = h_n f(t_n + \alpha h_n, \, y_n^2 + \beta K_1^3 + \delta K_2^3) \qquad \text{(RK3)}$$

$$y_{n+1}^3 = R_1^3 K_1^3 + R_2^3 K_2^3 + R_3^3 K_3.$$

The parallel character of the above formulas is based on the fact that RKi is independent of RKj if and only if $i < j$, i, j=1,2,3. This implies that if RK1 runs one step ahead of RK2 and RK2 runs one step ahead of RK3, then using Kopal's values of R's, the parallel third order RK formula is given by:

$$K_{1,n+2} = hf(t_{n+2}, \, y_{n+2}^1)$$

$$y_{n+3}^1 = y_{n+2}^1 + K_{1,n+2}$$

$$K_{2,n+1} = hf(t_{n+1} + \alpha h, \, y_{n+1}^1 + \alpha K_{1,n+1})$$

$$\qquad\qquad\qquad\qquad\qquad\qquad\qquad\qquad\qquad\qquad\text{(PRK3)}$$

$$y_{n+2}^2 = y_{n+1}^2 + (1-1/2\alpha)K_{1,n+1} + (1/2\alpha)K_{2,n+1}$$

$$K_{3,n} = hf(t_n + \alpha_1 h, \, y_n^2 + (\alpha_1 - 1/6\alpha)K_{1,n} + (1/6\alpha)K_{2,n})$$

$$y_{n+1}^3 = y_n^3 + ((2\alpha_1 - 1)/2\alpha)(K_{1,n} - K_{2,n}) + K_{3,n}$$

where

$$\alpha = 2(1 - 3\alpha_1^2)/(3(1 - 2\alpha_1)).$$

One value of α suggested by Kopal is $\alpha = 1$. This gives

$$\alpha_1 = 1/2 + 1/2\sqrt{3}.$$

The above 3rd order RK formula requires 3 processors to compute the three function evaluations in parallel.

The main drawback of the (PRK3) scheme mentioned above is that it is weakly stable. It is shown in [2] that the scheme leads to an error that grows linearly with n as $n \to \infty$ and $h \to 0$ for t_n = nh = constant. This problem is due to the basic nature of the one-step formulas with respect to their y-entries which are the only ones that contribute to the discussion of stability for $h \to 0$.

(iii)   Predictor-Corrector (PC) Methods

The serial one-step methods of Runge-Kutta type are conceptually simple, easy to code, self-starting, and numerically stable for a large class of problems. On the other hand, they are inefficient in that they do not make full use of the available information due to their one-step nature, which does not extend the numerical stability property to their parallel mode. It seems plausible that more accuracy can be obtained if the value of y_{n+1} is made to depend not only on y_n but also, say, on y_{n-1}, y_{n-2}, ... , and f_{n-1}, f_{n-2}, ... For this reason multi-step methods have become very popular. For high accuracy they usually require less work than one-step methods. Thus, deriving parallel schemes for such methods is reasonable.

A standard fourth order serial predictor-corrector (SPC) given by Adams-Moulton is:

$$y_{i+1}^p = y_i^c + h/24(55f_i^c - 59f_{i-1}^c + 37f_{i-2}^c - 9f_{i-3}^c) \qquad \text{(SPC)}$$

$$y_{i+1}^c = y_i^c + h/24(9f_{i+1}^p + 19f_i^c - 5f_{i-1}^c + f_{i-2}^c)$$

The following computation scheme of one PC step to calculate y_{i+1} called PECE is:

1.   Use the predictor equation to calculate an initial approximation to y_{i+1} set i = 0.
2.   Evaluate the derivative function f_{i+1}^p.
3.   Use the corrector equation to calculate a better

241

approximation to y_{i+1}.

4. Evaluate the derivative function f_{i+1}^C.

5. Check the termination rule. If it is not time to stop, increment i, set $y_{i+1} = y_{i+1}^C$ and return to 1.

Let T_f = total time taken by function evaluation done for one step of PC.

T_{PCE} = time taken to compute predictor (corrector) equation for a single equation.

Then the time taken by one step of SPC is

$$T_1 = 2(nT_{PCE} + T_f).$$

Miranker and Liniger developed formulas for PC method in which the corrector does not depend serially upon the predictor, so that the predictor and the corrector calculations can be performed simultaneously. The Parallel Predictor-Corrector (PPC) operates also in a PECE mode, and the calculation advances s steps at a time. There are 2s processors and each processor performs either a predictor or a corrector calculation. This scheme is shown in Figure 1. A fourth order PPC is given by:

$$y_{i+1}^P = y_{i-1}^C + h/3(8f_i^P - 5f_{i-1}^C + 4f_{i-2}^C - f_{i-3}^C) \qquad \text{(PPC4)}$$

$$y_i^C = y_{i-1}^C + h/24(9f_{i+1}^P + 19f_i^C - 5f_{i-2}^C + f_{i-3}^C).$$

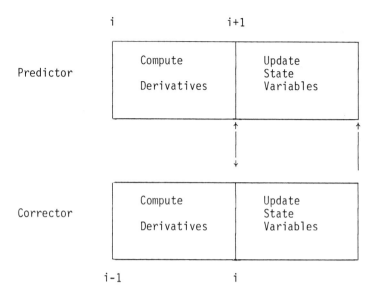

Figure 1. Parallel PC Scheme.

243

Thus, the parallel time for a single step of (PPC4) is given by

$$T_{PPC} = nT_{PCE} + T_f + 3nT_{DC} + 2T_S$$

Where

$T_{PCE} = T_f$ as defined before and

T_{DC} = time taken for data communication

T_S = time taken for synchronization.

Generally the high accuracy, less function evaluations of PC methods as compared to RK methods, is obtained at the cost of increase in complexity and some times numerical instability. The Parallel RK methods given in [2] do not inherit the stability of their serial counterparts. On the other hand, PCC methods in [2] as described above are as stable as their serial formulas. This is proved by Katz, et al., [7].

(iv)   Block-Implicit Methods

Sequential block implicit methods as described by Andria, et al., [8] and Shampine and Watts [9] produce more than one approximation of y at each step of integration. Shampine and Watts and Rosser [10] discuss block implicit methods for RK type and PC type schemes. A 2-point fourth order PC given in [9] is

$$y_{i+1}^p = 1/3(y_{i-2}^c + y_{i-1}^c + y_i^c) + h/6(3f_{i-2}^c - 4f_{i-1}^c + 13f_i^c)$$

$$y_{i+2}^p = 1/3(y_{i-2}^c + y_{i-1}^c + y_i^c) + h/12(29f_{i-2}^c - 72f_{i-1}^c + 79f_i^c)$$
$$\text{(BPC)}$$
$$y_{i+1}^c = y_i^c + h/12(5f_i^c + 8f_{i+1}^p - f_{i+2}^p)$$

$$y_{i+2}^c = y_i^c + h/3(f_i^c + 4f_{i+1}^p + f_{i+2}^p).$$

Worland in [3] describes the natural way to parallelize
(BPC) using the number of processors = number of block points
by the schemes shown in Figure 2. The parallel time for one
Block calculation given by Franklin [4] is

$$T_{BPC} = (2nT_{PCE} + 2T_f + 6nT_{DC} + 4T_S)/2.$$

A performance comparison of (PPC) and parallel (BPC) methods
is given by Franklin in [2] in case of two processors.

b.   Segmentation

Segmentation of a problem consists of partitioning that
problem into a number of tasks. A task is defined as a unit
of computational activity specified in terms of the input
variables it requires, the output variables it generates, and
its execution time. The specific transformation that it
imposes on its input to produce its output is not part of the
specification of a task. Thus, the task may be considered
uninterpreted. Let J = $(T_1, T_2, ..., T_n)$ be a set of tasks and
<. an irreflexive partial order (precedence relation) defined
on J. Then C = (J,<.) is called a task system. The
precedence relation means that if T <. T' then T must complete
execution before T' is started.

From this definition we introduce a graphical
representation, called a precedence graph, for a task system.
This consists of a directed graph whose vertices (nodes) are
the tasks J and which has an edge from T to T' if T <. T' and
there is no T" such that T <. T" <. T'. Thus, the set of
edges in the precedence graph represents the smallest relation
whose transitive closure is <..

245

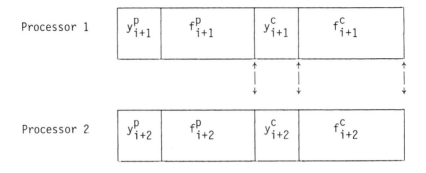

Processor 1 y^p_{i+1} f^p_{i+1} y^c_{i+1} f^c_{i+1}

Processor 2 y^p_{i+2} f^p_{i+2} y^c_{i+2} f^c_{i+2}

Figure 2. Parallel Scheme for BPC.

```
C*** TASK 15   COMPUTE THRUST
      NDX=ITHRUST-1
      IF(TIME .LT. THRUSTIME(ITHRUST)) GO TO 151
      NDX=ITHRUST
      IF (ITHRUST .LT. LTHRUST) ITHRUST=ITHRUST+1
151   THRUST=THRUSTAB(NDX)+THRUSTSL(NDX)
      :           *(TIME-THRUSTIME(NDX))
C*** TASK 23 COMPUTE LT
      NDX=ILT-1
      IF(TIME .LT. LTIME(ILT)) GO TO 231
      NDX=ILT
      IF (ILT .LT. LLT) ILT=ILT+1
231   LT=LTAB(NDX)+(TIME-LTIME(NDX))*LTSL(NDX)
C
C*** TASK 29 COMPUTE CMQS
      NDX=ICMQS-1
      IF(TIME .LT. CMQSTIME(ICMQS)) GO TO 291
      NDX=ICMQS
      IF(ICMQS .LT. LCMQS) ICMQS=ICMQS+1
291   CMQS=CMQSTAB(NDX)+(TIME-CMQSTIME(NDX))*CMQSSL(NDX)
C
C*** TASK 11   COMPUTE TIME
      CALL RK11(STEP)
C
C*** TASK 5   COMPUTE QS
      QDOT=$T(70)
      CALL RK5(STEP)
```

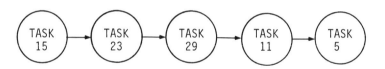

Figure 3.   Program Segment and Related Precedence Graph.

Many sequential programs and program segments can be viewed as precedence graphs. Figure 3 shows an example of a program segment and its related precedence graph. Since the relation <· is irreflexive, antisymmetric and transitive, the precedence graph is acyclic -- it represents only straight line code (or code that can be viewed as straight line). We can deal with data-dependent branches that fall entirely within a task, but not conditional branches to other tasks. Further, many loops can be "unrolled" (viewed as straight line code) and handled in an acyclic manner. In one instance, discussed later, we can deal with specific kinds of cyclic graphs.

With each task T, we associate two events: initiation and termination. An execution sequence of an n-task system $C = (J, <\cdot)$ is any string $\delta = \alpha_1, \alpha_2, \ldots, \alpha_{2n}$ of task events satisfying the precedence relation (this is, if $T <\cdot T'$ then the termination event of T must occur prior to the initiation event of T') and consisting of exactly one initiation and one termination event for each task. A task system that represents a sequential program has only one execution sequence; for other task systems (perhaps equivalent to the sequential task system) there may be several.

To discuss determinant task systems, let the physical system on which task systems execute be represented by an ordered set of memory cells $M = (M_1, M_2, \ldots, M_m)$. With each task T in a system C we associate two, possibly overlapping, ordered subsets of M: the <u>domain</u> D_T and the <u>range</u> R_T. When T is initiated it reads the values stored in its domain cells; when it terminates it writes values into its range cells. Given an execution sequence δ for a task system, we can define the value sequence $V(M_i, \delta)$ as the sequence of values written by terminating tasks in δ for which $M_i \in R_T$.

We can now define more rigorously the intuitive concept of determinant task systems:

A task system C is determinant if for any given initial state P_0, $V(M_i,\delta) = V(M_i,\delta')$, $1 \leq i \leq m$, for all execution sequences δ and δ'.

From this definition, it is clear that a task system that represents a sequential program is determinant since there is only one execution sequence. Given two task systems both consisting of the same tasks, they are said to be equivalent if they are determinant and, for the same initial state, produce the same value sequences.

Our goal now is to define a method by which, given a determinant task system (e.g., one representing a sequential program), we can derive another determinant task system equivalent to the first which has in some sense more parallelism. In fact, our method will derive one with maximum parallelism subject to the constraint that we have no knowledge of the internal transformations performed by the tasks. We begin with the following definition:

Given a task system C, then tasks T and T' are noninterfering if either

(i)   T <. T' or T' <. T
      or

(ii) $R_T \cap R_{T'} = R_T \cap D_{T'} = R_{T'} \cap D_T = \emptyset$.

A fundamental Theorem linking noninterfering tasks with determinancy is:

Task systems consisting of mutually noninterfering tasks are determinant.

A proof of this Theorem can be found in [11].

The final development falls naturally from the Theorem. Given a determinant task system C = (J,<•) we construct another task system C' = (J,<•') that is equivalent to C but whose precedence relation is constructed from <• on the basis that (T,T') ε <•' only if it is necessary to insure that T and T' are noninterfering. The resulting task system is, by the Theorem, determinant. Further, it is maximally parallel in that any further reduction of the precedence relation results in nondeterminancy. Finally, since <• $\supseteq$ <•', every execution sequence of C is an execution sequence of C' and, since C' is determinant, every execution sequence of C' produces the same value sequence. Therefore C' is equivalent to C. This is formally stated in the following Theorem:

From a given determinant task system C = (J,<•) construct a new system C' = (J,<•') where <•' is the transitive closure of the relation:

$$X = \{(T,T') <• \mid (R_T \cap R_{T'}) \cup (R_T \cap D_{T'}) \cup (R_{T'} \cap D_T) \neq \emptyset\}$$

Then C' is the unique, maximally parallel task system equivalent to C.

c. Scheduling

Given a determinant task system and the execution time of each task, the problem remains of assigning the tasks to p processors. More formally, we define the scheduling problem to be the following: we are given

(1) a set of tasks J = {$T_1, T_2, \ldots, T_n$}
(2) an irreflexive partial order <• on J,
(3) a weighting function W from S to the positive

250

integers, representing the execution time of each of the tasks, and

(4)   the number of processors p.

We may be executing in parallel as many as p tasks at any point in time. If task T is first executed at time t using processor K, then it is executed only at times t, t+1, ..., t+W(T)-1 using processor K each time. It is also required, for any task T' such that T' <. T, that T' complete execution at time t' when t' ≤ t. A schedule is an assignment of tasks to processors that satisfies the above conditions and has length tmax, where tmax is the maximum, over all tasks, of the times at which the termination events occur. The scheduling problem, then, is to determine an assignment that minimizes tmax. This problem has been shown to be NP-complete [12] and can be considered intractable. There are, however, polynomial time bound algorithms that produce good schedules. One such algorithm is critical path list scheduling.

The algorithm is defined as follows:

(1)   Given a task system and a list that orders the tasks, we require a scheduling strategy that assigns (to a free processor) the first unassigned task in the list whose precedence constraints have been met. Such a strategy is called demand list scheduling.

(2)   The critical time of a task is the execution time of that task plus the maximum critical times of any successor tasks.

(3)   If the list of tasks is ordered on non-increasing critical time, then the resulting list schedule is called critical path list scheduling.

Kohler [13] reports a preliminary evaluation in which 20 task systems, scheduled using critical path list scheduling, produced 17 optimal schedules. The worst-case schedule was only 3.4% longer than optimal. Using only limited back-tracking with a critical path list scheduler, Lord [14] found that in 100 randomly generated cases, 89 were scheduled optimally. He further found that for all cases, the schedules had an expected time of only .36% longer than optimal. The worst-case time was 5.6% longer. Thus, we conclude that critical path list scheduling is an acceptable technique for practical application.

d.   Cyclic Task Systems

As we have observed before, the standard task system represents an acyclic computational method. This method is applied to repetitious calculations such as solving ODE's by treating the calculation of derivatives and the updating of the state variable as a task system, scheduling those tasks, and then repeatedly executing that schedule. In some cases, however, shorter solution times can result if we consider precedence graphs which are cyclic. For example, consider the Van der Pol equation written as two first-order equations:

$$\dot{x}_1 = x_2$$
$$\dot{x}_2 = u(1 - x_1^2)x_2 - x_1$$

By using some suitable integration method (for example, 4th order Runge-Kutta as indicated by the function rk), the main part of a program for solving these equations is as follows:

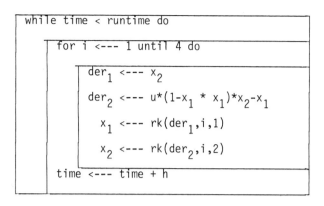

```
while time < runtime do

    for i <--- 1 until 4 do

        der₁ <--- x₂

        der₂ <--- u*(1-x₁ * x₁)*x₂-x₁

        x₁ <--- rk(der₁,i,1)

        x₂ <--- rk(der₂,i,2)

    time <--- time + h
```

The calculation interior to the "for" loop can be represented by the acyclic precedence graph shown in Figure 4. Assuming that each binary operation can be executed in one time unit and that the function rk can be evaluated in four units, the entire "for" loop can be represented by the cyclic precedence graph shown in Figure 4. T3 calculates $u * (1-x_1 * x_1)$, T4 calculates $* x_2 - x_1$, and T1 and T2 calculate the function rk.

Given two parallel processors, one way to schedule this solution is to assign the tasks interior to the "for" loop to processors. This should be done in such a way as to preserve the precedence relations and yet complete all tasks as quickly as possible. The solution to the problem is the repeated execution of this schedule. Such an assignment is shown by the Gantt chart in Figure 4. Note that this assignment is as good as possible -- the precedence graph has a maximum path length equal to the assignment period.

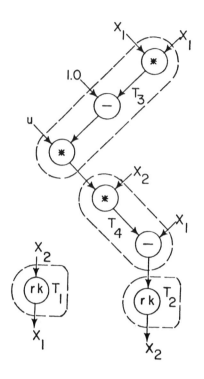

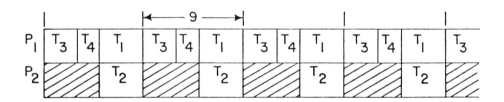

Figure 4. Acyclic Precedence Graph and Schedule.

The Gantt chart in Figure 5 shows the assignments made if we assume some initial values for X_1 and X_2 and then assign the tasks from the cyclic precedence graph while maintaining all precedence constraints. This assignment has a repetition period of seven units, as compared with nine units for assigning the acyclic precedence graph. This shorter schedule is the motivation for examining ODE's to determine their minimum solution period and to schedule them in that minimum period with as few processors as possible.

The method used constructs a task system representing the solution to a set of ODE's, where the tasks that update the state variables are flagged. The precedence graph of the task system is allowed to be cyclic so long as each cycle traverses at least one flagged task. The minimum solution period is then determined by examining all cycles in the graph.

Let the cycles be denoted by $C_1, C_2, \ldots, C_m$. For each cycle let $L(C_i)$ denote its length and $\#(C_i)$ the number of flagged tasks in the cycle. Then the minimum solution period t_{min} is:

$$t_{min} = \text{Max } \{ \lceil L(C_i)/\#(C_i) \rceil \mid 1 \leq i \leq m \}.$$

Once the minimum solution period is determined, a critical path list scheduler can, with only slight modifications, produce an efficient schedule whose repeated execution solves the set of ODE's. Algorithms for producing these schedules are given in [13].

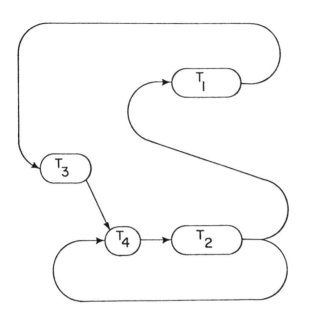

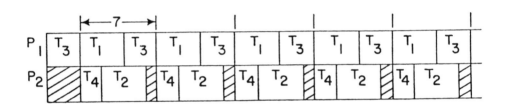

Figure 5. Cyclic Representation and Schedule.

e.   Synchronization

Once a schedule has been determined, there must be some way to ensure that the schedule is followed. A general assumption made regarding MIMD computing is that the precise execution rate of individual processors cannot be used to prove the correctness of a program. This assumption applies to HEP; although we know that execution rates of processes are generally the same, detailed knowledge of the progress of each process is beyond the scope of normal analysis of programs. Thus, having determined a schedule for computing the tasks, it now remains to implement it.

Much of the work on scheduling assumes, at least implicitly, that some mechanism external to the processors assigns the tasks to the processors. But our execution times are estimates only, so the scheduling mechanism would have to monitor the progress of all processors. Instead we seek a mechanism whereby all the tasks to be executed by a single processor are presented as a sequential program. Synchronization primitives, operating on semaphores, coordinate those tasks.

Dijkstra [15] introduced the primitives P and V, which operate uninterruptably on an event variable termed a semaphore, to control resource allocation among concurrent processes. For our purposes we may define P and V as:

$$P(E): \quad \underline{if} \ E \geq 1 \qquad\qquad V(E):$$
$$\underline{then} \ E \leftarrow E - 1 \qquad\qquad E \leftarrow E + 1$$
$$\underline{else} \ \text{wait}$$

P is normally used before a process uses a nonsharable resource; V is executed when the use of the resource is completed.

Denning [16] shows that these primitives can synchronize concurrent tasks. As an example, consider the task system and concurrent program shown in Figure 6. The program uses P and V operating on the suitably initialized semaphore X23. Clearly, the program correctly executes the task system. Since we are using task systems to represent computations, precedence constraints arise because one task computes data elements used by another task. If we were to consider a task system that represents a calculation loop, such as shown in Figure 7, we find that the first program still represents a valid solution to the problem. This is because it is implied that both stream 1 and stream 2 complete execution before beginning the second execution of these streams.

Such methods of computation have been previously proposed for handling looped and conditional execution using constructs named "fork" and "join". But if the alternate program executes the task system, then the P and V operations are no longer valid. This is so because if S2 runs more quickly than S1, at some point T2 completes the calculation before T3 has consumed the previous value. Even if we assume a queue for this data element, in any real implementation the queue would be of finite size and hence subject to overflow. To overcome this difficulty, we use two state semaphores associated with each data element or variable as indicated by:

```
1    VAR
     2    VALUE
     2    SEMAPHORE ['E','F']
```

where 'E' indicates empty and 'F' indicates full. We now define the P and V operations as:

258

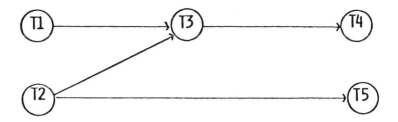

PARBEGIN

    S1: T1; P(X23); T3; T4

    S2: T2: V(X23); T5

PAREND

Figure 6. Task System and Concurrent Program.

259

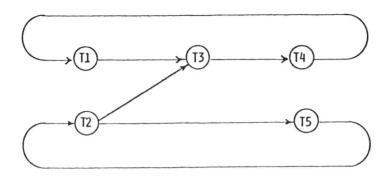

```
REPEAT N TIMES
     PARBEGIN
          S1: T1; P(X23); T3; T4
          S2: T2; V(X23); T5
     PAREND

ALTERNATE
     PARBEGIN
          S1:  REPEAT N TIMES
                    T1; P(X23); T3; T4
               END
          S2:  REPEAT N TIMES
                    T2; V(X23); T5
               END
     PAREND
```

Figure 7. Task System for Repeated Execution.

```
P(VAR):
    IF VAR.SEMAPHORE = 'F'
    THEN VAR.SEMAPHORE ← 'E'
    ELSE WAIT

V(VAR):
    IF VAR.SEMAPHORE = 'E'
        THEN VAR.SEMAPHORE ← 'F'
        ELSE WAIT
```

Then if we let X23 represent the variable responsible for the precedence constraints from T2 to T3, the alternate program correctly executes the task system.

To further simplify the programming aspects of such a synchronizing method, we note that, in a language involving assignment statements, context determines whether the operation is P or V. That is, any synchronizing operation on the left of the assignment symbol denotes a V operation. All others denote a P operation. In HEP Fortran, $ represents both P and V; context denotes which operation is implied. If some task T1 computes a value used by two other tasks, T2 and T3 (each in separate instruction streams), then the coordination problem between T1 and T3. Hence, two copies of the variable are required so that two separate semaphores are available.

4. Experimental Results

a. For the purpose of our computational analysis, the following problems of two specific instances of ODE's were investigated:

(i) The first problem was a set of 10 nonlinear first order equations which describe the flight characteristics of a ground launched guided missile. A sequential Fortran program of somewhat less than 1,000 source lines was available for its solution and was the starting point of our investigation.

(ii) The second problem was a set of six equations describing a reaction wheel stabilization device (for more details see [5]). A sequential Fortran program for the solution of this second problem was supplied to us by the authors of [5].

For both problems, the original solutions employed a fourth-order Runge-Kutta (RK-4) formula for performing integration, and we parallelized only the code for computing derivations and updating of the state variables. In addition, we coded both of these problems using the parallel predictor-corrector (PPC) method described by Miranker and Liniger [2] in order to evaluate this method. The code for reading initial conditions and parameters as well as the code for producing intermediate and final output was kept in its sequential form. Since, for both these problems, the amount of time devoted to these I/O activities is very low compared with the total solution time, the penalties for remaining sequential in this portion of the code was minimal.

For the first problem, a total of 40 tasks were identified, ten of which were updating of the dependent variables, one for updating the independent variable time, and the remaining 29 tasks were involved with evaluating the derivatives. For the most part, HEP executes all instructions in the same amount of time and thus instruction count is a good approximation to execution time. Figure 8 illustrates the task system for this problem with the task numbers and their expected execution times.

For our task selection, the shortest task was 2 instructions, the longest was 88 instructions and the total task system was 1,265 instructions for an average of slightly less than 32 instructions per task. For the second problem, a total of 19 tasks were selected with a minimum of 1 instruction time, a maximum of 43 instruction times and an

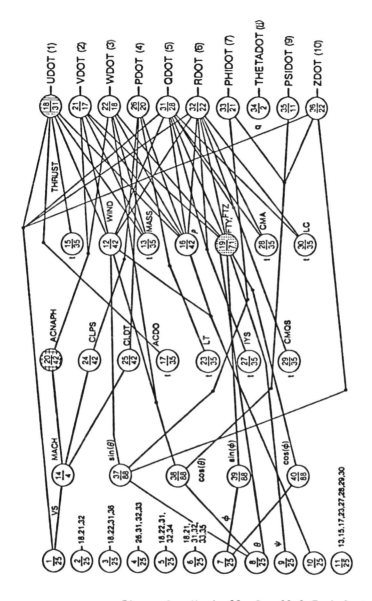

Figure 8. Maximally Parallel Task System.

average of just over 14 instruction times. Figure 9 illustrates the task system selected for the second problem. Following the selection of tasks, determination of their precedence constraints and estimating their execution time, our next step is to schedule these tasks for execution by p processors, using the methods described in section 3c and 3d. The final step in the process is to collect the code segments that constitute the various tasks into subroutines, one per processor, and add any required synchronization by utilizing asynchronous variables.

b. Performance

In this section, we present both the achieved results and an analysis of expected performance for the two sets of ODE's which we solved utilizing HEP.

For the methods we employed, there are a number of factors which contribute to achieving a speed-up of less than p (number of processors). The first of these factors has to do with scheduling inefficiencies. In general, one cannot expect that each processor can be kept totally busy during the entire execution period. For any particular task system, there is a limiting value for the execution time and as one approaches this limiting value the speed-up often departs significantly from p. For the task system we chose, speed-up versus p is shown in Figure 10 along with the limiting values of speed-up.

Another factor which causes efficiency (speed-up ÷ P) to depart from unity is the cost of synchronization. Since we do not have an external mechanism to enforce scheduling constraints, we must use asynchronous variables for this

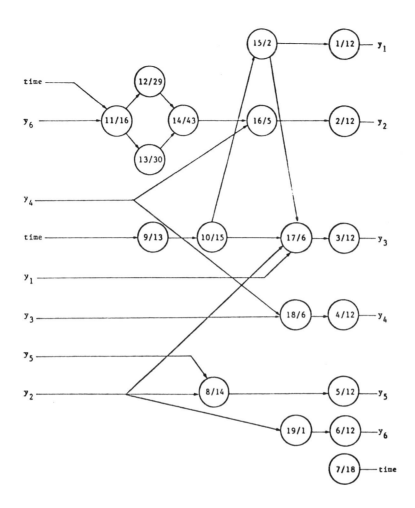

Figure 9. Graph illustrating task systems for reaction wheel where (i/j) is the i-th task of time duration j.

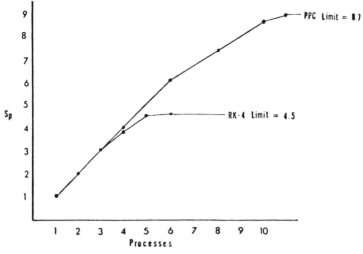

a.) Reaction Wheel Problem

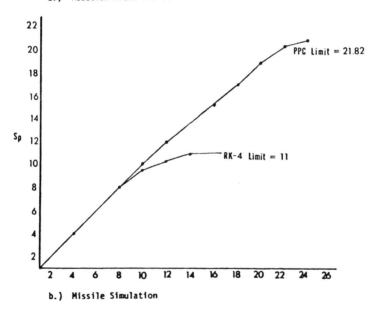

b.) Missile Simulation

Figure 10.   Speed-up vs. p Considering Only Scheduling.

purpose. In HEP, and probably in any MIMD design, there is some additional cost in ensuring that a task does not start execution until all of the variables in its domain are available. The method we employed to synchronize these calculations was for each variable in the range of some task to provide a separate semaphored copy of that variable to each processor that was assigned one or more tasks with that variable in their domain. For purposes of analysis, the extra instructions required to create these separate semaphored copies of the variable are termed "send penalties". We assume for all tasks, any execution results in a single store instruction for each variable in its range. This was true for all of the tasks which we selected and can easily be enforced for any code with only slight modifications. With the above assumption, the number of send penalties for a variable x is the number of processes less one, which are assigned tasks with x in their domain. For a given variable x, define dx (the degree) to be the number of tasks with x in its domain, and p to be the number of processors employed in a given schedule. Then the expected number of send penalties for the variable x is:

$$E = p - 1 - p \left(\frac{p-1}{p} \right)^{dx}.$$

For a complete schedule, the number of send penalties is the sum of the number of send penalties for each of the variables. Figure 11 gives the expected number of send penalties with various numbers of processors for variables with degree ranging from 1 to 8.

267

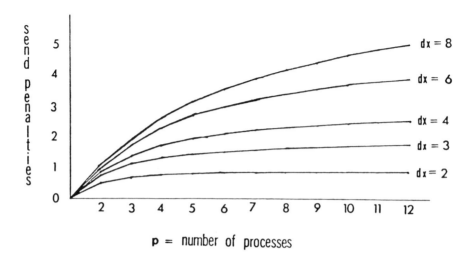

Figure 11. Send Penalties vs. p for Various Degrees.

The importance of the expected number of send penalties is not in their numeric value but is in their form. As Figure 11 illustrates, the synchronization penalty grows most rapidly with small values of p and grows less rapidly with larger values. That is, increasing the amount of parallelism in a particular problem solution does not yield a corresponding increase in synchronization penalty.

In addition to the synchronization send penalties, in some cases there will be "receive penalties" which arise in two ways: first, if a variable is in the domain of a task T which is assigned to a different processor than the task T_1 which had that same variable in its range, and, second, if T has multiple uses (load instruction) of the variable. In this case, a local copy of the variable is made and the transmitted copy is set empty so that T_1 can update it in a subsequent iteration. For similar reasons, if T_1 and T_2 both have x in their domains and are both assigned to a processor which is different than that to which the task that produces x (task with x in its range) is assigned, then a local copy of x is made prior to the execution of either T_1 or T_2. For the two problem solutions which we examined, the number of receive penalties was significantly less than the number of send penalties.

In addition to executions using only a single processor, both the problems were executed using multiple processors with the following results:

269

	Reaction Wheel RK-4	Missile RK-4	PPC
Number of processors	5	8	8
Predicted Results:			
Useful Work*	54	173	346
Scheduling Inefficiencies*	9	19	17
Synchronization*	7	23	58
Speed-up	3.85	6.44	6.57
Actual Results:			
Speed-up	3.60	5.76	6.48

*In HEP machine instructions for one cycle of innermost loop.

In all cases the actual speed-up was less than the predicted value. We believe this is because the average execution times were used for the tasks that had variable execution times. In general, a task running longer than average will result in additional execution time (decreased speed-up) while a task running shorter than average will often not result in shortening the problem execution time.

5. Conclusion

On the basis of the problems we examined, we can answer our original questions as follows:

a. Using sequential methods, i.e., RK-4, for updating the dependent variables, we were able to efficiently utilize approximately the same number of processes as the number of first order equations.

b. The parallel predictor-corrector method doubled the amount of parallel code that could be executed efficiently and the scheduling methods we used provided nearly twice the amount of parallelism as scheduling only the interior of the "While" loop.

c. It would seem quite difficult to have the original Fortran source mechanically translated into as efficient a parallel code as that which we produced. However, given some representation of the problem which identifies it as solving ODE's and a clear structure for identifying the derivatives such as is provided in the CSSL language [17], knowledge of the design of a translator is available. We expect that the efficiencies of such a translator would be as good as or better than the hand code which we produced.

We conclude from our experience in solving ODE's on the HEP parallel computer that the presented techniques offer a viable alternative to normal sequential computing and that the HEP computer is sufficiently fast to provide at least real time support for many cases. Further, should this type of computer become generally acceptable for solving differential equations, then support in the form of high level programming languages is feasible.

REFERENCES

1. J. Nievergelt, "Parallel Methods for Integrating Ordinary Differential Equations," CACM, Vol. 7, No. 12, December, 1964, pp. 731-733.

2. N. K. Miranker and W. M. Liniger, "Parallel Methods for the Numerical Integration of Ordinary Differential Equations," Math. Comput., Vol. 21, 1967, pp. 303-320.

3. P. B. Worland, "Parallel Methods for the Numerical Solution of Ordinary Differential Equations," IEEE Trans. Comp., Vol. C-25, October, 1976, pp. 1045-1048.

4. R. E. Lord and S. P. Kumar, "Parallel Solution of Flight Simulation Equations," Proceedings of the 1980 Summer Computer Simulation Conference, Seattle, WA, August, 1980, AFIPS Press.

5. W. O. Grierson, D. B. Lipski and N. O. Tiffany, "Simulation Tools: Where Can We Go?" Proceedings of the 1980 Summer Computer Simulation Conference, Seattle, WA, August, 1980, AFIPS Press.

6. Z. Kopal, "Numerical Analysis with Emphasis on the Application of Numerical Techniques to Problems of Infinitesimal Calculus in Single Variable," Wiley, New York; Chapman and Hall, London, 1955.

7. N. Katz, M. A. Franklin and A. Sen, "Optimally Stable Parallel Predictors for Adams-Moulton Correctors," Comp. and Maths. with Appls., Vol. 3, 1977, pp. 217-233.

8. F. D. Andria, G. D. Byrne, and D. R. Hill. "Natural Spline Block Implicit Methods," BIT, Vol. 13, 1973, pp. 131-144.

9. L. F. Shampine and H. A. Watts, "Block Implicity One Step Methods," Math. Comput., Vol. 23, 1964, pp. 731-740.

10. J. Rosser, "A Runge-Kutta for all Seasons," SIAM Rev., Vol. 9, 1967, pp. 417-452.

11. E. G. Coffman, and P. J. Denning, "Operating Systems Theory," Prentice Hall, Englewood Cliffs, NJ, 1974.

12. J. D. Ullman, "Polynomial NP-Complete Scheduling Problems," Operating Systems Review, Vol. 7, No. 4, 1973, pp. 96-101.

13. W. H. Kohler, "Preliminary Evaluation of the Critical Path Method for Scheduling Tasks on a Multiprocessor System," IEEE Trans. Comp. C24, 1975, pp. 1235-1238.

14. R. E. Lord, "Scheduling Recurrence Equations for Solution on MIMD Type Computers," Ph.D. Dissertation, Washington State University, Pullman, WA, 1976.

15. E. W. Dijkstra, "Cooperating Sequential Processes," Programming Languages, F. Genuys, Ed. (New York: Academic Press, 1968) pp. 43-122.

16. P. J. Denning, "Third Generation Computer Systems," Computing Surveys, Vol. 3, No. 4, 1971, pp. 175-216.

17. C. Strauss, Editor, "Continuous Systems Simulation Language," SIMULATION, Vol. 9, No. 6, 1976.

4.2 A Parallel Linear Algebra Library for the Denelcor HEP

J. J. Dongarra and D. C. Sorensen

Mathematics and Computer Science Division
Argonne National Laboratory
Argonne, Illinois

1. Introduction

One problem that always faces the scientific computing community when a new and exotic computer arrives is how to transport or efficiently redesign the numerical software libraries to take advantage of the computing power offered by the new machine. It is evident that the new computers arriving in this decade will offer some substantial degree of parallel processing capabilities. This situation presents a true challenge to software designers because the variety of ways to implement these parallel constructs are numerous indeed. It is imperative that we prepare now for this variety. We must learn to structure these software libraries in such a way that they are both transportable and efficient across a wide spectrum of architectures.

This paper describes a concept that we believe to be a viable method for structuring software libraries. We discuss the concept within the context of a library for solution of linear equations. However, we believe that the scheme described here could serve as a prototype for many software libraries (although certainly not all of them). The numerical software library we present has been developed to achieve transportability and high performance across a wide range of architectures. It has been successfully ported, to many machines including CRAY 1, CRAY X-MP, Fujitsu VP-200, Hitachi S-810, and CYBER 205. Performance figures for these machines are reported in [1].

Work supported in part by the Applied Mathematical Sciences subprogram of the Office of Energy Research, U.S. Department of Energy, under Contract W-31-109-Eng-38.

Here we describe the key features of this library in relation to the Denelcor HEP computer. We give some details concerning the implementation on the HEP. We also present computational results indicating the performance of the library on this machine. These results were obtained on Denelcor HEP computers located at Argonne National Laboratory, Los Alamos National Laboratory, and the Ballistics Research Laboratory. The Denelcor HEP is the first commercially available machine of the MIMD variety. It supports tightly coupled parallel processing and large, globally shared memory. Synchronization is accomplished through the use of a few basic extensions to the FORTRAN language. (See papers by B. Smith [9] and H.F. Jordan [7] for more details on the architecture.)

2. Algorithms Based on Modules

The algorithms discussed here are implementations of standard procedures in linear algebra. They include LU, Cholesky, and QR factorizations as well as the appropriate triangular solvers. These algorithms have been reformulated in terms of a few relatively high- level constructs such as matrix-vector or $O(n^2)$ operations.

The concept of structuring a library in terms of basic modules is not new. LINPACK, for example, has been written in terms of a set of low-level constructs called the Basic Linear Algebra Subprograms (BLAS). The BLAS operations [8] are functions such as inner product, a scalar multiple of a vector added to another vector, vector scaling, etc. The BLAS are well suited for operations that occur on some of the vector processors, but they are not the best choice for certain other vector processors, multiprocessors, or parallel processing computers [3].

The next level up from simple vector operations are the matrix-vector operations. These include such operations as a matrix times a vector and a rank one change to a matrix. Of course these matrix vector operations can be coded in terms of the BLAS. However, efficiency may gained by coding them directly since they provide enough computational granularity to make use of the more powerful capabilities of the most advanced architectures. In most cases performance is vastly improved through the ability to accumulate results in vector registers and avoid unnecessary data movement between main memory and register memory. The details of this technique for the HEP are presented in Section 4.

The module concept has already proven to be very successful in transporting these linear algebra routines across various architectures. They have been run on a variety of machines, as reported by Dongarra in [1]. Designing the algorithms in terms of such operations is the hard part of an implementation. This can require considerable rethinking of the structure of the algorithms. However, restructuring the algorithms in terms of these modules is more than just a challenging exercise. It tends to unify the structure of library far more than the coding in terms of the BLAS. Moe allows us to avoid locking the structure of the algorithms into one computer's architecture.

As we show in Section 3, it is possible to express all of the primary subroutines mentioned above in terms of just three basic modules. This places us in a very fortunate situation. In order to retarget the library for a new machine, we are faced with replacing only three very simple modules: matrix-vector multiplication ($y \leftarrow y + Ax$), vector-matrix multiplication ($y^T \leftarrow y^T + x^T A$), and a rank-one-update to a matrix ($A \leftarrow A + xy^T$). These modules represent a high level of granularity in the algorithm in the sense that they are based on matrix-vector operations, $O(n^2)$ work, not just vector operations, $O(n)$ work.

Our reasons for embracing the module concept are twofold: first, to avoid specifically designing the primary algorithms for high performance on a particular computer architecture, however fast that one may be; and second, to structure the library in such a way that the fundamental modules need only be replaced to gain reasonable performance on any given machine. The success of this approach in achieving high performance from the library across a wide spectrum of computers depends on how well the modules can be chosen. They must be at a high enough level to embody a significant number of floating point operations and yet remain at a level that is fundamental enough that all of the primary routines can be expressed in terms of them. In the case of software for the solution of linear systems and linear least squares problems these goals have clearly been met. It remains to see if this approach will extend to other more complicated settings.

3. Structure of the Algorithms

Restructuring the algorithms in terms of the basic modules described above is not so obvious in the case of LU decomposition. The approach is inspired by the work of Fong and Jordan [5]. They produced an assembly language code for LU decomposition for the CRAY-1. This code differed significantly in structure from those commonly in use because it did not modify the entire k-th reduced submatrix at each step but only the k-th column of that matrix. This step was essentially matrix-vector multiplication operation.

Dongarra and Eisenstat [3] showed how to restructure the Fong and Jordan implementation explicitly in terms of matrix-vector operations and were able to achieve nearly the same performance from a FORTRAN code as Fong and Jordan had done with their assembly language implementation.

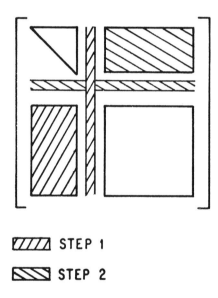

▨ STEP 1

▧ STEP 2

Figure 1. LU Data References

At the k-th step of this algorithm, a matrix formed from columns 1 through $k-1$ and rows k through n is multiplied by a vector constructed from the k-th column, rows 1 through $k-1$, with the results added to the k-th column, rows k through n. The second part of the k-th step involves a vector-matrix product, where the vector is constructed from the k-th row, columns 1 through $k-1$, and a matrix constructed from rows 1 through $k-1$ and columns $k+1$ through n, with the results added to the k-th row, columns $k+1$ through n. A diagram of the data references with respect to the original array A is depicted in Figure 1.

To see that the LU decomposition can be computed in this way, let us denote the k-th reduced submatrix by A_k and its elements by $\alpha_{ij}{}^{(k)}$. Then (in the absence of pivoting)

$$L_k^{-1}A = \begin{bmatrix} U_k & S_k \\ 0 & A_k \end{bmatrix},$$

and the subdiagonal elements of the first $k-1$ columns L_k are stored in the place of the zeroed elements of A. The formula for taking the factorization one step further is

$$\alpha_{ij}{}^{(k+1)} = \alpha_{ij}{}^{(k)} - \frac{\alpha_{ik}{}^{(k)}\alpha_{kj}{}^{(k)}}{\alpha_{kk}{}^{(k)}}$$

for $i,j = k+1, k+2, \cdots n$. Thus, the first column of A_k is

$$\alpha_{ik}{}^{(k)} = \alpha_{ik} - \sum_{l=1}^{k-1} \frac{\alpha_{il}{}^{(l)}\alpha_{lk}{}^{(l)}}{\alpha_{ll}{}^{(l)}}$$

for $i = k,k+1,...,n$ and this is just the matrix- vector product described as part one of step k above. Similarly, the first row of A_k is

$$\alpha_{kj}{}^{(k)} = \alpha_{kj} - \sum_{l=1}^{k-1} \frac{\alpha_{kl}{}^{(l)}\alpha_{lj}{}^{(l)}}{\alpha_{ll}{}^{(l)}}$$

for $j = k+1, k+2, ...,n$. This is the vector-matrix product described as part two of step k above. The algorithm that results is essentially the Crout reduction, which is described with more detail in [11,p.134].

The same ideas for use of high-level modules can be applied to other algorithms, including matrix multiply, Cholesky decomposition, and QR factorization.

For the Cholesky decomposition the matrix dealt with is symmetric and positive definite. The factorization is of the form

$$A = LL^T ,$$

where $A = A^T$ and is positive definite. If we assume the algorithm proceeds as in LU decomposition, but reference only the lower triangular part of the matrix, we have an algorithm based on matrix-vector operations which accomplishes the desired factorization.

The final method we shall discuss is the QR factorization using Householder transformations. Given a real $m \times n$ matrix A, the routine must produce an $m \times m$ orthogonal matrix Q and an $n \times n$ upper triangular matrix R such that

$$A = Q \begin{bmatrix} R \\ 0 \end{bmatrix} .$$

Householder's method consists of constructing transformations of the form

$$I - 2ww^T ,$$

with the unit vector w constructed to transform the first column of a given matrix into a multiple of the first coordinate vector e_1. At the k-th stage of the algorithm one has

$$Q_{k-1}^T A = \begin{bmatrix} R_{k-1} & S_{k-1} \\ 0 & A_{k-1} \end{bmatrix} ,$$

and w_k is constructed such that

$$\left[I - 2w_k w_k^T \right] A_{k-1} = \begin{bmatrix} \rho_k & s_k^T \\ 0 & A_k \end{bmatrix} .$$

The factorization is then updated to the form

$$Q_k^T A = \begin{bmatrix} R_k & S_k \\ 0 & A_k \end{bmatrix} ,$$

with

$$Q_k^T = \begin{bmatrix} I & 0 \\ 0 & I - 2w_k w_k^T \end{bmatrix} Q_{k-1}^T .$$

This is the basic algorithm used in LINPACK [2] for computing the QR

factorization of a matrix. This algorithm may be coded in terms of two of the modules. To see this, just note that the operation of applying a transformation may be broken into two steps:

$$z^T = w^T A \qquad (vector \times matrix)$$

and

$$\hat{A} = A - 2wz^T \qquad (rank\ one\ modification)$$

As we have seen, all of the main routines of LINPACK can be expressed in terms of the three modules described in Section 2. It remains to show how to code these operations efficiently for the HEP.

4. Efficient Modules for the Denelcor HEP

To produce the three basic modules described above for the HEP, we found it necessary to construct vector operations in software, since no vector operations are hardwired into the HEP. Certainly the capability to construct these operations should exist, since MIMD is more general than SIMD. The key idea in recovering these vector operations is prompted by the fact that the HEP has 2048 registers available on each PEM. Most of these are not used within a normal FORTRAN job. However, they may be put to very good use indeed. A block of these registers may be used as a local memory to a process. Efficiency may be gained through accumulation of results in registers to reduce data movement and through reduction of integer arithmetic associated with index calculations. These are very important issues concerning efficiency on the HEP, in particular, because every instruction emitted from the task queue has equal weight in terms of clock cycles once the pipelines are full enough to achieve a 10-MIP rate of execution. (See [7] for a diagram of the internal instruction flow on a PEM.)

To illustrate the idea, let us consider the computation required for the matrix-vector multiplication module

(4.1) $$y \leftarrow y + Ax \ ,$$

where y is a real vector of length n_1, A is an $n_1 \times n_2$ real matrix, and x is a real vector of length n_2. The vector y is to be overwritten with the result $y + Ax$.

281

The natural parallelism in matrix-vector multiplication is exploited by performing n_1 independent inner products between the matrix rows and the vector x in (4.1). In FORTRAN on the HEP one might simply self-schedule the inner products

(4.2) $\qquad y(i) \leftarrow y(i) + A(i, *)x(*)$ for $i = 1,2,...,n_1$

in parallel. However, even though a substantial speedup could be achieved, the FORTRAN DO LOOP that would be used to express the inner product would of necessity be very inefficient because it would reference one storage location in each of the arrays at a time instead of in blocks. In fact, the data movement and indexing operations will completely dominate this calculation if the present HEP FORTRAN 77 compiler is used.

On a vector machine one would accumulate the desired result in y by adding in appropriate multiples of the columns of A in the following fashion

(4.3) $\qquad y(*) \leftarrow y(*) + A(*,j)x(j)$ for $j = 1,2,...,n_2$.

This operation is inappropriate for an MIMD machine because one would have to synchronize the access to y by each of the processes, and this would block processes that could be doing useful work. One would do better to partition the vector y and the rows of the matrix A into blocks

(4.4) $\qquad \begin{bmatrix} y_1 \\ y_2 \\ \cdot \\ \cdot \\ \cdot \\ y_k \end{bmatrix} = \begin{bmatrix} y_1 \\ y_2 \\ \cdot \\ \cdot \\ \cdot \\ y_k \end{bmatrix} + \begin{bmatrix} A_1 \\ A_2 \\ \cdot \\ \cdot \\ \cdot \\ A_k \end{bmatrix} x$

and self-schedule individual vector operations on each of the blocks in parallel:

(4.5) $\qquad y_i \leftarrow y_i + A_i x$ for $i = 1,2,...,k$.

If a vector operation such as (4.3) were available to compute each of the blocks on (4.5), there would be nothing left to do. Synchronization costs at the outer loop would be reduced from requirements of (4.2), and we would have very efficient vector operations at the inner loop level.

As previously mentioned, there is no vector operation in hardware on the HEP. However, it is possible to construct such a vector operation in software that effectively uses the pipelined arithmetic functional units.

One way to achieve this is to set up a contiguous block of registers designated as a buffer vector-register and another block of registers designated as a result vector-register. If the length of the buffer is l, then we want k in (4.5) to satisfy $n_1 = (k-1)l + r$ with y_i of length l for $i < k$. Then for each i, y_i is loaded into the result vector-register and then the columns of A_i are successively loaded into the buffer vector-register, multiplied by the appropriate component of x, and added to the result vector-register. Since storage of the result register is deferred until the computation is completed, data movement is minimal.

This may be described in the following pseudo-code:

program matvec (ldm,n,A,x,y)

   comment: ldm the leading dimension of A is needed for column indexing;
   comment: initialize the result register;

   begin
   result $\leftarrow y$;
   for $j = 1$ *step* 1 *until* n *dc*

      begin
      comment: load the next column of A into buffer;
      buffer $\leftarrow A(*,j)$;

      comment: multiply by $x(j)$ *and add to result register;*
      buffer $\leftarrow$ *buffer*$\times x(j)$;
      result $\leftarrow$ *result* $+$ *buffer*;
      end

   comment: store result into y before exit;
   $y \leftarrow$ *result*;
   end.

Unfortunately this code cannot be implemented in FORTRAN. It is possible to implement it in assembly language, though, and an example of such a code is available in [10]. The essential idea is to compute the index offsets at assembly time so that the only index operation needed at run time in MATVEC is to calculate the address of the first element in the next column to be buffered in. That element together with the contiguous block of data that follows it are loaded into the buffer using the precomputed offsets.

The performance of a matrix-vector product coded in this way is easily predicted. If an appropriate number (10 per PEM say) of MATVEC routines operate in parallel on the matrix-vector product so that the peak rate of 10 million instructions per second are issued from the task queue, then roughly two out of three of these instructions are floating point operations. This is evident upon examination of the body of the loop in the pseudo-code for MATVEC given above. Therefore, the peak performance expected would be 6.7 megaflops. Computational results verifying this prediction are presented here in Section 6 and with more detail in [10].

Assembly language routines for the other two modules have also been provided using the same ideas. The vector-matrix product

$$y^T \leftarrow y^T + x^T A$$

is performed in the same way as the matrix-vector product, except that the partition is by columns of A instead of rows. There is a bit more overhead with this routine since the increments for buffering in a portion of a row within one of these column partitions need to be computed once at run time. The asymptotic performance rate is the same as for MATVEC though. The rank-one-update

$$A \leftarrow A + xy^T$$

is partitioned by rows as follows

$$(4.6) \qquad \begin{bmatrix} A_1 \\ A_2 \\ \cdot \\ \cdot \\ A_k \end{bmatrix} = \begin{bmatrix} A_1 \\ A_2 \\ \cdot \\ \cdot \\ A_k \end{bmatrix} + \begin{bmatrix} x_1 y^T \\ x_2 y^T \\ \cdot \\ \cdot \\ x_k y^T \end{bmatrix}.$$

The indexing scheme is similar to the one for MATVEC. The vector x_i is held in registers throughout the computation for the i-th partition in (4.6) while the columns of A_i are buffered in as they are in MATVEC along with the corresponding component of y. The peak performance obtainable for rank-one-update is 5 megaflops since there is a load, two floating point operations, and a store associated with each column update.

5. Library Issues

The notion of introducing parallelism at the level of the modules we have just discussed presents an unpleasant situation. When designing a library, one wishes to conceal machine dependencies as much as possible from the user. Also, in the case of transporting existing libraries to new machines, one wishes to preserve user interfaces in order to avoid unnecessary modification of existing code that references library subroutines. These important considerations seem to be difficult to accommodate if we are to invoke parallelism at the level described above. It would appear that the user must be conscious of the number of parallel processes required by the library subroutines throughout his program. This is the result of physical limitations on the total number of processes allowed to be be created. Should the library routines be called from multiple branches of a parallel program, the user could inadvertently attempt to create many more processes than is allowed.

A solution to this dilemma is to construct a scheduler that is capable of handling numerous requests from many processes. In our case on the HEP this scheduler takes the form of parallel work processes, each of which are capable of performing all of the requests coming from the linear algebra library routines, such as matrix vector multiplication. These matrix vector routines in turn do not actually carry out the floating point computation, rather they place requests for work to be performed on a queue. Each of the work processes polls an asynchronous variable which indicates work is waiting on the queue. The asynchronous variable takes on a value of full in this case. When work is pending, the first process to poll the asynchronous variable and receive a full status is assigned to carry out the task. These work processes are created at the outset and exist throughout the computation. The service requests are data-activated as described above. This is important on multi-PEM systems, as the overhead for issuing intertask creates under HEP-OS is substantial.

The diagram in Figure 2 illustrates schematically how such a server mechanism might be structured. We have constructed a prototype of such a scheduler to implement the linear algebra library as described in Sections 2 and 3 above. In fact, problems are assigned to the WORK routines through a self scheduling mechanism. In this prototype, we have not implementated the queue mechanism. The subroutine issuing the work request simply waits until one of the WORK routines has the appropriate addresses before issuing another request. The WORK routines compete for new problems as they complete old problems as we describe now.

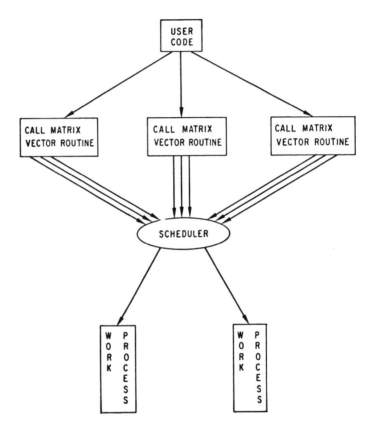

Figure 2. Library Scheduler

The three modules described in Section 2 each require support from one or more assembly language programs. The names of the modules are: SMXPY for matrix-vector multiplication ($y \leftarrow y + Ax$), SXMPY for vector-matrix multiplication ($y^T \leftarrow y^T + x^T A$), and SRANK1 for a rank-one-update to a matrix ($A \leftarrow A + xy^T$). These modules are FORTRAN subroutines; they issue requests to the server routines WORK for work to be performed by the FORTRAN-compatible assembly language programs MATVEC, INPROD, VECMAT, VINPRD, R1UPDT. For example, SMXPY performs the matrix-vector product (4.1) by partitioning the problem as described in (4.4) and issuing simultaneous requests to the assembly routines MATVEC and INPROD. Several (NPROC) copies of WORK are created in advance. These routines poll the asynchronous variable $START for a signal to call one of the assembly language routines. A local copy of the appropriate addresses is made and then a signal is returned to the requesting module by filling the asynchronous variable $IHAVE. In the case of SMXPY this call will be either to MATVEC to perform a matrix vector product on one of the partitions in (4.4) or to INPROD to perform an inner product on one of the rows in the k-th partition of (4.4). The assembly routine MATVEC performs the operations described in the above pseudo-code on one of the partitions in (4.4). The assembly routine INPROD is required because the k-th block in the partition (4.4) will not be the same length as the buffer for MATVEC in general. INPROD calculates the inner product of a single row of a matrix and a vector. A HEP-FORTRAN version of the work routine is available in the Appendix.

6. Performance

The performance gain through the use of these modules is striking. In this section we give sample results for the matrix vector product assembly language routine MATVEC, and for the LU decomposition based upon the modules SMXPY and SXMPY. Each of these has results of HEP FORTRAN routines both parallel and serial versions running on one PEM. The parallel FORTRAN results were obtained using the routines described in [4]. The matrix size required to achieve efficiency is $n_1 \geq 150$ using this implementation. The reason for this is that the buffer length was set at 15, and the number of copies of WORK was 10. This means that all 10 of the WORK routines could not be kept busy unitil the matrix order exceeded 150. This also accounts for the jagged appearance of the graph. Note the peaks at orders 150 and 300 where the buffer length 15 evenly

divides the order of the matrix. Performance degrades when this is not the case since inner products are done to clean up the last few rows.
Figure 3.

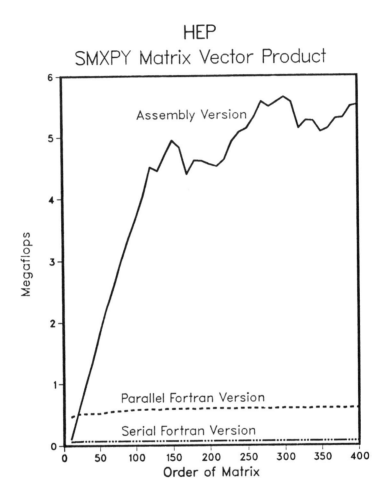

HEP
SMXPY Matrix Vector Product

The performance curve is smoothed out when the modules are used within the various factorizations. The performance shown below for LU decomposition is typical.

Figure 4.

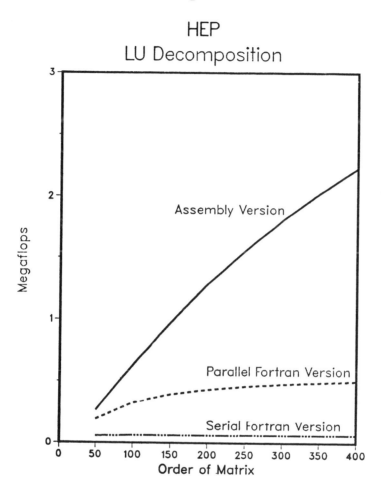

Since the matrix-vector and vector-matrix products range in size from $n_1 = 1,2,...,n/2$ in the decomposition of a matrix of order n, we effectively see the average performance of the modules in this application. The performace curve is not close to peaking in this example. While we expect to see better performance from the new FORTRAN compiler that will be included as part of the new HEP/UPX operating system, these results give some indication of the potential for the module concept.

7. Acknowledgements

We would like to thank the people at Los Alamos National Laboratory, the Ballistic Research Laboratory, and Denelcor for their help and support in this work.

References

[1] J. J. Dongarra, *Performance of Various Computers Using Standard Linear Equations Software in a Fortran Environment*, Argonne National Laboratory Report MCS-TM-23 (updated August 1984)

[2] J.J. Dongarra, J.R. Bunch, C.B. Moler, and G.W. Stewart, *LINPACK Users' Guide*, SIAM Publications, Philadelphia, 1979.

[3] J.J. Dongarra and S.C. Eisenstat, "Squeezing the Most out of an Algorithm in CRAY Fortran," *ACM Trans. Math. Software*, Vol. 10, No. 3, (1984).

[4] J.J. Dongarra and R. Hiromoto, *A Collection of Parallel Linear Equations Routines for the Denelcor HEP*, Argonne National Laboratory Report MCS-TM-15 (September 1983), to appear in Parallel Computing, Vol. 1 No. 2, 1984.

[5] J.J. Dongarra, E.L. Lusk, R.A. Overbeek, B.T. Smith, and D.C. Sorensen, *New Directions in Software for Advanced Computer Architectures*, Argonne National Laboratory Report MCS/TM 32 (August, 1984).

[6] Kirby Fong and Thomas L. Jordan, *Some Linear Algebra Algorithms and Their Performance on the CRAY-1*, Los Alamos Scientific Laboratory Report, UC-32, June 1977.

[7] H.F. Jordan, *Section 1.2*, This Volume.

[8] C. Lawson, R. Hanson, D. Kincaid, and F. Krogh, *Basic Linear Algebra Subprograms for Fortran Usage. ACM Trans. Math. Software*, 5 (1979), 308-371.

[9] B. Smith, *Section 1.2*, This Volume.

[10] D. C. Sorensen, *Buffering for Vector Performance on a Pipelined MIMD Machine*, Argonne National Laboratory Report MCS-TM-29 (April 1984), to appear in Parallel Computing, Vol. 1 No. 2, 1984.

[11] G.W. Stewart, *Introduction to Matrix Computation*, Academic Press, New York, 1973.

```
      SUBROUTINE WORK(TAG)
C ** CALLS ASSEMBLY LANGUAGE ROUTINES THAT  WORK
C    IN PARALLEL TO ACCOMPLISH LINEAR ALGEBRA TASKS.
C
C    MATV ...  MATRIX VECTOR PRODUCT.
C
C    Y <-- Y + A*X
C
C    VMAT ...  VECTOR MATRIX PRODUCT.
C
C    Y' <-- Y' + X'*A
C
C    UPD  ...  RANK ONE UPDATE.
C
C    A <-- A + X*Y'
C
C    INPD ...  INNER PRODUCT MATRIX ROW TIMES VECTOR.
C
C    Y <-- Y + A(I,.)*X
C
C    VNPD ...  INNER PRODUCT VECTOR TIMES MATRIX COLUMN.
C
C    Y <-- Y + X'*A(.,J)
C
C    A IS AN M X N REAL ARRAY.
C    X AND Y ARE VECTORS OF APPROPRIATE DIMENSIONS.
C    ADDRESSES AND STRIDES ARE PASSED THROUGH COMMON BLOCK /SYNC/.
C
C    THIS ROUTINE WAITS TO READ $START AT LABEL 10.
C    $START MUST CONTAIN ONE OF THE INTEGERS SET UP
C    IN THE COMMON BLOCK /MYTASK/ AND WILL PERFORM THE
C    APPROPRIATE TASK UPON READING $START.  $IHAVE IS FILLED
C    ONCE LOCAL POSSESSION OF ADDRESSES HAS BEEN ASSURED.
C    THE HOST MAY RESUME WHEN $IHAVE IS FILLED BY THIS ROUTINE.
C    UPON COMPLETION OF THE REQUEST CONTROL RETURNS
C    TO LABEL 10 TO RECIEVE A NEW REQUEST FROM $START.
C    A REQUEST OFF IN $START IS A REQUEST TO FILL $IHAVE ONLY.
C
C***************
```

```
C
C      D.C. SORENSEN
C      MCSD
C      ARGONNE NATIONAL LABORATORY
C      ARGONNE, ILLINOIS 60439
C
C****************
C
       INTEGER TAG
C
C      DECLARE SHARED SYNCHRONIZATION VARIABLES.
C
       INTEGER $IHAVE,$START,NPROC,ADDA,ADDX,ADDY,M,N,LDA
       INTEGER OFF,MATV,VMAT,UPD,INPD,VNPD
       INTEGER LBUFMV,LBUFVM,LBUFUD
       COMMON/SYNC/ $IHAVE,$START,NPROC,ADDA,ADDX,ADDY,M,N,LDA
       COMMON/MYTASK/OFF,MATV,VMAT,UPDT,INPD,VNPD
       COMMON/BLENG/LBUFMV,LBUFVM,LBUFUD
C
C      DECLARE LOCAL VARIABLES.
C
       INTEGER IDUMMY,MYTAG,A,X,Y
       MYTAG = TAG
       LBUFMV = 15
       LBUFVM = 10
       LBUFUD = 10
       OFF = 1
       MATV = 2
       VMAT = 3
       UPDT = 4
       INPD = 5
       VNPD = 6
       $IHAVE = 1
   10  CONTINUE
       IDUMMY = $START
C
C      WAIT FOR SIGNAL TO START.
C
         A = ADDA
         X = ADDX
         Y = ADDY
C
C      SIGNAL POSSESSION OF PARAMETERS.
C
       $IHAVE = 1
C
```

```
C     TASK IS
C               OFF  MATV  VMAT  UPD   INPD  VNPD  STOP
      GO TO (10,  100,  200,  300,  400,  500,  600),IDUMMY
C
C
  100 CONTINUE
C
C     $START CONTAINED MATV.
C
              CALL MATVEC(LDA,N,A,X,Y)
              GO TO 10
C
  200 CONTINUE
C
C     $START CONTAINED VMAT.
C
              CALL VECMAT(LDA,N,A,X,Y)
              GO TO 10
C
  300 CONTINUE
C
C     $START CONTAINED UPDT.
C
              CALL R1UPDT(LDA,N,A,X,Y)
              GO TO 10
C
  400 CONTINUE
C
C     $START CONTAINED INPD.
C
              CALL INPROD(LDA,N,A,X,Y)
              GO TO 10
C
  500 CONTINUE
C
C     $START CONTAINED VNPD.
C
              CALL VINPRD(LDA,N,A,X,Y)
              GO TO 10
C
  600 CONTINUE
C
C     SHUT OFF THIS ROUTINE.
C
      RETURN
C
C     LAST CARD OF WORK
C
      END
```

4.3   PARALLEL ALGORITHMS FOR RECURRENCE AND TRIDIAGONAL
        EQUATIONS

J. S. KOWALIK
Boeing Computer Services
Artificial Intelligence Center
Bellevue, Washington

S. P. KUMAR
Department of Computer Science
Colorado State University
Fort Collins, Colorado

INTRODUCTION

Systems of tridiagonal equations frequently arise in practical applications related to solving ordinary or partial differential equations by discrete numerical methods. Sets of such equations or a large single tridiagonal system of equations constitute a large fraction of many problems in physics and engineering. The conventional Gaussian elimination method leads to sequential recurrences that have to be evaluated term by term. Several attempts have been made to remedy this difficulty and to design alternative algorithms suitable for parallel multiprocessors or pipeline vector computers. A recent review of the methods that allow vectorization is given in Gentzsch [1984]. Our interest is in exploring a modification of the Gaussian method suitable for a MIMD computer with the number of processors p much smaller than the number of equations n, i.e. $p \ll n$. The method is simple conceptually and lends itself to a straightforward implementation on such MIMD computer as the Heterogeneous Element Processor discussed in this book. First we consider a set of first order recurrence equations.

RECURRENCE EQUATIONS

A set of recurrence equations

$$x_1 = d_1$$

$$b_j x_{j-1} + x_j = d_j \quad \text{for} \quad 2 \le j \le n$$

can be represented by a matrix equation $A\,\mathbf{x} = \mathbf{d}$ where A is bidiagonal.

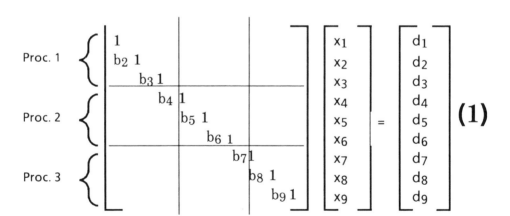

To illustrate the method we have assumed that $n = 9$, $p = 3$ and $k = n/p = 3$;
see (1). In the first phase of the method for obtaining the vector x we eliminate
b_2, b_3, , b_5, b_6, b_8, and b_9 using three processors simultaneously. In general, Phase 1
is:

Processor i, $1 \le i \le p$

$f_{(i-1)k+1} := b_{(i-1)k+1}$,   not computed for $i = 1$

For $j := (i-1)k + 2$ to ik do

begin

$f_j := -b_j f_{j-1}$,   not computed for $i = 1$

$d_j := d_j - b_j d_{j-1}$

end

After Phase 1 the system of equations is almost diagonalized but the new non zero
elements f_5, f_6, f_8, and f_9 have been created; see (2).

$$
\begin{bmatrix}
1 & & & & & & & & \\
& 1 & & & & & & & \\
& & 1 & & & & & & \\
& & f_4 & 1 & & & & & \\
& & f_5 & & 1 & & & & \\
& & f_6 & & & 1 & & & \\
& & & & & f_7 & 1 & & \\
& & & & & f_8 & & 1 & \\
& & & & & f_9 & & & 1 \\
\end{bmatrix}
\begin{bmatrix}
x_1 \\ x_2 \\ x_3 \\ x_4 \\ x_5 \\ x_6 \\ x_7 \\ x_8 \\ x_9
\end{bmatrix}
=
\begin{bmatrix}
d_1 \\ d_2 \\ d_3 \\ d_4 \\ d_5 \\ d_6 \\ d_7 \\ d_8 \\ d_9
\end{bmatrix}
\quad \textbf{(2)}
$$

Note that the vectors d in (1) and (2) are different.

To decouple the system we have to find the values of x_3 and x_6 by solving evuations 3 and 6. Since in general there are only p - 1 of them we can solve these equations using one processor.

In general in Phase 2 we solve the following set:

$$x_k = d_k$$

$$f_j x_{j-k} + x_j = d_j \quad , \quad j = 2k, 3k, ..., (p-1)k$$

Now the remaining system of equations is decoupled and can be solved in parallel by p - 1 processors as Phase 3:

$$\text{Processor} \quad i, \quad 2 \le i \le p$$

$$\text{For} \quad j := (i-1)k + 1 \quad \text{to} \quad ik - 1 \quad \text{do}$$

$$x_j := d_j - f_j x_{(i-1)k}$$

Processor 1 can compute the value $x_{pk} := d_{pk} - f_{pk} x_{(p-1)k}$

TRIDIAGONAL EQUATIONS

The method presented in the previous Section can be extended to solve a single set of tridiagonal equations:

$$b_j x_{j-1} + a_j x_j + c_j x_{j+1} = d_j \quad , \quad 1 \le j \le n$$

$$b_1 = c_n = o$$

Again for the purpose of illustration we assume n = 9 and p = 3. Since we deal with an MIMD processor it is not necessary that k = n/p is an integer, but this choice simplifies our notation. The initial matrix is partitioned as shown in (3).

$$
\begin{bmatrix}
a_1 & c_1 & & & & & & & \\
b_2 & a_2 & c_2 & & & & & & \\
& b_3 & a_3 & c_3 & & & & & \\
& & b_4 & a_4 & c_4 & & & & \\
& & & b_5 & a_5 & c_5 & & & \\
& & & & b_6 & a_6 & c_6 & & \\
& & & & & & b_7 & a_7 & c_7 \\
& & & & & & & b_8 & a_8 & c_8 \\
& & & & & & & & b_9 & a_9
\end{bmatrix}
\begin{bmatrix}
x_1 \\ x_2 \\ x_3 \\ x_4 \\ x_5 \\ x_6 \\ x_7 \\ x_8 \\ x_9
\end{bmatrix}
=
\begin{bmatrix}
d_1 \\ d_2 \\ d_3 \\ d_4 \\ d_5 \\ d_6 \\ d_7 \\ d_8 \\ d_9
\end{bmatrix}
\qquad \textbf{(3)}
$$

For equations (3) Phase 1 consists of two steps and reduces (3) to equations (4).

$$
\begin{bmatrix}
a_1 & & g_1 & & & & & & \\
& a_2 & g_2 & & & & & & \\
& & a_3 & & & g_3 & & & \\
& & f_4 & a_4 & & g_4 & & & \\
& & f_5 & & a_5 & g_5 & & & \\
& & f_6 & & & a_6 & & & g_6 \\
& & & & & f_7 & a_7 & & g_7 \\
& & & & & f_8 & & a_8 & g_8 \\
& & & & & f_9 & & & a_9
\end{bmatrix}
\begin{bmatrix}
x_1 \\ x_2 \\ x_3 \\ x_4 \\ x_5 \\ x_6 \\ x_7 \\ x_8 \\ x_9
\end{bmatrix}
=
\begin{bmatrix}
d_1 \\ d_2 \\ d_3 \\ d_4 \\ d_5 \\ d_6 \\ d_7 \\ d_8 \\ d_9
\end{bmatrix}
\qquad \textbf{(4)}
$$

Note that the vectors **d** and the values of a_j's in (3) and (4) are different.

For example, processor 2 eliminates b_5, b_6, c_4, and c_3, in this order. In general Phase 1 is as follows:

PHASE 1

STEP 1

Processor i, $\quad 1 \le i \le p$

$f_{(i-1)k+1} := b_{(i-1)k+1}$, not computed for $i = 1$

For $j := (i-1)k+2$ to ik do

begin

$m_j := b_j / a_{j-1}$

$a_j := a_j - m_j c_{j-1}$

$f_j := -m_j f_{j-1}$, not computed for $i = 1$

$d_j := d_j - m_j d_{j-1}$

end

STEP 2

Processor i, $\quad 1 \le i \le p$

$g_{ik-1} := c_{ik-1}$

For $j := ik-2$ down to $(i-1)k+1$ do

begin

$m_j := c_j / a_{j+1}$

$g_j := -m_j g_{j+1}$

$f_j := f_j - m_j f_{j+1}$, not computed for $i = 1$

$d_j := d_j - m_j d_{j+1}$

end

$m_i := c_{(i-1)k} / a_{(i-1)k+1}$

$g_{(i-1)k} := -m_i g_{(i-1)k+1}$

$a_{(i-1)k} := a_{(i-1)k} - m_i f_{(i-1)k+1}$ $\left.\right\}$ not computed for $i = 1$

$d_{(i-1)k} := d_{(i-1)k} - m_i d_{(i-1)k+1}$

In Phase 2 we solve the following p tridiagonal equations using Gaussian elimination and one processor:

PHASE 2

$$f_j x_{j-k} + a_j x_j + g_j x_{j+k} = d_j$$

where $j = k, 2k, 3k, ..., pk$

and $f_k = g_{pk} = 0$

Phase 2 decouples system of equations (4) into p subsystems.

In Phase 3 we calculate the remaining n - p variables.

PHASE 3

Processor i, $\quad 1 \le i \le p$

For $j := (i-1)k + 1 \quad$ to $ik - 1$ do

$x_j := (d_j - f_j x_{(i-1)k} - g_j x_{ik})/a_j$

In the formula for x_j the product $f_j x_{(i-1)k}$ is not computed for $i = 1$. If we assume that the execution time for division is twice the time for multiplication, or addition or subtraction then the total solution time for solving n equations with using p processors is proportional to $T_p = 20k + 10p + $ constant. On the other hand a single processor requires $T_1 = 10n + $ constant.

Thus the theoretical speedup is approximately

$$S_p = \frac{T_1}{T_p} \approx \frac{n}{2k + p} \tag{5}$$

or assuming that p is much smaller than n and k we get

$$S_p \approx 0.5p \tag{6}$$

The presented algorithm is numerically safe for diagonally dominant matrices. Also, the value of S_p would somewhat increase for such systems since the values of f's and g's become progressively smaller and their computation can be avoided when they drop below certain numerical value. Actual program runs on HEP did confirm this type of increase in the speedup values.

Finally, we would like to mention two references where algorithmic ideas with similar objectives have been investigated. Wang [1981] designed a partition algorithm for solving tridiagonal systems on SIMD machines. Dongarra and Sameh [1984] presented a partitioning algorithm for solving a banded diagonally dominant system of equations.

COMPUTATIONAL RESULTS

For the purpose of our computational analysis, the parallel algorithm (which we shall refer to as PTRD) composed of Phase 1, Phase 2, and Phase 3 was programmed using HEP FORTRAN and was executed on the HEP machine. This program was written for any values of n and p. Thus, speedup can be determined from the execution time for various values of p. To obtain experimental results, the program was run on randomly generated coefficient matrix A of different sizes n, for $100 \leq n \leq 10,000$. The generated matrix was made diagonally dominant for reasons of numerical stability. Table 1 presents the results for achieved speedup and efficiency of some of these programs runs for different values of n and p, $2 \leq p \leq 12$. Since eight task status words can be created on one Processor Element Module (PEM) of HEP, during one clock period (100 nsec), the performance of 10 million operations per second can be obtained when at least 8 instruction streams are active. In reality, depending on the data memory access delays, on the average between 8 and 12 parallel streams may give the same performance. Hence, the obtained numerical results up to p = 12 are useful to compare. Figure 1 shows the performance variation of PTRD as the number of processors varies.

N	P	S_p	E_p
1000	2	1.266444	.633222
	4	2.474079	.618519
	5	3.033750	.606750
	10	5.084461	.508446
5000	2	1.274462	.637231
	4	2.530474	.632618
	5	3.136509	.627301
	8	4.852678	.606584
	10	5.588169	.558816
10000	2	1.275488	.637744
	4	2.540851	.635212
	5	3.147782	.629556
	8	4.896047	.612005
	10	5.656060	.565606

Table 1. Actual speedup and efficiency for PTRD on HEP.
(time is measured in seconds)

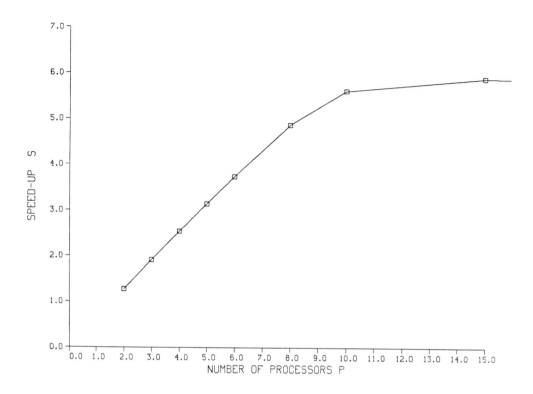

Figure 1 . Number of processors vs. actual speedup on HEP.

The program required a negligible amount of synchronization. To demonstrate this, let

T_1^i : Computation of Phase 1, for the i-th block of (3), i = 1, 2, ..., p

T_2 : Computation of Phase 2

T_3^i : Computation of Phase 3 for the i-th block of (3), i = 1, 2, ..., p

be definition of program tasks of PTRD. The first step in the program, then, is to create p parallel instruction streams corresponding to p blocks of (3), where the i-th stream executes T_1^i . Next, these p streams are joined and only one stream executes T_2 sequentially. Finally, p parallel instruction streams are created again to compute the tasks T_3^1 T_3^2 ,..... T_3^p in parallel yielding the solution vector x.

As shown in Figure 2, synchronization is required only at two points in the complete process which was achieved by using one semaphored variable (based on Full/Empty principle implemented on HEP). Since the time complexity of each of the tasks T_1^i , i = 1, 2, ..., p is the same, the time taken to join p tasks is negligible. The same holds for joining the p streams at the end of tasks T_3^i , i = 1, 2,....p.

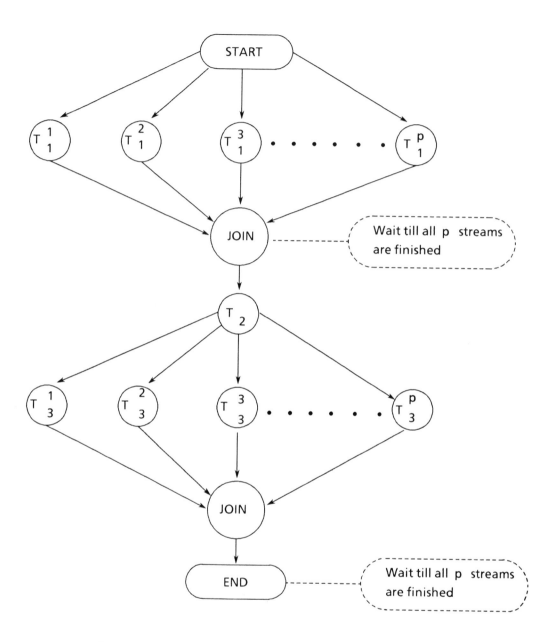

Figure 2 Synchronization points of PTRD.

References:

1. W. Gentzsch, Vectorization of Computer Programs with Applications to Computational Fluid Dynamics, Notes on Numerical Fluid Mechanics, Vol. 8, Vieweg, Braunschweig -- Wiesbaden, 1984.

2. H. H Wang, A Parallel Method for Tridiagonal Equations, ACM Transactions on Mathematical Software, Vol. 7, 1981, pp. 170 - 183.

3. J. J. Dongarra and A. Sameh, On Some Parallel Banded System Solvers, Argonne National Laboratory, Mathematics and Computer Science Division, Technical Memorandum No. 27, March 1984.

4.4 HYDROCODES ON THE HEP

D. L. HICKS
Department of Mathematical and Computer Sciences
Michigan Technological University
Houghton, Michigan

INTRODUCTION

As is well known, the motion of a continuum (solid, liquid, gas, plasma or multiphase material) is governed by the conservation laws of continuum dynamics. Since the very first hydrocode (proposed by von Neumann in 1944), programs for computational continuum dynamics have suffered from computer limitations. Indeed the hydrocodes, wavecodes and magnetohydrocodes have provided a strong motivation for the development of super computers. These "super codes" have many applications on a variety of "super problems" arising in meteorology, aeronautics, dynamic structural analysis, reactor safety, weapons effects, fusion reactor research, etc. (see the bibliography). Limitations on computational power obviate the simulation of many complicated continuum dynamic phenomena. Concurrent computations on parallel processors appear to be the only possible way to achieve sufficient computational power to simulate these complicated phenomena.

In an explicit, single-phase, one-dimensional Lagrangean hydrocode the restructuring of the algorithm to achieve block-by-block parallelization is straightforward. Thus for this case, the simplest hydrocode, the optimal parallelization problem is evidently easily solved.

But is it? Is this the best restructuring of the algorithm? If so, then how do we prove it? Can we automate this parallelization of a serial algorithm? What do the answers to these questions imply about the best architecture for super computers?

309

The next case we consider is the extension from an explicit to an implicit code; it involves the inversion of a tridiagonal array. It appears that this case can essentially be reduced to the previously solved case by an a priori, symbolic inversion of the inherent tridiagonal matrix. Block implicit methods may prove to be optimal here.

Extensions to Eulerian codes can be achieved by the Harlow-Johnson rezone (see Hicks and Walsh (1976)) technique. This technique can also form the basis for the parallelizations of other rezoning (also known as adaptive mesh) schemes.

The extension to two-phase or two-material flow codes in Eulerian coordinates appears to be straightforward (see Hicks (1983)).

Finally, to extend to multidimensions the method of operator splitting (see Hicks and Madsen (1976)) can be used.

Thus it appears that through stages of increasing complexity one can achieve the block-by-block parallelization of multiphase (or multimaterial) and multidimensional hydrocodes. It appears that block-by-block parallization or some variation thereon will lead to the optimal parallel algorithm.

Block-by-Block Parallelization

Smith (1981) and Jordan (1981) recommend a top down approach to the parallelization of a program from peak performance on parallel processors such as the HEP. In a hydrocode this appears to mean block-by-block parallelization. However, we remain open to the consideration and comparison of alternatives. Also we would like to be able to prove (or disprove) that block-by-block parallelization leads to the best algorithms for hydrocodes on the HEP.

The construction of a multimaterial, multidimensional hydrocode can get quite complicated. We approach the problem of the block-by-block parallelization of hydrocodes and the proof that this leads to the optimal algorithm in the following stages:

Stage 1:   Explicit, single-material, one-dimensional, Lagrangean hydrocode

Stage 2:   Implicit extension

Stage 3:   Eulerian extension

Stage 4:   Two-phase flow extension

Stage 5:   Multidimensional extension

This stage-by-stage approach was first documented in an Idaho National Engineering Laboratory research report (Hicks (1983)).

Stage-by-Stage Approach

Stage 1. Let X be the Lagrangean spatial coordinate and μ be the Lagrangean mass coordinate related by:

$$d\mu = \rho^\circ dX$$

where ρ° is the initial mass density. Let V be the specific volume related by

$$V = 1/\rho$$

μ be the specific momentum, E be the specific (total) energy, e be the specific internal energy, related by

$$E = e + u^2/2$$

p be the pressure and q be the viscosity. The conservation laws
are represented by

$$\partial \underset{\sim}{U}/\partial t = \partial \underset{\sim}{F}(\underset{\sim}{U})/\partial \mu$$

where

$$\underset{\sim}{U} = (V, u, E)^T$$

and

$$\underset{\sim}{F}(\underset{\sim}{U}) = (u, -(p + q), -u(p + q))^T$$

Consider the von Neumann–Richtmyer (1950) scheme. This scheme
is the basis for many hydrocodes and wavecodes used in the national
laboratories (e.g., PUFF at AFWL; WONDY, TOODY, CHARTD, CSQ at SNLA;
HEMP at LLNL; etc.) Their discretization of the conservation of volume

$$\partial V/\partial t = \partial u/\partial \mu$$

law is

$$\frac{V_{j+\frac{1}{2}}^{n+1} - V_{j+\frac{1}{2}}^{n}}{t^{n+1} - t^{n}} = \frac{u_{j+1}^{n+\frac{1}{2}} - u_{j}^{n+\frac{1}{2}}}{\mu_{j+1} - \mu_{j}}$$

Similarly they discretize the conservation of momentuum

$$\partial u/\partial t = -\partial(p + q)/\partial \mu)$$

law as

$$\frac{u_j^{n+\frac{1}{2}} - u_j^{n-\frac{1}{2}}}{t^{n+\frac{1}{2}} - t^{n-\frac{1}{2}}} = - \frac{\left(p_{j+\frac{1}{2}}^n + q_{j+\frac{1}{2}}^{n-\frac{1}{2}}\right) - \left(p_{j-\frac{1}{2}}^n + q_{j-\frac{1}{2}}^{n-\frac{1}{2}}\right)}{\mu_{j+\frac{1}{2}} - \mu_{j-\frac{1}{2}}}$$

Instead of discretizing the conservation of energy

$$\partial E/\partial t = - \partial u(p + q)/\partial \mu$$

law von Neumann and Richtmyer (1950) discretized the internal energy equation

$$\partial e/\partial t = -(p + q)\partial V/\partial t$$

as follows:

$$e_{j+\frac{1}{2}}^{n+1} - e_{j+\frac{1}{2}}^n = -\left[\left(p_{j+}^{n+1} + p_{j+\frac{1}{2}}^n\right)/2 + q_{j+\frac{1}{2}}^{n+\frac{1}{2}}\right]\left(V_{j+\frac{1}{2}}^{n+1} - V_{j+\frac{1}{2}}^n\right)$$

The material law (or equation of state) gives $p_{j+\frac{1}{2}}^n$ as a function of $V_{j+\frac{1}{2}}^n$ and $e_{j+\frac{1}{2}}^n$. One well-known example of an equation of state is the ideal gas law

$$p = (\gamma - 1)e\rho$$

where $\gamma > 1$ is a constant. A slight generalization of this is the Mie-Grüneisen law

$$p = f(\rho) + \Gamma e\rho$$

where $\Gamma > 0$ is the Gruneisen parameter. This form is often used in work involving shock waves in solids. Observe that for the Mie-Grüneisen law it is easy to reduce von Neumann and Richtmyer's implicit discretization of the internal energy equation to an explicit equation for

$e_{j+\frac{1}{2}}^{n+1}$. However, when the material law is not so tractable the discretized internal energy equation will require an iteration procedure and the parallelization of this requires further work.

One of the advantages of the parallel computer (MIMD architecture) over the vector computer (SIMD architecture) is in dealing with the parallelization of the material law routine. Material law routines do not in general vectorize and a large portion (often over 75%) of the time is spend there in calculations with complicated material laws.

Note that for mechanical material laws (i.e., where p is a function of ρ only) the energy equation is not needed and it may be omitted. This is convenient for preliminary testing and debugging procedures.

Consider the data structure for the discretized conservation of momentuum law:

$$u_{new} = u_{old} - (\sigma_{right} - \sigma_{left})*r$$

where

$$r = \Delta t/\Delta \mu$$

and

$$\sigma = p + q .$$

Observe the same simple structure in the discretized conservation of volume

$$V_{new} = V_{old} + (u_{right} - u_{left})*r$$

The momentum may be advanced in time by constructing a subroutine to implement the discretized conservation of momentum law. We let the main program CREATE the optimal number of copies of this routine and use the fork-join structure of parallel programming. Similarly the discretized conservation of volume law can be programmed in a fork-parallel-join fashion. Further if the discrete internal energy equation can be reduced to an explicit equation for e^{n+1} then it and the equation of state evaluations may be done with the same zone-by-zone parallel programming structure. For further details see Hicks (1983).

Generally explicit schemes lead to conditional stability with a timestep restruction of the CFL form (see Hicks and Walsh (1976)). On the other hand, implicit schemes can lead to unconditionally stable schemes.

Various necessary and sufficient conditions for the stability of hydrocodes with classical material laws (ideal gas, etc.) may be found in Richtmyer and Morton (1967). More recent results on nonequilibrium, rate dependent materials and related computational techniques such as subcycling may be found in Hicks (1978a, 1981, 1982). For a discussion of the hydrocode convergence problem see Hicks (1978b, 1979).

Stage 2. The extension to an implicit scheme involves the inversion of a certain tridiagonal matrix. It appears that this can be accomplished by the a priori, symbolic inversion of the inherent tridiagonal array. This allows us to essentially reduce the implicit parallelization case to the explicit parallelization case which we

discussed in Stage 1. For further details see Hicks (1983). Block
implicit methods look good for this purpose (see Evans (1983)).

Stage 3. The Eulerian extension can be achieved by a rezone
technique whose precursors may be seen in the work of F. Harlow (in his
Particle in Cell codes) and the work of W. Johnson (in his "continuum-
ized" versions of the PIC codes). We refer to this rezone technique
as the Harlow-Johnson rezone technique. It can be modified to achieve
dynamic rezone methods (also known as adaptive mesh methods). See
Hicks (1983) and Hicks and Walsh (1976) for further details.

Stage 4. Two-phase flow extensions are readily accomplished once
the coordinate system is rezoned to Eulerian. Discussion of two-phase
flow models and their relevance to reactor safety may be found in Hicks
(1979, 1980, 1981b, 1983, 1984) and Ransom and Hicks (1984). One of
the important problems in reactor safety is the need for fast simu-
lator/predictors to assist operators in handling situations such as
the event at Three-Mile-Island.

Stage 5. The extension to multidimensions may be achieved by
operator splitting. See Hicks and Madsen (1976) for further details.

Test Problems

To simplify the testing and debugging we use a simple test problem (whose exact solution is known) involving shock and rarefaction
waves:

-The material law is the linear p-V law.

-The boundary data are $u = 0$ at both ends.

-The initial data is two states with left state at 2 atmospheres and right state at 1 atmosphere.

The exact solution has a rightward traveling shock and a leftward traveling rarefaction wave. The reader desiring further details should consult Hicks, Scott and Treadway (1984).

Parallel Algorithms

1. <u>Zone-by-Zone</u>. WUNDEE8 is the name of this algorithm. It utilizes a zone-by-zone parallelization with self-scheduling as follows:

-fork - compute viscosities - join

-fork - compute momenta - join

-fork - compute volumes - join

-fork - compute pressures - join

Within each fork-join the calculations are done with parallel processes that advance single zones using self-scheduling of the parallel processes.

2. <u>Block-by-Block</u>. WONDEE7 is the name of this algorithm. It utilizes a block-by-block parallelization as follows:

-fork - compute viscosities - join

-fork - compute momenta - join

-fork - compute volumes - join

-fork - compute pressures - join

Within each fork-join the calculations are done with N_p (number of processes) parallel processes that advance a block of N_B (number of zones in a block) contiguous zones. N_p and N_B are related by

$$N_B * N_p = \text{Total number of zones}$$

For further details see Hicks, Scott and Treadway (1984).

DATA FROM COMPUTATIONAL EXPERIMENTS ON THE LANL HEP

We ran the following computational experiments on the LANL (Los Alamos National Laboratories) HEP in the summer of 1984:

(1) WONDY8 (zone-by-zone, self-scheduling) on 21 zones for 4,000 cycles;

(2) WONDY7 (block-by-block) on 4,200 zones for 1,000 cycles.

We ran these experiments with number of processes ranging from one to twenty-one. The WONDY8 results are plotted in FIGURE 1 and the WONDY7 results are plotted in FIGURE 2.

WONDY 7 Block-By-Block Parallelization.

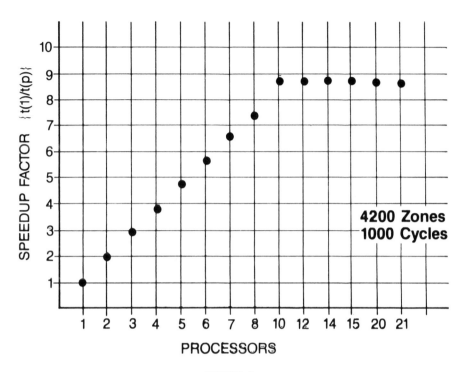

FIGURE 1

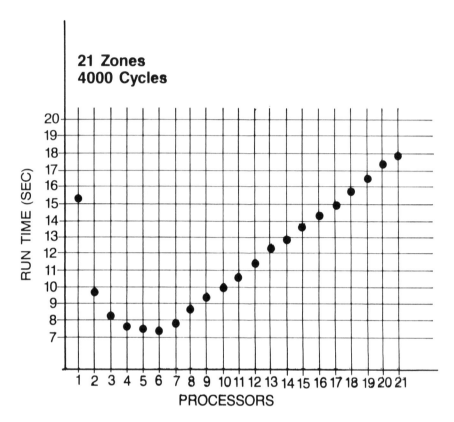

FIGURE 2

Discussion and Conclusion

The data presented in Figure 1 can be understood by considering the following model for parallel processing times. Let the time to compute with n parallel processes be $T(n)$ and suppose

$$T(n) = T(1)/n + (n - 1)*C_T$$

where C_T is a coefficient that includes the time lost to creation of parallel processes and communication and contention between parallel processes. If we plot $T(n)$ versus n we get a curve qualitatively similar to that displayed in Figure 1. By curve fitting one could determine the effective C_T for this calculation.

The WONDY8 calculation was done with too fine a granularity. That is, the "computational chunks" were too small. We can increase the size of the computational chunks by going to blocks of zones instead of advancing a single zone at a time. This, of course, leads us to the block-by-block parallel structure of WONDY7.

The results of the WONDY7 experiments are shown in Figure 2. Note that the speed up factor peaks at a value just under nine somewhere in the range of 10-14 processes. The reason the speed up factor gets up almost to nine is that in the single process calculation there are essentially nine segments in the calculation: eight of the segments are in the pipe and the ninth segment is the store operation. This peaking phenomena in the range of 10-14 processes has been observed by many previous investigators (e.g. Smith, Jordan, Lubeck, etc.)

The (rather obvious) conclusion that we have reached is that it is a good idea to minimize the C_T coefficient as much as is possible. One way to reduce C_T is to minimize the number of creates. We have under development an algorithm which seems to be the best approach to reducing the number of creates. We call this approach the method of immortal subroutines. Basically the immortal subroutines method involves creating and never "killing" (returning at the end of the subroutine) copies of the subroutines. This approach will apparently lead to the optimal parallel algorithm for hydrocodes on the HEP.

Acknowledgements

I have been helped in many ways by many people on this project. I wish to thank: B. J. Smith, D. Carstensen, J. Middleton, and L. Wolf of Denelcor; B. Buzbee, A. Hayes and O. Lubeck of Los Alamos National Laboratory; K. Ottenstein and D. Poplawski of Michigan Technological University; R. Detry, M. Scott, J. Tischauser and A. Treadway of Sandia National Laboratories; V. Ransom and J. Trapp of Idaho National Engineering Laboratory; H. Jordan, S. Lett and B. J. Lord of the University of Colorado; and J. Larsen, L. Liebrock and J. McGrath of KMS Fusion, Inc.

Bibliography

L. M. Adams (1983), "Experiences using the Finite Element Machine", pres. at SIAM Conf. Parallel Proc. (1983).

G. Alaghband and H. F. Jordan (1983), "Parallelization of the MA28 Sparse Matrix Package for the HEP", pres. at SIAM Conf. Parallel Proc. (1983).

J. L. Baer (1982) "Techniques to Exploit Parallelism", pp. 75-100 of Parallel Processing Systems Ed. by D. J. Evans, Cambridge University Press.

R. H. Barlow (1982) "Performance Measures for Parallel Algorithms", pp. 179-192 of Parallel Processing Systems, Ed. by D. J. Evans, Cambridge University Press.

S. W. Bostic (1983), "Solution of tridiagonal systems of equations on the finite element machine", pres. at SIAM Conf. Parallel Proc. (1983).

J. C. Browne (1983), "Parallel Algorithms for a Dynamically Reconfigurable Computer Architecture" pres. at SIAM Conf. Parallel Proc. (1983).

M. Ciment (1984), "News from NSF: Reorganization, Supercomputers", SIAM NEWSLETTER V17, N1 (Jan. 1984) p. 6.

R. Courant, K. O. Friedrichs and H. Lewy (1982) "Uber die partiellen Differenzengleichungen der mathematische Physic", Math. Ann., V100, pp. 32-74.

G. Dallaire (1984), American Universities Need Greater Access to Super-computers Communs. of the ACM, V27, N4 (May 1984) pp. 292-298.

Denelcor (1981), HEP (Heterogeneous Element Processor) Principles of Operation, Denelcor Publication No. 9000001, April 1981, Denelcor, Inc., 17000 East Ohio Place, Aurora, Colorado 80017.

Denelcor (1982a), <u>HEP Concepts and Facilities</u> Denelcor Publication No. 9000005, 15 February 1982.

Denelcor (1982b), <u>HEP FORTRAN 77 User's Guide</u>, Denelcor Publication No. 9000006, 15 February 1982.

P. H. Enslow, Jr. and T. G. Saponas (1982) "Parallel Control in Distributed Systems", pp. 43-74 of <u>Parallel Processing Systems</u>, Ed. by D. J. Evans, Cambridge University Press.

D. J. Evans (1982), "Parallel Numerical Algorithms for Linear Systems", pp. 357-384 of <u>Parallel Processing Systems</u>, Ed. by D. J. Evans, Cambridge University Press.

D. J. Evans (1983), "New Parallel Algorithms for Partial Differential Equations" pp. 3-56 of <u>Parallel Computing 83</u>, M. Feilmeier, J. Joubert, and V. Schendel (eds.) Elsevier Science Publishers B. V. (North-Holland).

D. J. Evans et al. (1982), <u>Parallel Processing Systems</u>, Ed. by D. J. Evans, Cambridge University Press.

M. Feilmeier (1982) "Parallel Numerical Algorithms", pp. 285-338 of <u>Parallel Processing Systems</u> by D. J. Evans, Cambridge University Press.

D. C. Fisher (1983), "Numerical Computations on Multiprocessors with only Local connections", pres. at SIAM Conf. on Parallel Proc. (1983).

D. Gannon and J. Panetta (1983), "Restructuring SIMPLE for the CHIP system" pres. at SIAM Conf. Parallel Proc. (1983).

G. Girault (1982), "Proof of Protocols in the Case of Failures", pp.

121–142 of <u>Parallel Processing Systems</u>, Ed. by D. J. Evans, Cambridge University Press.

W. Handler (1982), "Innovative Computer Architecture-How to increase Parallelism But Not Complexity", pp. 1–42 of <u>Parallel Processing Systems</u>, Ed. by D. J. Evans, Cambridge University Press.

F. H. Harlow (1957), "Hydrodynamic Problems Involving Large Fluid Distortions", pp. 137–142, J. Assoc. Comp. Math. V4.

M. Hatzopoulos (1982), "Parallel Linear System Solvers for Tridiagonal Systems", pp. 385–394 of <u>Parallel Process Systems</u>, Ed. by D. J. Evans, Cambridge University Press.

E. F. Hayes (1984), "Access to Supercomputers: An NSF Perspective", Communs. of the ACM, V27, N4 (May 1984), pp. 299–303.

D. L. Hicks (1978a), "Stability Analysis of WONDY (A Hydrocode Based on the Artificial Viscosity Method on von Neumann and Richtmyer) for a Special Case of Maxwell's Material Law", pp. 1123–1130 of <u>Mathematics of Computation</u>, V32, N144.

D. L. Hicks (1978b), "The Hydrocode Convergence Problem-Part 1", <u>Comp. Meth. in Appl. Mech. and Eng.</u>, <u>13</u>, 79.

D. L. Hicks (1979a), "The Hydrocode Convergence Problem-Part 2", <u>Comp. Meth. in Appl. Mech. and Eng.</u>, <u>20</u>, 303.

D. L. Hicks (1979b), "Well-Posedness of the Two-Phase Flow Problem, Part 1: Theory and Procedures Developed and applied to Mechanical EOS with Equal Pressures", Sandia Natl. Labs., SAND-79-1435.

D. L. Hicks (1980), "Well-Posedness of the Two-Phase Flow Problem, Part 2: Stability Analyses and Microstructural Models", Sandia Natl. Labs., SAND-80-1276

D. L. Hicks (1981a), "Hydrocode Subcycling Stability", Math. Comp. V37, N155, pp. 69–78.

D. L. Hicks (1981b), "Hyperbolic Models for Two-Phase or Two-Material Flow", Sandia National Laboratories Research Report, SAND-81-0253, Aug. 1981.

D. L. Hicks (1982), "Stability Concepts Relevant to Discrete Schemes for the Partial Differential Equations of Initial Value Problems", Idaho Natl. Engr. Lab. Report, AMO-82-6.

D. L. Hicks (1983), "Parallel processing algorithms for hydrocodes on a computer with MIMD architecture (Denelcor's HEP) Idaho National Engr. Lab., EGG-SAAM-6452.

D. L. Hicks (1984), "Microstructural models for immiscible mixtures: mathematical modelling methods", pp. 467–472 of Mathematical Modelling in Science and Technology, Eds. X. Avula, R. Kalman, A. Liapis and E. Rodin, Pergamon Press.

D. L. Hicks and M. M. Madsen (1976), "Operator Splitting, Method of Characteristics and Boundary Value Algorithms", Sandia National Laboratories in Albuquerque, SAND-76-0436.

D. L. Hicks, J. Middleton and A. Stokes (1983b), "Hydrocodes on the HEP", pres. at SIAM Conf. Parallel Proc. (1983).

D. L. Hicks and R. Pelzl (1968), "Comparison between a von Neumann-Richtmyer Hydrocode and a Lax-Wendroff Hydrocode", AFWL-TR-68-112 (1968).

D. L. Hicks, M. R. Scott and A. H. Treadway (1984), "Parallel Algorithms for Computational Continuum Dynamics on the HEP, ELXSI and CRAY-XMP Parallel Processors, Part 1: HEP Results", to appear as an SNLA research report.

D. L. Hicks and R. T. Walsh (1976), "Numerical and Computational Analysis of the Partial Differential Equations in Hydrocodes and Wavecodes", SAND-75-0448.

R. Johnsonbaugh and T. Murata (1982), "Petri Nets and Marked Graphs-Mathematical Models of Concurrent Computation", pp. 552-566, Amer. Math. Monthly V89, N8 (October 1982).

H. F. Jordan (1981a), "Parallelizing a Sparse Matrix Package", Report of the Computer Systems Design Group, Dept. of E. E., University of Colorado at Boulder (January 1981).

H. F. Jordan (1981b), "Parallel Programming on the HEP Multiple Instruction Stream Computer", Denelcor report, 20 August 1981.

H. Jordan (1984), "HEP-1 Architecture", Computer Architecture Technical Committee Newsletter (Feb. 1984) pp. 54-55.

G. Kaplan (1983), "Nuclear-Power-Plant Malfunction Analysis", pp. 53-58 of IEEE Spectrum (June 1983).

J. S. Kowalik (1983), "Examples of Multiple-instruction Multiple-data (MIMD) Computations, pres. at SIAM Conf. Parallel Proc. (1983).

J. S. Kowalik and Y. K. Bushnag (1983), "Parallel Solution of Banded Linear Equations", pres. at SIAM Conf. Parallel Proc. (1983).

D. J. Kuck (1982), "High-Speed Machines and Their Compilers", pp. 193-214 of Parallel Processing Systems, Ed. by D. J. Evans, Cambridge University Press.

D. J. Kuck (1983), "Performance Potentials of Various Parallel Architectures", pres. at SIAM Fall Mtg. (1983).

H. T. Kung (1982), "Notes on VLSI Computation", pp. 339–356 of <u>Parallel Processing Systems</u>, Ed. by D. J. Evans, Cambridge University Press.

R. Landshoff (1955), "A Numerical Method for Treating Fluid Flow in the Presence of Shocks", LASL Report LA-1930.

R. E. Lord, J. S. Kowalik and S. P. Kumar (1983), "Solving Linear Algebraic Equations on an MIMD Computer", to appear in the Journal of the ACM.

O. M. Lubeck (1983), "Experiences with the Denelcor HEP", pres. at SIAM Conf. Parallel Proc. (1983).

R. H. Mendez (1984), "Supercomputer Benchmarks Give Edge to Fujitsu", SIAM News, V17, N2 (March 1984), p. 3.

J. W. Moore (1983), "PμPS: Parallel Microprocessor System", pres. at SIAM Conf. on Parallel Proc. (1983).

NASA (1975), "Aerodynamic Analyses Requiring Advanced Computers, Parts I and II", Scientific and Technical Information Office, NASA report.

J. von Neumann and R. D. Richtmyer (1950), "A Method for the Numerical Calculation of Hydrodynamic Shocks", J. Appl. Physics, V21, N3, pp. 232-237.

K. W. Neves (1983), "Vector algorithms as a function of hardware architecture", pres. at SIAM Conf. on Parallel Proc. (1983).

I. A. Newman (1982), "The Organization and Uses of Parallel Processing Systems", pp. 143-160 of <u>Parallel Processing Systems</u>, Ed. by D. J. Evans, Cambridge University Press.

V. H. Ransom and D. L. Hicks (1984), "Hyperbolic Two Pressure Models for Two Phase Flow", <u>J. of Comp. Phys.</u>, <u>53</u>, 124-151.

R. D. Richtmyer and K. W. Morton (1967), <u>Difference Methods for Initial</u>

Value Problems, Interscience pub.

G. Rodrique (1983), "Large scale numerical simulations and parallel computers", pres. at SIAM Fall Mtg. (1983).

G. Roucairol (1982), "Transformations of Sequential Programs into Parallel Programs", pp. 101-114 of Parallel Processing Systems", Ed. by D. J. Evans, Cambridge University Press.

SIAM Conf. Parallel Proc. (1983), SIAM Conference on Parallel Processing for Scientific Computing, 10-11 Nov. 1983 in Norfolk, VA. Abstracts of presentations will appear in SIAM Review.

SIAM Fall Mtg. (1983), SIAM 1983 Fall Meeting Nov. 7-9, 1983 in Norfolk, VA. Abstracts of presentations will appear in SIAM Review.

J. Schwartz (1983), "Present status and future direction of parallel computers", SIAM Fall Mtg. (1983).

A. J. Slade (1982), "Implementing Parallel Processing on a Production Minicomputer System", pp. 161-172 of Parallel Processing Systems, Ed. by D. J. Evans, Cambridge University Press.

B. J. Smith (1978), "A Pipelined, Shared Resource MIMD Computer", pp. 6-8, Proceedings of the 1978 International Conference on Parallel Processing, Bellaire, Michigan, August 1978.

B. J. Smith (1981), "Architecture and Applications of the HEP Multiprocessor Computer System", pp. 241-248 of Proceedings of SPIE-The International Society for Optical Engineering, SPIE Vol. 298, Real-Time Signal processing IV.

H. S. Stone (1984), "Computer Research in Japan", Computer, Mar. 1984, pp. 26-32.

P. N. Swarztrauber (1979a), "A Parallel Algorithm for Solving General Tridiagonal Equations", <u>Math. Comp. 33, 145 (1979), 185-199</u>.

P. N. Swarztrauber (1979b), "The Solution of Tridiagonal Systems on the CRAY-1", pp. 344-358 of <u>Infotech State of the Art Report on Super-</u> <u>computers, Vol. 2: Invited Papers</u>, Published by Infotech International Limited, Maidenhead, Berkshire, England.

P. N. Swarztrauber (1983), "Vector FFT algorithms", pres. at SIAM Conf. on Parallel Proc. (1983).

J. C. Syre (1982), "The Data Flow Approach for MIMD Multiprocessor Systems", pp. 239-274 of <u>Parallel Processing Systems</u>, Ed. by D. J. Evans, Cambridge University Press.

P. C. Treleaven (1982), "Parallel Models of Computation", pp. 275-284 of <u>Parallel Processing Systems</u>, Ed. by D. J. Evans, Cambridge University Press.

J. Trulio, L. Riley and S. Wilson (1966), "Development of an automatic device for solving continuum mechanics problems", Air Force Weapons Labs. Report AFWL-TR-65-165 (Feb. 1966).

S. A. Williams (1982), "Representation of Parallelism in Computer Programs", pp. 115-120 of <u>Parallel Processing Systems</u>, Ed. by D. J. Evans, Cambridge University Press.

M. C. Woodward (1982), "Coordination", pp. 173-178 of <u>Parallel Pro-</u> <u>cessing Systems</u>, Ed. by D. J. Evans, Cambridge University Press.

4.5 LOS ALAMOS EXPERIENCES WITH THE HEP COMPUTER

O. M. Lubeck
P. O. Frederickson
R. E. Hiromoto
J. W. Moore
Computing and Communications Division
Los Alamos National Laboratory
Los Alamos, New Mexico

1. INTRODUCTION

Los Alamos National Laboratory became interested in the HEP Heterogeneous Element Processor) architecture in 1981. At that time, we began tests on a machine at the Denelcor plant in Aurora, Colorado, that culminated in the acquisition of a one PEM (process execution module) configuration in July 1983. This acquisition has allowed many researchers, both within the Laboratory and across the nation, to extend research in parallel processing from theory to experiment and, ultimately, to a mature technology. But why are we involved in the search for advanced architectures with increasing amounts of parallelism, and, in particular, why have we become interested in the HEP?

The answer to the first question is that the yearly speedups caused by the components that make up supercomputers is slowing. This point was illustrated by Jack Worlton of Los Alamos [1] and is the topic of discussion among numerous engineers[2, 3]. Dramatic gains in the density of components and the speedups they caused were the rule in the 1960s and 1970s. However, the complexity of state-of-the-art VLSI components is causing design difficulties that are slowing the rate at which new performance milestones are attained.

The inevitable conclusion, therefore, is that we must get more performance from the logical structure in which these components are assembled. Most supercomputer architects and users, in fact, are convinced that the next generation of machines will be architectures with multiple processors.

This conclusion brings us to the second question, why have we become interested in the HEP? The answer is that the Denelcor HEP was designed from the start with multiprocessor parallelism in mind. As a result, we believe that the HEP architecture has made giant gains toward solving three major problems that are introduced by multiprocessor architectures. These remarkable innovations are:

- Low overhead synchronization is fundamental to the efficient use of multiprocessors. The Denelcor HEP has a synchronization bit on every data memory word. This synchronization is enforced in hardware and, in particular, it obviates the need for operating system intervention. This means that users are able to partition their problems at finer granularity and still obtain efficient use of every PEM.

- Low overhead process creation is also a hallmark of the HEP. The act of creating another process is a hardware instruction. Context information that is normally managed by operating system queues is built into the hardware of the HEP.

- Memory latency, which is inevitable as machines grow larger, can defeat most of the speedup gains from a multiprocessor architecture. The HEP's solution to this problem is to allow many separate instruction streams (processes) to be simultaneously active in a single PEM. A process waiting for data memory is isolated in a separate queue until its memory access is satisfied, thereby allowing other processes to execute. The result of this innovation is that each PEM can run at virtually peak speed.

331

Although the speed of a single PEM in the HEP is slow by today's standards, we believe that the architecture has an important property—that of "scaleability." Scaleability has two advantages. First, we believe that the increase in speed of a single PEM, brought about by the use of state-of-the-art componentry, will not be masked by any bottlenecks in the architecture of the machines. Second, many PEMs (up to 256 on the HEP II) can be added to the system and used efficiently. (Assuming that the algorithm or problem size is not the bottleneck.)

2. OVERVIEW OF OUR WORK ON THE HEP

To date we have implemented four 1000- to 5000-line Fortran codes on a single PEM HEP. The codes represent simulations important to Laboratory programmatic goals and, also, represent very different algorithms in computational physics. The PIC code is a particle-in-cell algorithm that is widely used at Los Alamos and elsewhere. TRAC is a nuclear reactor simulation developed at Los Alamos and used by the Nuclear Regulatory Commission (NRC). TRAC has simulated the major behavior of the Three Mile Island incident[4]. The performance goal for TRAC is to run in real time, a goal that will not be met without parallel processing. SIMPLE is a generic example of the type of hydrodynamics algorithms that make up a large part of our computer workload at Los Alamos. The code was developed at Lawrence Livermore National Laboratory. GAMTEB is an example of a Monte Carlo algorithm that simulates gamma-ray transport.

Although the four codes simulated different physical systems and were based on very different computational approaches, we successfully applied a common strategy to their parallel implementations. Amdahl's Law [5], dictates that the serial portions of each code must be minimized and that the effective parallelism of the concurrent portions must be maximized. We attempted to minimize the number of synchronization points and used the simplest and most efficient communication constructs because these points represent code that can reduce the effective parallelism in the program. We used the technique of domain decomposition to find independent computational tasks that were then processed using the self-scheduled DO loop construct. In subdividing the problem, we first obtained a global view of the program and found partitions of large granularity that were computationally independent. Usually, this strategy reduced to partitioning the code in outer DO loops among different processes. Two points should be made about this strategy. First, outer loop parallelization can be contrasted with the vectorization effort, which is an inner loop problem. This contrast is the reason why obtaining a global view of the computational algorithm is more important in partitioning for MIMD (Multiple Instruction/Multiple Data) machines than in vectorizing for SIMD (Single Instruction/Multiple Data) architectures. Second, partitioning at outer loops (or any large grain partitioning) complements inner loop vectorization. Of course, we expect interactions and tradeoffs between the two strategies, but, generally, the two efforts occur at different levels and will not interfere with each other. In fact, a process partitioned at an outer loop can be further sped up by vectorization over purely scalar code.

It should be noted that the HEP is capable of achieving vector performance [6]. In [6], Sorensen observed that the HEP's MIMD architecture can encompass the capabilities of a SIMD machine. His paper, for example, points to the possibility of MIMD compilers "parallelizing" inner loops, just as SIMD compilers "vectorized" them. What makes this practical, in our opinion, is the HEP's low overhead process creation and synchronization capability. We mention this interaction of inner (vectors) and outer loop parallelization throughout this chapter.

3. PIC

The PIC algorithm models the collisionless, electrostatic interaction between two superimposed plasma beams with a relative drift velocity[7]. In the simulation, the magnetic field was purely external, whereas the electric field was partly a result of the charged particles themselves. The code uses the PIC method for studying the interaction and resulting motion of the charged particles. This method discretizes the field and charge distribution over a grid (Figure 1). An initialization stage sets up two ensembles of charged particles making up the two superimposed plasma beams. Initially, the particles are distributed uniformly in space and randomly in velocity. During each computational time step, cell-centered charges are calculated by linearly weighting each particle's charge contribution to the four nearest-neighbor cell centers. This charge distribution is used in solving Poisson's equation for the electric potential with periodic boundary conditions. The electric field is computed from the resulting potential, and under the influence of this field the particles are accelerated.

The key to the parallel implementation of this algorithm is the computational independence of each particle while it is accelerated by the electric field. Using the self-scheduling construct, the algorithm places particles in a queue. Each process picks particles one at a time out of the queue and accelerates them for one time step. Their charges are then summed to a global grid in a critical section of the code, and Poisson's equation is solved.

Figure 2 illustrates the multithread and single-thread implementation of our PIC code, with accompanying definitions of the respective calculations done by each thread. This parallel implementation of PIC is a refinement of a previous version, which was designed for a distributed multiple-processor system[8, 9]. The current PIC implementation was designed for a shared-resource environment (i.e., a common-memory type architecture). In this environment, only a single copy of the mesh quantities is used. We note that the parallel implementation is only partially parallel. (Although there is no reason to prevent this algorithm from being made totally parallel.) Our initial interest in constructing this particular implementation was to determine the optimum parallel speedup gained with the minimum amount of recoding.

Given that the PIC code is implemented with a single charge distribution mesh, and that all parallel particle push processes must contend for this one mesh, a critical section of code is unavoidable. Two strategies are used for forcing synchronization of parallel processes during any update of the mesh. The first blocks all but one process from the critical charge updating section of the code (Figure 3), whereas the second uses the resources of the HEP's extra bit in each data memory word allowing for the synchronization to be done on each individual array element of the charge mesh (Figure 4). Figures 3 and 4 make it clear that forming a critical section of code may substantially reduce the parallelism (as each parallel process is in some sense serialized) as compared with the synchronization on elements of the mesh array.

Figure 5 shows the speedup of both implementations, whereas Figure 6 represents their execution times. In this implementation, 37,000 particles were processed using a mesh size of 32x32. The code is about 92% parallelized.

4. TRAC

TRAC is a simulation of the hydrodynamics and heat transfer in a nuclear reactor[10]. The program has been designed so that building full-scale pressurized water reactors in an erector set style is possible. The code models the flow of water and steam through the numerous components of a pressurized water system (Figure 7). TRAC has been designed to simulate loss-of-coolant accidents that have time scales from a few minutes for a large break, to a few hours for a small one. Los Alamos and the NRC are working toward increasing the performance of the code so that it can run in real time. To obtain real-time performance speedup must be increased tenfold for small breaks and 1,000-fold for large breaks.

TRAC is composed of two levels of modules. The first level is made up of reactor-component subprograms. These modules simulate the geometry, connectivity, and function of various reactor components, such as pipes, pumps, tees, and accumulators. The component subprograms, in turn, access the second level of modules. These second-tier subroutines simulate the major physical processes occurring within each component.

The code that was implemented on the HEP is a subset of the complete program. It simulates one-dimensional flow and heat transfer in pipes. However, about half of the functional subroutines were used.

The equations used in the code model two-phase hydrodynamics [11], but for simplicity we present a form dealing with a single phase that still illustrates how the code was partitioned. The continuous equations used in TRAC are statements of mass, energy, and momentum conservation:

$$\frac{\delta \rho}{\delta t} + \nabla \cdot \rho V = 0 \, , \tag{1}$$

$$\frac{\delta \rho e}{\delta t} + \nabla \cdot \rho e V = -P \nabla \cdot V + h(T_w - T) \, , \tag{2}$$

$$\frac{\delta V}{\delta t} + V \cdot \nabla V = -\frac{1}{\rho} - kV|V|, \tag{3}$$

where k is the wall friction coefficient, h is the heat transfer coefficient, and T_w is the wall temperature.

By discretizing the equations and eliminating the velocity in equations (1) and (2) by using equation (3) we get a set of two coupled equations in P, T, ρ, and e. Thermodynamic relationships give the internal energy and density as functions of P and T: $\rho(P,T)$ and $e(P,T)$. Using these equations, expanding in a Taylor series, and neglecting all but first order terms, we can obtain the following coupled equation in the pressure and temperature tendencies δP and δT:

$$B_j \begin{Bmatrix} \delta P_j \\ \delta T_j \end{Bmatrix} = b_j + c_j(\delta P_{j+1} - \delta P_j) - d_j(\delta P_j - \delta P_{j-1}) \tag{4}$$

where B_j is a matrix of cell j quantities, b_j, c_j, and d_j are coefficients of cell j quantities.

The matrix B_j and coefficients b_j, c_j, and d_j are calculated from cell j quantities. Thus these computations are independent of each other and can be self-scheduled during this portion of the calculations. Once B_j is known at each cell for the one-phase flow, the matrix can be easily solved analytically. (In the two-phase flow, however, the matrix is larger and is solved by LU decomposition.) During this phase of the calculations, N (where N is the number of cells) serial linear equations solvers can be executed concurrently. The decoupled equations now involve unknowns in δP that form a tridiagonal matrix over all cells. In this portion of the computation, the cells are not independent and the tridiagonal system must be solved simultaneously.

In summary, we note that the semi-implicit scheme used by TRAC leads to the conclusion that the computations to advance each cell in time are not entirely independent, but rather that they exhibit nearest-neighbor interaction. The interaction, however, is localized in the code and, in the one-dimensional case, is evidenced by a tridiagonal matrix of order equal to the number of cells that must be solved at each time step. The computations leading up to the tridiagonal matrix are a major part of the total time in TRAC and, thus, 93% of the code was parallelized by self-scheduling cell computations across processes. The tridiagonal solution is currently done serially. Figure 8 shows the speedup for this implementation of TRAC.

5. SIMPLE

To further explore computationally intensive numerical simulations we used a hydrodynamics simulation program known as SIMPLE [12]. With this generic program, we studied the inherent parallel structure of this class of algorithm.

Specifically, the SIMPLE code models the hydrodynamic and thermal behavior of fluids. The code uses a two-dimensional Lagrangian finite difference formulation of the equations of hydrodynamics with an explicit time scheme and an Alternating Direction Implicit (ADI) method on a five-point difference operator in solving the heat diffusion equations. Initially, SIMPLE (Lawrence Livermore National Laboratory, version 5) was about 70% vectorized. The parallel implementation was done with little effort by parallelizing the existing outer loops, while leaving intact the inner loops. In all but one case, the parallelization of SIMPLE was straightforward. The only exception was the ADI scheme used in computing the heat diffusion of the fluid system. In this instance, the vector implementation of the implicit iteration scheme was abandoned in favor of a non-vector, parallel implementation. The independence of each row (column) iteration led us to treat these sweeps as separate self-scheduled parallel processes. In the ADI method the progression of implicit iterations proceeds along rows in the forward direction (i.e., from left to right) and returns in the reverse, or backward, direction. A similar iteration sweep is then begun up columns. In Figure 9 these parallel processes are labelled P_i with corresponding arrows indicating the rows and direction of their iteration sweep. The forward row sweeps proceed chronologically from C_0 to C_n, whereas the reverse sweeps go from C_n to C_0. Although our implementation removed the vector nature of the computations and reduced it to a typically sequential algorithm, it would have been equally feasible to have retained the original vectorized scheme by partitioning the rows (columns) for assignment to each of the various parallel processes. This implementation would have the advantage of running on a vector multiprocessor system [13].

Because of the computational methods used in SIMPLE, its parallelization sometimes allowed concurrent processing of computationally different loops. For example, boundary calculations done during the hydrodynamics portion of each time step were processed in parallel with the interior mesh computations. Appropriate synchronization was implemented to ensure that boundary values were calculated only after the corresponding interior points were updated. The parallel processes would either do the boundary calculations or continue with their parallel interior updating. This strategy was used not only across loops but also across different subroutines. Figure 10 shows the resulting speed up for SIMPLE. The grid size reflected in the performance graphs includes a boundary of "ghost cells" included to aid boundary calculations. The mesh is two fewer in each direction in all cases. This explains the points at which the "saw-tooth" effect, shown in Figure 10, occurs. For example, there is no speedup gain realized from 13 to 15 processes for a problem with 62x62 interior points. This results because the longest processes will compute five columns. This effect is typical of medium granularity parallelism. It is also an artifact of the particular scheme used in partitioning the code.

The scheme that was chosen uses barrier synchronization between the join of one set of processes and the fork of another. Additionally, barriers are used to synchronize between loops in the same set of processes. This has the advantage of simplicity and is relatively transparent. However, this scheme is also inefficient.

There are methods to remove this inefficiency, and we partially implemented one such technique. In one of the subroutines there are three loops, the third dependent on the second and the second dependent on the first. In addition, part of the boundary processing is dependent on the first loop. The boundary calculation can be completed only after the first loop finishes. But half of the calculation can be done when the first and last interior column are complete.

We created processes to do the computation for this subroutine using the self-scheduling technique. As each process finds no further work to do on the current loop it proceeds to the next, checking for completion of the individual array columns it requires from the previous loop, and waiting for completion if the columns are not done. Figure 11 shows the dependencies between the loops. The ability of the programmer to declare large arrays of synchronization variables makes this a straightforward procedure. This technique avoids the ramp down and back up at synchronization points, which is inefficient and leads to the "saw-tooth" effect.

In our implementation of the code, the technique was applied only to one subroutine; but there is no reason why it could not be applied to the code as a whole with full synchronization only at output stages (every 10 cycles in the test problem).

Although providing a high sustained degree of parallelism, this technique leads to obscure coding, especially with the constructs available at the time. On machines with many processes, reducing the amount of code not executed with high parallelism is crucial to effective use. We need to devise appropriate syntax to support this type of use.

Another useful property of the HEP is its insensitivity to adding short-lived processes. In particular the boundary calculations, while consisting of large amounts of code, execute for only a short time. They can be slipped in while other processing is being done with little effect on the central processing unit. The process creation and scheduling overhead is small, in contrast to other more rigid architectures, allowing more freedom in structuring problems for the machine.

The SIMPLE code has been extended to multiple PEM machines. The performance results tend to follow a generally linear path but with a lower slope than the single PEM results. This is a result of the rigid partitioning method and the concentration of control, boundary, and output processing in a single PEM. This reduces the overall parallelization (98% in the single PEM case) in an environment in which such a reduction is even more important. However, the overall speed is much improved.

6. A MONTE CARLO ALGORITHM

GAMTEB is a gamma-ray (photon) transport simulation using the Monte Carlo method [14]. This method attempts numerical simulation of the statistical behavior of a given physical or mathematical problem. The Monte Carlo method may be thought of as a branch of "experimental" mathematics concerned with experiments based on random numbers in which a stochastic model is set up by sampling from appropriate probability distributions. As in any statistical sampling study, Monte Carlo applications require statistical techniques designed to enhance both the efficiency of the algorithm and the reliability of the resulting statistical estimate.

GAMTEB tracks the interaction of gamma-rays passing through two carbon cylinders joined end to end. During the gamma-ray's lifetime, various physical processes (selected on the basis of a random number) are allowed to affect the progress of the particles (photons); these processes include Compton scattering (the collision of a photon with a free electron), pair production (the absorption of a photon in the presence of a nuclear or electron field producing an electron-positron pair with a total energy equal to that of the photon), and photoelectric absorption (the absorption of a photon by a bound electron, which then is ejected as a free electron from its orbit). A much more detailed account of each of these physical processes may be found in [15].

In the application of the Monte Carlo method, various sampling techniques are used. In GAMTEB, a sequence of pseudo-random numbers are generated for sampling the photon energy, the distance to next collision within the carbon geometry, the isotropic scattering of the photon under Compton scattering, the probability of photon absorption due to the photoelectric effect, and numerous other processes. Statistical importance sampling techniques are used by assigning significant (weights) to the occurrence of various physical processes. Particle splitting with Russian roulette are two such sampling techniques [15] used in GAMTEB. Particle splitting increases the particle sample size where a particle of weight w may be replaced with n identical particles but with weights $w_1, \ldots, w_n$, where $w_1 + , , , + w_n = w$. These particles are then processed independently. On the other hand, if the number of particles becomes too large, the Russian roulette technique selects a particle and, with some probability, p discards it from the sample. If the selected particle is not discarded but allowed to proceed, its weight is multiplied by $(1-p)^{-1}$. This process is repeated until the number of particles is brought to a manageable, computational size. Furthermore, particle cutoff techniques, in the form of weight cutoff and energy cutoff routines, are employed to reduce particle tracking time. Although the Monte Carlo model may not be an exact realization of the physical problem, the techniques mentioned above provide for a more convenient and efficient computational implementation. In general, the Monte Carlo problems represent a sophisticated method for the solution of many intractable problems [16].

The problem that we have chosen to examine is a very simple photon transport simulation. Although the problem contains only a few of the common sampling techniques, it presents enough structure to provide details of more elaborate particle transport problems as well as providing insight into the parallel processing of probabilistic Monte Carlo algorithms.

Central to any Monte Carlo calculation is the accuracy of the resulting statistically derived values. This usually involves an estimate of the statistical errors in these values. Forming the variance, σ, for a particular history of sample values $x_1, x_2, \ldots, x_n$ of the random variable x, the confidence of the Monte Carlo results are provided by the evaluation of the standard deviation of the mean, σ_m, given by

$$\sigma_m = \sigma / \sqrt{n} ,$$

where n is the number of histories sampled. The confidence in the correctness of results is determined through the minimization of σ_m. This minimization procedure is guided by numerous results from probability theory, use of exact analytical results when possible, and the application of reliable variance reduction techniques (see [15] for a comprehensive bibliography). For example, in GAMTEB the collection of the statistics regarding the histories of various particle interactions, the amount of biasing introduced, and the total number of particle tracks terminated (to name a few) are of interest in determining the accuracy of the Monte Carlo results.

Figure 12 illustrates the computational flow of GAMTEB. The simulation is almost completely parallel. The tracking of each particle and their daughter particles is independent of all other histories. Only the accumulation of statistics used in sample biasing couples one particle history to another. This process is shown by the Global Tally which forms a critical section of code, thereby allowing for only one process at a time to update this region of the program. The individual tallies (statistics) for each particle history are accumulated in each of the local parallel processes as indicated by the Subtallies. As implemented on the HEP, each photon history is begun by available processes using the self-scheduling technique.

An important consideration in this parallel implementation was to guarantee reproducible results from one parallel execution to the next. As the nature of asynchronous parallel processing adds a significant level of random ordering, the classical approach to Monte Carlo calculations (using a single, long, statistically valid sequence of random numbers) will produce answers (for which the statistics are acceptable) that differ at the level of events processed within a single particle history. By fixing the problem size but varying the number of parallel processes, the correctness of the implementation can be checked if reproducible statistics are generated (up to roundoff errors). For this reason we have implemented an orthogonal (non-overlapping) set of random number generators to form a Pseudo-Random Tree [17]. Under this implementation each particle is given a unique random "particle seed," which in turn is used to generate a unique sequence of random numbers used in doing the appropriate physics of the problem. Using this tree structured scheme for the production of a particle seed and a corresponding sequence of unique random numbers (based on the particle seed), the simulation is guaranteed that the particle history track is independent of the order in which the particle seed is obtained and thus reproducible.

We followed the work described in [17], and implemented a Lehmer tree, a simple generalization of the linear congruential pseudo-random sequence introduced by Lehmer [18]. As a by-product of our strict demand for reproducibility, a logical error was detected in the sequential version of GAMTEB from which our parallel code was developed. Without resorting to an important level of parallel complexity (the introduction of the Pseudo-Random Tree for reproducibility of particle history), the debugging of GAMTEB would have been next to impossible considering the inherently random nature of the sequential algorithm. It becomes clear then that the concept of the Pseudo-Random Tree in a parallel processing environment is a very important tool for developing parallel Monte Carlo algorithms.

Figure 13 indicates the parallel processing performance attained under our initial implementation. Not only does the parallel speedup increase with increasing number of processes but as the total number of particles (photons) increase we see a corresponding increase in parallel speedup.

7. CONCLUSIONS

We have been able to convert serial implementations of different computational algorithms to the HEP architecture making few changes to the original codes. We believe this suggests it is possible for current application programs to evolve to MIMD machines that have relatively few processors. We do not mean to suggest that current problems will not benefit significantly from a total reanalysis with parallelism in mind, but the conversion of existing codes may be a successful short-term solution with significant speedup gains.

During this research we have gained confidence that the use of MIMD architectures can be worthwhile for important laboratory problems and that the programming difficulty, although significant when compared with serial machines, is acceptable considering the payoff.

We suggest that the need for programmer productivity tools in a MIMD environment is immediate. By far the largest amount of time in parallelizing serial codes was spent in debugging problems arising from global data dependencies. While the long-term solution to this problem may lie in language development or automatic parallelization of Fortran programs, we see an immediate need for an interactive diagnostic tool that will exhaustively search for these dependencies.

REFERENCES

[1] Jack Worlton, "A Philosophy of Supercomputing," Los Alamos National Laboratory report LA-8849-MS (June 1981).

[2] V. L. Rideout, "Limits to Improvement of Silicon Integrated Circuits," Digest of Papers, IEEE Compcon (San Francisco, California, 1980).

[3] Charles Seitz and Juri Matisoo, "Engineering Limits on Computer Performance," Physics Today (May 1984).

[4] J. R. Ireland, J. H. Scott, and W. R. Stratton, "Three Mile Island and Multiple-Failure Accidents," Los Alamos Science, Vol. 2, No. 2 (1983).

[5] G. M. Amdahl, AFIPS Conference Proceedings (1967), pp. 483-485.

[6] D. C. Sorensen, Buffering for Vector Performance on a Pipelined MIMD Machine, Argonne National Laboratory Technical Report, ANL/MCS-TM-29, (April 1984).

[7] R. L. Morse and C. W. Nielson, "One-, Two-, and Three-Dimensional Numerical Simulation of Two Beam Plasmas," Phys. Rev. Lett., Vol. 23 No. 19, pp. 1087-1090 (November 10, 1969).

[8] I. Y. Bucher, P. O. Frederickson, and J. W Moore, "Experience with a Multiprocessor Based on Eight FPS 120B Array Processors," Los Alamos National Laboratory document LA-UR-81-1082 (1981).

[9] R. E. Hiromoto, "Parallel-Processing a Large Scientific Problem," NCC Conference (1982), pp. 233-237.

[10] J. C. Vigil and R. J. Pryor, "Accident Simulation with TRAC," Los Alamos Science, Vol. 2, No. 2 (1983).

[11] J. H. Mahaffy and D. R. Liles, "A Numerical Solution Package for Transient Two-Phase Flow Equations," Los Alamos National Laboratory document, LA-UR-82-1483 (November 1982).

[12] W. P. Crowley, C. P. Hendrickson, and T. E. Rudy, "The SIMPLE Code,ρq Lawrence Livermore National Laboratory report, UCID-17715 (1978)

[13] T. S. Axelrod, P. F. Dubois, and P. G. Eltgroth, "Proceedings of the 1983 International Conference of Parallel Processing," Bellaire, Michigan (August 1983), pp. 350-358.

[14] N. Metropolis and S. Ulam, "The Monte Carlo Method," J. Amer. Stat. Assoc., 44, 335-341 (1949).

[15] L. L. Carter and E. D. Cashwell, "Particle-Transport Simulation with the Monte Carlo Method," Technical Information Center Energy Research and Development Administration (1975).

[16] J. M. Hammersley and D. C. Handscomb, "Monte Carlo Methods," (John Wiley & Sons, Inc., New York, 1964).

[17] P. O. Frederickson, R. E. Hiromoto, T. L. Jordan, B. Smith, and T. Warnock, "Pseudo-Random Trees in Monte Carlo," Parallel Computing , Vol. 1, No. 2 (1984).

[18] D. H. Lehmer, "Proc. 2nd Symp. on Large-Scale Digital Calculating Machinery," Harvard University Press, Cambridge, Mass. (1951).

339

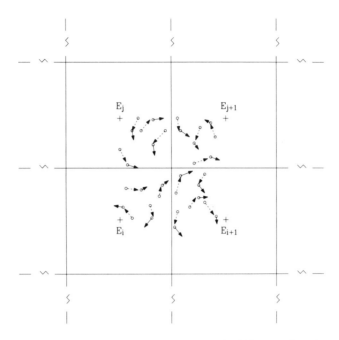

Figure 1. The PIC algorithm. Charged particles moving under the influence of an electrostatic field. The field and charge distribution are discretized on grid points.

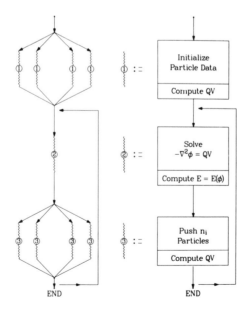

Figure 2. The multithread flow of PIC.

```
      -  -  - SET LOCK FOR CRITICAL SECTION  -  -  -

C      JLOCK IS LOCAL VARIABLE
C
       JLOCK=$ILOCK

          QV(IJ)=QV(IJ) + FXC*FYC
          QV(IJ+1)=QV(IJ+1) + FX*FYC
          QV(IK)=QV(IK) + FXC*FY
          QV(IK+1)=QV(IK+1) + FX*FY


       $ILOCK=JLOCK
C
```

SELF–SCHEDULED SYNCHRONIZATION SCHEME

Figure 3. PIC strategy implementing a critical section to update the charge distribution on a global grid.

```
      -  -  - DATA LOCK FOR CRITICAL SECTION  -  -  -

       C


          $QV(IJ)=$QV(IJ) + FXC*FYC
          $QV(IJ+1)=$QV(IJ+1) + FX*FYC
          $QV(IK)=$QV(IK) + FXC*FY
          $QV(IK+1)=$QV(IK+1) + FX*FY


       C
```

SELF–SCHEDULED SYNCHRONIZATION SCHEME

Figure 4. PIC strategy implementing data synchronization to update the charge distribution on a global grid.

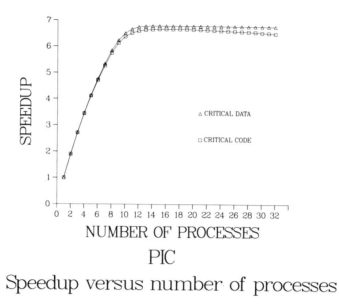

PIC

Speedup versus number of processes

Figure 5. Speedup for two implementations of PIC.

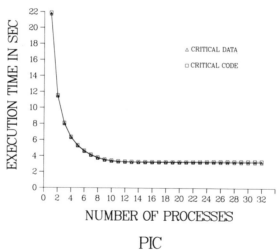

PIC

Execution time versus number of processes

Figure 6. Execution times for two implementations of PIC.

342

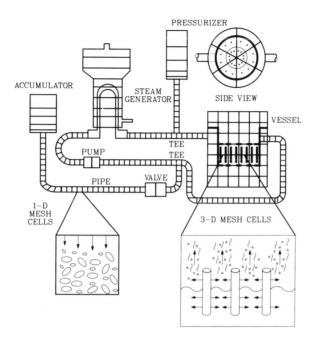

Figure 7. TRAC, which simulates the hydrodynamics in a nuclear reactor, models the flow of water and steam through the many components of a pressurized water system.

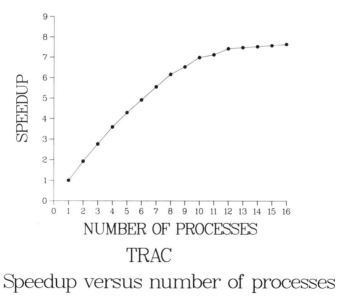

TRAC

Speedup versus number of processes

Figure 8. Speedup for the implementation of TRAC described in the text.

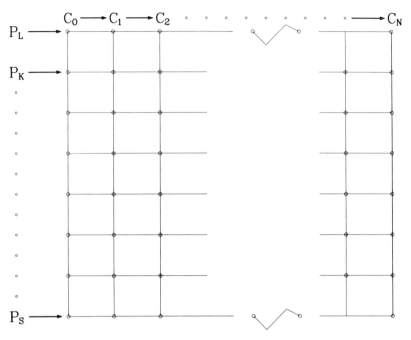

Figure 9. Flow of the parallel ADI algorithm.

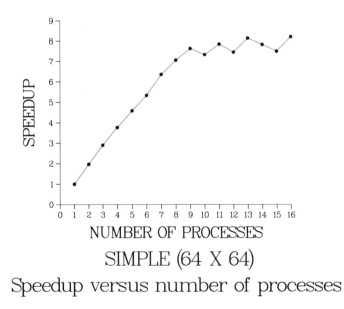

Figure 10. Speedup results for SIMPLE.

ENTRY

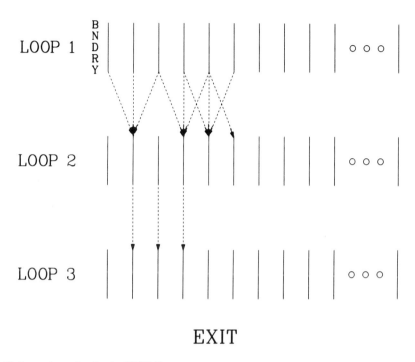

Figure 11. Loop dependencies in SIMPLE.

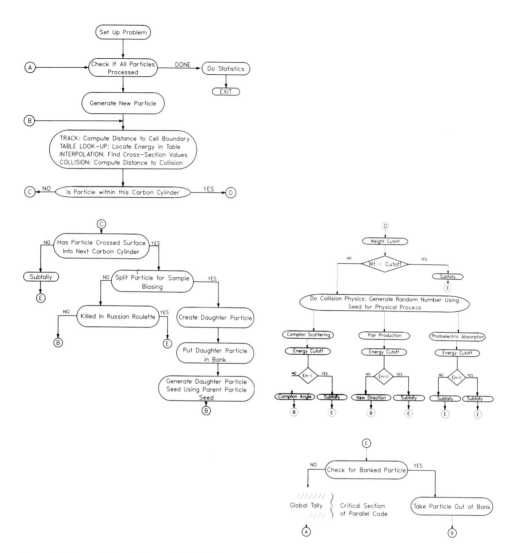

Figure 12. Computational flow of GAMTEB.

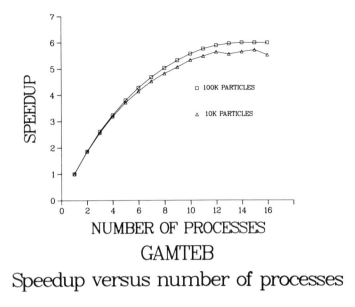

Figure 13. Speedup results for GAMTEB.

4.6 SOLUTION OF BOUNDARY-VALUE PROBLEMS ON HEP

M. R. SCOTT
Applied Mathematics Division
Sandia National Laboratories
Albuquerque, New Mexico 87185

1. INTRODUCTION

Over the past few decades, the computational speed of computers has increased a thousandfold, due primarily to the development of faster circuitry. Now, however, advances in the speeds of electronic circuits are beginning to be limited by the fundamental physical properties, such as the propagation speed of electronic currents. As a result, the most recent generation of high-performance computers has turned to architectural schemes which permit a number of computational steps to proceed simultaneously so that a larger total number of computations can be accomplished in a given time. Although these computers are theoretically much faster than computers which perform each operation in a serial sequence, algorithms must be specifically developed so that many parts of the computation can be run in parallel or so that new steps in the computation can begin before previous steps are complete.

The research and development of programmatic goals at Sandia National Laboratories depend critically on the availability and the ability to utilize the latest in large, high-speed computers. As a result, the Applied Mathematics Division for several years has been involved in the evaluation of the architecture of new computers and the research and development of software and algorithms for such machines. The purpose of this research is to obtain a fundamental knowledge of the underlying principles of high-performance computers. This knowledge will then be applied to the development of algorithms which can utilize the basic architecture of parallel machines. It seems clear that all future generation computers must apply some type of vector, parallel, array, or multiprocessor technique in order to obtain improved performance.

This is a preliminary report which is devoted to the multitasking cababilities of a computer code on three parallel processing computers. The three computers used were the CRAY X-MP/48, the ELXSI System 6400, and the Denelcor HEP-1. Section 2 is devoted to a discussion of the levels of parallel processing. Sections 3-5 provide a short description of each machine. The next section describes the code in some detail and some of the multitasking techniques utilized. The last section describes some preliminary conclusions and future directions of study.

2. LEVELS OF PARALLELISM

Various levels of parallelism have been available in computer systems for many years [3]. In this paper, we shall define levels of parallelism in terms of the software processes that are done in parallel.

Level 1: Jobs; independent jobs. Each has a CPU

Level 2: Job steps; related parts of the same job

Level 3:   Routines/Subroutines

Level 4:   Loops

Level 5:   Statements

Level 1 traditionally refers to classical multiprocessing where two or more processors are operating at the same time on different and independent job streams. In this case, the processors are sharing memory and peripherals to help in load leveling and, hopefully, improvement of total system throughput. Level 2 traditionally refers to multiprogramming where multiple, independent jobs or processes are sharing processor resources. Multiprogramming has been used for many years to improve system throughput on a single central processing unit (CPU). If one process needs to perform input/output (I/O), another process can have access to the CPU.

Levels 4 and 5 of parallelism have been available for several years in machines such as the CRAY-1S, the CYBER 205, and to a lesser extent in machines such as the CDC 6600 and the CDC 7600. Vector processing is the parallel processing of iterations of loops (Level 4). The compilers have the ability to schedule instructions in such a manner as to exploit the independence and different speeds of the hardware functional units; this leads to parallel execution of different statements or Level 5 parallelism.

It is interesting to note the effects of the various levels of parallelism upon the system and the individual user. Levels 1 and 2 are under control of the operating system and are not generally under the control of the user. These tend to improve system throughput and have no effect on decreasing CPU cycles of a user program. Levels 4 and 5 are under the control of the user and any optimization obtained by the user results in reduced CPU cycles for the program and, hence, also better system throughput. Level 3 is also at the disposal of the user. However, the purpose of multitasking is to improve individual throughput. In fact, multitasking will always introduce some increase in CPU cycles used by the code. Just how much improvement in individual throughput that is achieved may vary widely from run to run. This will depend upon the demand other users are putting on the system. As a result, we generally think of multitasking in a dedicated environment.

Another interesting aspect of the multitasking of Level 3 and the vectorization of Levels 4 and 5 is that the gains achieved in the two types of parallelization tend to be multiplicative. This is strongly illustrated in Section 6.

This report will concentrate on the parallelism represented by Level 3. One of the major drawbacks to the use of multiprocessors is the amount or number of times that data must be passed between processors. The term granularity refers to the amount or length of tasks that can be performed in parallel without the necessity of communicating with one another. Notice that the higher the number of the level, the smaller the granularity. Our interest in this research is to distribute as much work as possible and to sustain that work as long as possible on a few processors. This will tend to reduce the interprocessor communication time.

3. CRAY X-MP/48

The CRAY X-MP is a four processor machine with each processor similar to the CRAY-1S, but with a 9.5 nanosecond clock period, as compared to a 12.5 nanosecond clock period on the CRAY-1S. In addition, there have been a number of architectural changes which have contributed to an improved performance in each processor over the CRAY-1S. The number of memory ports per processor has been increased from one to four. This allows two memory reads, one memory write, and I/O to proceed simultaneously in each processor. Finally, the "chaining" mechanism, which allows results of previous operations to enter the computational pipeline, is improved by eliminating the fixed chain slot time (clock period when links are put together). These are extremely important changes for codes which are highly vectorized.

4. ELXSI SYSTEM 6400

The ELXSI System 6400 is a modular multiple processor computer. The central processing system is a 64-bit byte addressable multiprocessor that performs high-speed processing of variable length instructions supporting a wide range of data formats. The modular system architecture accommodates up to 10 central processing units interfaced to a high-speed central bus. The central bus is an extremely high-speed, proprietary system bus, the GIGABUS. All functional elements of the system communicate via this bus. It accommodates multiple CPUs, memory modules, I/O processors, and a service processor.

The GIGABUS is a synchronous, 64-bit bus with a bandwidth of 320 Mbytes/sec. Taking into account all bus overheads for memory access, usable data rates range from 160 to 213 Mbytes/sec. depending on the relative proportion of reads and writes to memory. The GIGABUS modules can be configured in various quantities to provide the performance and availability a user requires.

5. DENELCOR HEP-1

The HEP-1 is a pipelined multiple processor machine with an eight-stage pipe, and most instructions execute in eight cycles. The system is designed to accommodate up to 16 processors (Process Execution Modules-PEMS), each capable of executing up to 50 user processes in a time-sliced manner at the instruction level. Thus, on each succeeding machine cycle, an instruction for a new process is executed until all ready processes have been serviced in a round robin fashion. A single processor HEP requires at least eight concurrently executing processes to fully utilize the PEM. Interconnection of additional PEMs will further increase the parallelism available to the user. In addition, synchronization on the HEP is achieved by utilizing an extra full/empty bit on each word in memory. This allows a process to "read when full" and "write when empty," which achieves the desired low-overhead synchronization.

6.   SUPORT

SUPORT is a large code and uses the methods of super-position and orthonormalization for the solution of linear, two-point, boundary-value problems [1]. The method of superposition is conceptually a very simple method for solving linear boundary-value problems and is ideally suited for use on a multitasking machine. However, there are some well-known stability problems with superposition, and the orthonormalization proce-dure is introduced in order to stablize the algorithm. Unfortunately, as we shall see, the introduction of the orthonormalization procedure makes the algorithm sightly less attractive for the multitasking environment.

Before describing the algorithm in a multitasking environment, we shall review the methods of super-position and orthonormalization. We consider linear two-point boundary-value problems of the form

$$y' = F(x) * y(x) + g(x), \tag{1}$$

$$A * y(a) = alpha, \tag{2}$$

$$B * y(b) = beta, \tag{3}$$

where y and g are vector functions with n components, F is an n x n matrix, A is an (n - k) x n matrix of rank n - k, B is a k x n matrix of rank k, and alpha is a vector with n - k components, and beta is a vector with k components.

The method of superposition is conceptually very simple. Any solution of Eq (1) can be written as a linear combination of n linearly independent solutions $u_1(x),\ldots,u_n(x)$ of the homogeneous equation

$$u'(x) = F(x) \ u(x), \qquad\qquad\qquad (4)$$

and a particular solution $v(x)$ of the inhomogeneous equation

$$v'(x) = F(x) \ v(x) + g(x). \qquad\qquad\qquad (5)$$

Because the boundary conditions are separated, we need examine only a subspace of dimension k or n - k for the homogeneous solutions. This is possible by suitably choosing initial values for these solutions at one or the other end point. In this paper, we shall assume the initial point to be a, so the integration proceeds from a to b. In practice, the choice of the initial point is made by the user of the code. This can be important in achieving an efficient solution. Thus, instead of the classical superposition approach, we use the reduced algorithm allowed by separated boundary conditions and compute

$$y(x) = v(x) + U(x) \, c \, , \tag{6}$$

where c is a k-dimensional vector and U is a matrix consisting of k independent solutions of Eq (4). The initial conditions for the $u_i(x)$ and $v(x)$ are chosen to satisfy

$$A \, U(a) = 0, \tag{7}$$

$$A \, v(a) = alpha, \tag{8}$$

so that Eq (6) satisfies Eq (2). In [1], we discuss how these initial conditions are computed by the code. In order to specify the constant vector c, we evaluate Eq (6) at x = b and substitute into Eq (3), thus obtaining

$$B \, y(b) = B \, U(b) \, c + B \, v(b) = beta. \tag{9}$$

This represents a system of k linear equations for the k unknowns defining c. The solution of the original boundary-value problem, Eqs (1-3), is now completely specified. Notice that all of the equations to be integrated, namely Eqs (4) and (5), along with Eqs (7) and (8), can now be treated as initial-value problems. Thus, we can put to good use the sophisticated integrators already developed for solving initial-value problems.

Although the superposition method is conceptually simple and works in many instances, it has some major drawbacks. In order for the method to yield accurate results, it is important that $v(x)$ and the columns of $U(x)$ be linearly independent for all x. The initial conditions, as given by Eqs (7) and (8), theoretically ensure that $v(x)$ and the columns of $U(x)$ are linearly independent. However, due to the finite word length used by computers, the solutions may lose their numerical independence. When this happens the resulting matrix in Eq (9) may be so poorly conditioned that c cannot be determined accurately. Another problem, also related to the finite word length of the computer, is a loss of significance and can occur even if the linear combination vector c has been computed accurately. This will occur if the base vectors are large compared to the desired solution; that is, accuracy is lost in the recombination of Eq (6).

The orthonormalization procedure is designed to overcome the above difficulties. Each time the linearly independent solutions of the homogeneous and inhomogeneous equations "start to lose their numerical independence," the solution vectors are reorthonormalized before integration proceeds. Thus, if z_i represents an orthonormalization point, the superposition solution becomes

$$y(x) = v_m(x) + U_m(x)c_m, \text{ for } x \epsilon [z_m, z_{m+1}]. \tag{10}$$

At $x = z_m$, a new orthonormal set of vectors is formed and becomes the initial conditions on the integration interval $[z_m, z_{m+1}]$;

358

$$U_{m-1} = U_m P_m \quad \text{and} \tag{11}$$

$$v_m = v_{m-1} - U_m w_m \ , \quad v_m = v_m / \|v_m\| , \tag{12}$$

where P_m and w_m contain the Gram-Schmidt information. Continuity of y is achieved by matching the solutions over successive orthonormalization subintervals. This leads to the basic recursion relation

$$P_m c_{m-1} = c_m - w_m . \tag{13}$$

The process is, therefore, a two pass affair. The first constitutes the integration sweep from a to b while storing the orthogonalization information at the points of orthonormalization and homogeneous and particular solution values at all the designated output points. The second involves the computation of the c_m vectors from the boundary conditions at b and use of the recursion equation so that the solution values of y may be determined at the output points.

For this particular test, the SUPORT code was used to solve Poisson's equation in two dimensions.

$$\nabla^2 \phi = \frac{\partial^2 \phi}{\partial x^2} + \frac{\partial^2 \phi}{\partial y^2} = g(x,y)$$

for (x,y) in the open rectangle

$$R = \{(x,y) : 0 < x < a, \ 0 < y < b\} ,$$

satsifying the Dirichlet boundary conditions

$$\phi(x,y) = f(x,y)$$

for (x,y) on the boundary Γ enclosing R. Let us now discretize with respect to the y variable. (In practice one would want to choose the discretization variable which exhibits the least variation and greatest smoothness in the solution, thereby letting the integrator in the two-point boundary value technique resolve any difficulties such as boundary layers occurring with the remaining independent variable.) Thus, let us define $\phi_k(x) = \phi(x,y_k)$ for the N points $0 = y_0 < y_1 < \ldots < y_{N-1} = b$. Then we obtain N - 2 equations of second order,

$$\frac{d^2\phi(x)}{dx^2} = \frac{-1}{(\Delta y)^2}\left\{\phi_{k-1}(x) - 2\phi_k(x) + \phi_{k+1}(x)\right\} + g_k(x) \quad,$$

$$\phi_k(0) = f(0,y_k), \quad \phi_k(a) = f(a,y_k) \quad,$$

for $k = 1,\ldots,N-2$. $\phi_0(x) = f(x,0)$ and $\phi_{N-1}(x) = f(x,b)$ are specified and $\Delta y = y_{i+1} - y_i = \frac{b}{N-1}$. Letting

$$\psi = \begin{bmatrix} \phi_1 \\ \cdot \\ \cdot \\ \phi_{N-2} \\ \phi'_1 \\ \cdot \\ \cdot \\ \phi'_{N-2} \end{bmatrix}$$

our problem becomes $\psi'(x) = M\psi(x) + G(x)$ where

$$M = \begin{bmatrix} 0 & I \\ \dfrac{1}{(\Delta y)^2} T & 0 \end{bmatrix} \quad ,$$

$$T = \begin{bmatrix} 2 & -1 & & \\ -1 & 2 & -1 & \\ & & & -1 \\ & & -1 & 2 \end{bmatrix} \quad \text{and} \quad G = \begin{bmatrix} 0 \\ \cdot \\ \cdot \\ 0 \\ g_1 - \dfrac{\phi_0}{(\Delta y)^2} \\ g_2 \\ \cdot \\ \cdot \\ g_{N-3} \\ g_{N-2} - \dfrac{\phi_{N-1}}{(\Delta y)^2} \end{bmatrix}$$

The boundary conditions are now expressed as

$$[I \quad 0]\psi(0) = \begin{bmatrix} f(0,y_1) \\ \cdot \\ \cdot \\ f(0,y_{N-2}) \end{bmatrix} \quad ,$$

$$[I \quad 0]\psi(a) = \begin{bmatrix} f(a,y_1) \\ \cdot \\ \cdot \\ f(a,y_{N-2}) \end{bmatrix} \quad .$$

Hence, we obtain a two-point boundary value problem with 2N-4 equations.

For our illustration we use the following parameter values: $a = 0.3$, $b = 0.1$, $N = 27$, 30 equally spaced output points $x\epsilon[0,a]$ for the two-point boundary value problem, $f(x,y) = 0$ on Γ, and $g(x,y) = 4\rho x(a-x)/a^2$ with $\rho = -10^5$. The choice of the 30 x 27 grid presents the code with a fairly large problem--50 differential equations with a solution constructed at 30 output points.

Lastly, let us compute an approximation to the maximal length of the orthonormalization subintervals for this problem. We note that the eigenvalues of M are $\lambda = \pm \frac{1}{\Delta y} \sqrt{\mu}$ where μ is an eigenvalue of the tridiagonal matrix T,

$$\mu_j = 2\left(1 - \cos \frac{j\pi}{N-1}\right) \text{ for } j=1,\ldots,N-2 \quad .$$

Thus, the spectral width for M is

$$\frac{2}{\Delta y} \sqrt{\mu_{max}} \doteq \frac{4}{\Delta y}$$

for N sufficiently large. This produces the interval restriction of

$$x - x^* < \frac{\mu - \tau}{1/2(\text{Re } \lambda_n - \text{Re } \lambda_1)} \quad .$$

where μ is the number of significant digits carried by the computer being used, τ is the desired digits of accuracy in the solution, $\text{Re}(\lambda_n) - \text{Re}(\lambda_1)$ is the spectral width of the matrix M. For details of the derivation of this formula, see [2]. For the CRAY, we use $\mu = 14$ and for the ELXSI, we use $\mu = 7$, which yields, respectively, 10 and 30 orthonormalization points.

Approximately 90 percent of the total computing time is spent in integrating the differential equations and less than 10 percent in performing the orthonormalization. Thus, it is natural to devote the effort in multitasking to the solutions of the differential equations. Since each solution of the homogeneous equation and the inhomogeneous are independent, the multitasking is achieved by spreading the differential equations across several tasks. For this particular example, there are 26 differential equations. Figure 1 illustrates how the equations were spread across four tasks. At each orthonormalization point, the tasks must be synchronized and the orthonormalization process is performed on one task. This process is then repeated over each interval.

It is surprising how few changes are required to run the code on the three machines although there is a world of difference in their architectures. Due to some time constraints on the preparation of this manuscript, results only for the CRAY and the ELXSI are presented in Table I.

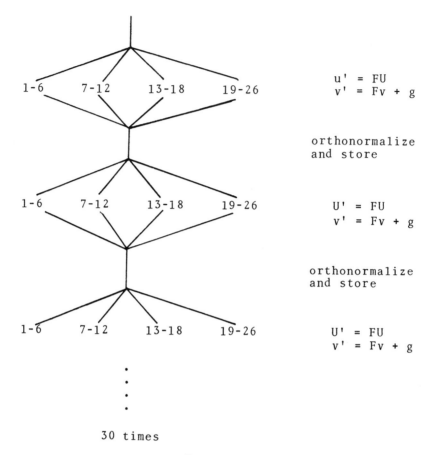

u' = FU
v' = Fv + g

orthonormalize
and store

U' = FU
v' = Fv + g

orthonormalize
and store

U' = FU
v' = Fv + g

30 times

Figure 1

Table I

Speedup Factors

Number of Tasks (CPUs)	CRAY-XMP	ELXSI**	Theoretical Maximum*
2	1.41	1.26	1.54
3	1.85	1.68	2.00
4	2.35	2.12	2.55
5		2.24	2.96
5		2.47***	

*The theoretical maximum was obtained by using a particular subdivision of equations across tasks. For example, for two tasks, the subdivision was 13 and 13 and for four tasks, the subdivision is given in Figure 1. This does not give the best balance of CPU utilization.

**The speedup factors on the ELXSI are somewhat lower than might first be expected. Each processor on the ELXSI has 16 K of very high speed (100 ns) cache memory when no multitasking is performed. These results were obtained by not utilizing the cache memory when more than one task was performed and hence memory access time is a factor of four slower than using the cache memory. With some redesign of the code, these results can be significantly improved.

***This result was obtained by adjusting the number of differential equations on each task to obtain a better balance of CPU utilization.

7. CONCLUSIONS AND FUTURE PLANS

Future plans are to design tests to determine what is the smallest level of granularity that is feasible for each machine. This will certainly be problem dependent but perhaps some rough guidelines can be given. Other plans for SUPORT are to multitask some of the I/O portions of the code.

8. REFERENCES

1. M. R. Scott and H. A. Watts, "Computational Solution of Linear Two-Point Boundary-Value Problems via Orthonormalization," *SIAM J. Num. Anal. 14*, p 40-70 (1977).

2. B. L. Darlow, M. R. Scott, and H. A. Watts, *SAND77-1328, Modifications of SUPORT, A Linear Boundary-Value Solver: Part I*, Sandia National Laboratories, Albuquerque, NM, Pre-Assigning Orthonormalization Points, Auxiliary Initial Value Problem, Disk or Tape Storage.

3. "Multitasking User Guide, SN-0222," (Mendota Height, MN: CRAY Research, Inc., 1984).

Appendix: Use of Monitors in FORTRAN:

A Tutorial on the Barrier,

Self-scheduling DO-Loop,

and Askfor Monitors

E. L. Lusk and R. A. Overbeek

Argonne National Laboratory
Argonne, Illinois

1. Introduction

Monitors have been used for many years as a basis for process synchronization[1, 3, 4, 5, 6, 9]. After some experimentation, we have found that portable programs for use on multiprocessors can be written using monitors implemented by means of macros. Furthermore, once a programmer is familiar with the use of the macros, they offer a relatively convenient mechanism for writing programs that require the synchronization of multiple processes.

Two of our earlier publications[7, 8] discussed the basic concept of macros and briefly described their use. This document is intended as a tutorial for anyone who wishes to write portable FORTRAN for multiprocessors. Our earlier reports are not prerequisites to this document, but can be be accessed for more of the implementation details.

One problem faced by a person beginning to code for multiprocessors is a choice of "synchronization primitives". A large number of primitives have grown up from applications in systems programming, telecommunications, and shared databases. The set of proposed alternatives may well appear bewildering to the uninitiated, and arguments between advocates of the different primitives can become quite heated. Unquestionably, the

This work was supported in part by National Science Foundation grant MCS82-07496 and in part by the Applied Mathematical Sciences Research Program (KC-04-02) of the Office of Energy Research of the U.S. Department of Energy under Contract W-31-109-Eng-38.

particular synchronization primitives that you select will have important consequences. Choosing primitives that are too "low-level" will almost inevitably lead to avoidable errors. On the other hand, utilizing primitives that are too "high-level" can preclude efficient implementation on many machines.

This second point is somewhat controversial, so let us briefly amplify our position. The use of a rendezvous mechanism of the sort included in Ada will (we believe) prevent the efficient implementation of an algorithm based on small-granularity parallelism. That is, the cost of your synchronization mechanism determines a lower bound on the size of the "work units" that are done in parallel.

We believe that monitors offer a reasonable conceptual framework for writing FORTRAN code for multiprocessors, without introducing overhead that unnecessarily restricts the class of algorithms that can be implemented.

Before offering a precise definition of what we mean by a monitor, we present a few programming examples that illustrate common synchronization patterns. These examples can then be used as a basis for forming a precise notion of the concept. Please note that our examples are (for the most part) relatively trivial. They are intended to clarify synchronization patterns and use of our macros; they are not considered of interest in themselves. The examples all illustrate "small-granularity" parallelism. That is, the computational tasks that are executed in parallel are very small. However, exactly the same synchronization patterns would be used in programs that capitalized on "large-granularity" parallelism.

To make our discussion concrete, we may occasionally discuss some aspect of a specific machine. We usually reference the Denelcor HEP, although our techniques are equally applicable to most multiprocessors that feature a number of processors operating on a globally shared memory.

In the programs covered in this tutorial, we use lowercase names to represent macro invocations. In addition, after each listing we briefly comment on each example.

2. Example 1: Self-scheduling DO-loops

Our first program illustrates a number of important concepts. The task is to read in two vectors of integers, add the two vectors, and write out the resulting vector. To illustrate the use of parallelism, we coordinate a number of processors that add different elements of the vectors in parallel. That is, one process computes C(1) = A(1) + B(1), while a separate process adds A(2) and B(2). (Adding two integers is a very small task; that is why our example illustrates small-granularity parallelism. If, instead, each element in the vector C were set to the smallest prime number greater than the product of the corresponding elements in the A and B vectors, the granularity would be considerably larger.) The program used to add the two vectors is as follows:

```
1    **********************************************************************
2    *
3    * THIS PROGRAM DEMONSTRATES THE "SELF-SCHEDULING DO-LOOP"
4    * SYNCHRONIZATION PRIMITIVE.  IT READS IN TWO VECTORS, ADDS THEM,
5    * AND PRINTS THE RESULT.
6    *
7    **********************************************************************
8    *
9          PROGRAM ADDTWO
10   *
11   * COMMON AREA VARIABLES
12   *
13         INTEGER A(1000), B(1000), C(1000)
14         INTEGER NPROCS, N
15         COMMON /MAINC/ A, B, C, N, NPROCS
16   *
17   **********************************************************************
18   *
19   *    DECLARE THE VARIABLES AND COMMON TO SUPPORT THE MONITOR
20   *
21   **********************************************************************
22   *
23         gsdec(GS)
24   *
25         INTEGER I
26   *
27   **********************************************************************
28   *
```

369

```
29    *    INITIALIZE THE ENVIRONMENT (ON HEP THIS MEANS SET THE TIMEBOMB)
30    *
31    ************************************************************************
32    *
33         initenv
34    *
35    ************************************************************************
36    *
37    *    INITIALIZE THE SELF-SCHEDULING DO-LOOP MONITOR
38    *
39    ************************************************************************
40    *
41         gsinit(GS)
42    *
43    ************************************************************************
44    *
45    *    READ IN THE NUMBER OF PROCESSES TO RUN IN PARALLEL
46    *
47    ************************************************************************
48    *
49         READ (5,10) NPROCS
50    10   FORMAT(I4)
51         WRITE(6,20) NPROCS
52    20   FORMAT(' NPROCS = ',I4)
53    *
54    ************************************************************************
55    *
56    *    READ IN THE TWO INPUT VECTORS
57    *
58    ************************************************************************
59    *
60         READ (5,10) N
61         READ (5,10) (A(I), I = 1,N)
62         READ (5,10) (B(I), I = 1,N)
63    *
64    ************************************************************************
65    *
66    *    CREATE THE SLAVE PROCESSES
67    *
68    ************************************************************************
69    *
70         DO 30 I=1,NPROCS-1
71            create(SLAVE)
```

```
72   30    CONTINUE
73   *
74         CALL WORK
75   *
76         WRITE (6,10) (C(I), I = 1,N)
77         STOP
78         END
79   *
80   **************************************************************************
81   *
82   *    THE SLAVE PROCESSES JUST CALL THE WORK SUBROUTINE TO ADD UP
83   *    ELEMENTS UNTIL THE END OF THE VECTOR IS REACHED.  THE PROCESSES
84   *    THEN EXIT (WHICH IS ASSUMED TO DESTROY THEM).
85   *
86   **************************************************************************
87   *
88         SUBROUTINE SLAVE
89   *
90         CALL WORK
91         RETURN
92         END
93   *
94   **************************************************************************
95   *
96   * THE WORK SUBROUTINE JUST CAUSES A PROCESS TO GRAB AVAILABLE
97   * SUBSCRIPTS UNTIL ALL OF THE WORK HAS BEEN COMPLETED.  AT THAT
98   * POINT THE SUBROUTINE EXITS.  NOTE THAT IF THERE IS A SINGLE
99   * PROCESS (I.E., NO SLAVES), THE ALGORITHM STILL WORKS JUST
100  * FINE.
101  *
102  **************************************************************************
103  *
104        SUBROUTINE WORK
105  *
106  * COMMON AREA VARIABLES
107  *
108        INTEGER A(1000), B(1000), C(1000)
109        INTEGER NPROCS, N
110        COMMON /MAINC/ A, B, C, N, NPROCS
111  *
112        gsdec(GS)
113  *
114        INTEGER I
```

```
115    *
116    10    CONTINUE
117    *
118    **********************************************************************
119    *
120    *     CLAIM THE NEXT AVAILABLE SUBSCRIPT (RETURNED IN I)
121    *
122    **********************************************************************
123          getsub(GS,I,N,NPROCS)
124    *
125          IF (I .EQ. 0) GO TO 20
126    *
127          C(I) = A(I) + B(I)
128          GO TO 10
129    *
130    20    CONTINUE
131          RETURN
132          END
133    *
134    **********************************************************************
135    *
136    *     THE FOLLOWING MACRO GENERATES THE ROUTINES REQUIRED AS PART
137    *     OF THE "ENVIRONMENT".  ON THE HEP THIS AMOUNTS TO THE TIMEBOMB
138    *     SUBROUTINE, WHICH CAUSES ABNORMAL TERMINATION AFTER SOME
139    *     SPECIFIED NUMBER OF MINUTES (A VALUE THAT GETS READ FROM AN
140    *     INPUT RECORD.
141    *
142    **********************************************************************
143    *
144          env
```

A number of features of this program require discussion:

1. The user creates a COMMON area that will be shared between the
   processes. At this point, there is not complete agreement
   between vendors as to how to distinguish between COMMON that
   is common only to routines in one process (i.e., multiple copies
   exist for multiple processes) and COMMON that is globally
   shared. In our examples, we assume that COMMON is globally
   shared. To protect yourself, you could code a small macro that
   simply converted some word like "globcommon" to the

appropriate wording for whichever machine you intend to run on. For experiments, this hardly seems necessary. For large production code development, such measures seem only prudent.

2. The program uses two macros, *initenv* and *env*, to perform initialization functions appropriate to a given environment.

3. The *gsdec* macro is used to define a monitor that can be used to coordinate a "self-scheduling DO-loop". We will show you exactly what that means later in the code; for now all you really need to know is that the *gsdec(GS)* is used to generate the COMMON blocks required to coordinate processes to work on a self-scheduling DO-loop. It should be used in your main program and in any routines that include *gsinit* or *getsub* macro invocations. The GS is an arbitrary two-character "name" of the monitor. It can be anything, but the names used in the *gsdec*, *gsinit*, and *getsub* invocations must agree. Note that we included *gsdec(GS)* in the main routine and in the WORK subroutine.

4. Line 41 contains *gsinit(GS)*, which initializes the variables that will be used to maintain proper synchronization between the processes. It must be invoked before more processes are created (i.e., before the other processes that will utilize the monitor begin to try acquiring subscript values from it).

5. Lines 49-52 represent the code that reads in the number of processes desired and prints it back out. It is quite useful to make the number of processes an input value. It is highly desirable that the code run properly with a value of 1, which allows the code to be (more or less) debugged on a uniprocessor.

6. Lines 70-72 create the extra processes that have been requested. Line 71 illustrates the use of the *create* macro. In this case, no parameters are passed to the "slave" processes. Execution of the *create* will cause a new process to be created, with execution beginning at the routine specified (in this case, SLAVE).

7. The created processes all start at SLAVE, which simply calls WORK. After creating the "slaves", the master process immediately calls WORK. If you examine the subroutine WORK, you will see the code that all of the processes are simultaneously

executing. The "heart" of the self-scheduling DO-loop is given in lines 116-128. Each process executes the macro command *getsub(GS,I,N,NPROCS)*. Think of this command as executing instantaneously. This is, of course, not true; but because it is a monitor command it is indivisible. Only one process will be allowed to execute the command at any point in time. The result of the command is to return in I the next available subscript in the range 1-N. The first parameter is just the name of the monitor (to connect the *getsub* with the uses of the *gsdec* and *gsinit* macros), and the last parameter is the number of processes that will be competing for the subscripts. Each process claims a subscript (line 123). If there are no more, I will be returned as 0 (causing a GO TO 20). Otherwise, the subscript is processed (line 127), and the process returns to claim another available subscript. This continues until the processes exhaust the subscripts in the range 1-N.

There are a few fine points worth noting. First, no process will be returned a value of 0 before all processes have reached the point where they are requesting a subscript and there is none available (that is why NPROCS must be a parameter to the request -- it allows the monitor command *getsub* to be able to determine when all of the processes have completed their last tasks). This ensures that no process will actually return before the last subscript has been processed.

Second, it is assumed that when the slave processes exit from SLAVE (after returning from WORK) that they will "die"; furthermore, it is assumed that the slaves may exit either before or after the master returns (to line 74) to complete its functions. This assumption may, in fact, not be valid for some implementations (which would make the code fail to port properly). Please note that our development of these tools is still at a preliminary state. Once we have run experiments on several more machines, we are confident that a (more or less) complete set of macros will evolve leading to a high probability of portability.

Let us now pause and consider why this pattern of synchronization is called a "self-scheduling DO-loop". Note that the illustrated logic is used to replace a DO-loop of the following form (which would occur in the uniprocessing version of the code):

```
        DO 10 I = 1,N
            <body of loop>
10      CONTINUE
```

The pattern will work only when executions of the body of the loop can be done in parallel.

3. Barrier Synchronization

Now let us introduce a second pattern of synchronization called *barrier* synchronization. This type of synchronization is quite simple: the execution of

```
        barrier(B1,N)
```

will cause a process to "hang" in the monitor command until N processes are all "hanging". Then they are all released from the barrier and allowed to continue.

One common use of barrier synchronization occurs when multiple processes must be coordinated to perform a sequence of tasks, where the individual tasks must be executed stricly in order. To illustrate, suppose that we wished to perform a two-stage computation. The first stage is just as in our previous example, where C is set to A + B. The second stage involves creating a new vector D, where each value in D is a 0 or 1. The values in D are 0 exactly when the corresponding value in C is identical to the value that precedes it in C. That is, if A = (1,4,2,5,6) and B = (3,2,4,2,1), then C would be set to (4,6,6,7,7) and D would then be set to (1,1,0,1,0). This example is obviously contrived. Clearly, both C and D could be created in a single loop. But suppose that the creation of C is a complex task calling for parallelism and that the creation of D could then be done most efficiently after creating C. In this case, the following code might be used:

```
1       ***************************************************************************
2       *
3       * THIS PROGRAM READS IN TWO VECTORS A AND B.  IT THEN CREATES
```

```
4        * C = A + B.  THEN D IS CREATED AS A VECTOR IN WHICH EACH ELEMENT
5        * IS SET AS FOLLOWS: D(I) = 0 IFF (C(I) = C(I-1).  THOSE ELEMENTS
6        * OF D WHICH ARE NOT SET TO 0 ARE SET TO 1.  D(1) IS ALWAYS SET
7        * TO 1.
8        *
9        ****************************************************************
10
11             PROGRAM GETDUPS
12       *
13       * COMMON AREA VARIABLES
14       *
15             INTEGER A(1000), B(1000), C(1000), D(1000)
16             INTEGER NPROCS, N
17             COMMON /MAINC/ A, B, C, D, N, NPROCS
18       *
19             gsdec(G1)
20             gsdec(G2)
21             bardec(BA)
22       *
23             INTEGER I
24       *
25             initenv
26       *
27       ****************************************************************
28       *
29       *    INITIALIZE THE MONITORS
30       *
31       ****************************************************************
32       *
33             gsinit(G1)
34             gsinit(G2)
35             barinit(BA)
36       *
37             READ (5,10) NPROCS
38       10    FORMAT(I4)
39             WRITE(6,20) NPROCS
40       20    FORMAT(' NPROCS = ',I4)
41       *
42       ****************************************************************
43       *
44       *    READ IN THE TWO INPUT VECTORS
45       *
46       ****************************************************************
```

```
47      *
48              READ (5,10) N
49              READ (5,10) (A(I), I = 1,N)
50              READ (5,10) (B(I), I = 1,N)
51      *
52              DO 30 I=1,NPROCS-1
53                  create(SLAVE)
54      30      CONTINUE
55      *
56              CALL WORK
57      *
58              WRITE (6,40)
59      40      FORMAT(' THE VALUES IN THE C VECTOR ARE AS FOLLOWS:')
60              WRITE (6,10) (C(I), I = 1,N)
61              WRITE (6,50)
62      50      FORMAT(' THE VALUES IN THE D VECTOR ARE AS FOLLOWS:')
63              WRITE (6,10) (D(I), I = 1,N)
64              STOP
65              END
66      *
67      ***********************************************************************
68      *
69      *   THE SLAVE PROCESSES JUST CALL THE WORK SUBROUTINE TO ADD UP
70      *   ELEMENTS UNTIL THE END OF THE VECTOR IS REACHED.  THE PROCESSES
71      *   THEN EXIT (WHICH IS ASSUMED TO DESTROY THEM).
72      *
73      ***********************************************************************
74      *
75              SUBROUTINE SLAVE
76      *
77              CALL WORK
78              RETURN
79              END
80      *
81      ***********************************************************************
82      *
83      * THE WORK SUBROUTINE PERFORMS A 2-STAGE COMPUTATION.  FIRST,
84      * C = A + B IS COMPUTED.  THEN A BARRIER IS USED TO MAKE SURE THAT
85      * NO PROCESS BEGINS THE SECOND STAGE UNTIL THE FIRST STAGE IS
86      * COMPLETED.  THE SECOND STAGE THEN USES ANOTHER SELF-SCHEDULING
87      * DO-LOOP TO CALCULATE D.
88      *
89      ***********************************************************************
```

```
90      *
91            SUBROUTINE WORK
92      *
93      * COMMON AREA VARIABLES
94      *
95            INTEGER A(1000), B(1000), C(1000), D(1000)
96            INTEGER NPROCS, N
97            COMMON /MAINC/ A, B, C, D, N, NPROCS
98      *
99            gsdec(G1)
100           gsdec(G2)
101           bardec(BA)
102     *
103           INTEGER I
104     *
105     10    CONTINUE
106           getsub(G1,I,N,NPROCS)
107     *
108           IF (I .EQ. 0) GO TO 20
109     *
110           C(I) = A(I) + B(I)
111           GO TO 10
112     *
113     20    CONTINUE
114     *
115           barrier(BA,NPROCS)
116     *
117     30    CONTINUE
118           getsub(G2,I,N,NPROCS)
119     *
120           IF (I .EQ. 0) GO TO 40
121     *
122           IF (I .EQ. 1) THEN
123               D(I) = 1
124           ELSE
125               IF (C(I) .EQ. C(I-1)) THEN
126                   D(I) = 0
127               ELSE
128                   D(I) = 1
129               ENDIF
130           ENDIF
131     *
132           GO TO 30
```

```
133     *
134    40   CONTINUE
135     *
136         RETURN
137         END
138     *
139         env
```

Again, several points should be mentioned:

1. Two self-scheduling DO-loops are used in WORK. We used two monitors G1 and G2. Actually, since the *getsub* command reinitializes itself before releasing all of the processes at the end, a single monitor would suffice. We used two to illustrate the use of similar monitors with distinct names.

2. The barrier monitor is declared with *bardec(BA)* in a way completely analagous to the declaration for self-scheduling DO-loops. Similarly, *barinit(BA)* initializes the barrier.

3. The *barrier(BA,NPROCS)* in line 115 sets a barrier between the two stages of computation.

4. Since self-scheduling DO-loops do not release any process with a subscript of 0, the barrier is actually unnecessary.

In some sense, the above example is awful. It uses two monitors (G1 and G2) where one would suffice, and it uses an unnecessary barrier. However, it should help you to become more familiar with the statements required to declare, initialize, and use monitors. Furthermore, it does illustrate in a fairly simple manner how a barrier can be set.

4. A More Challenging Example

Let us proceed to a more challenging example. The next program constructs vectors in descending order and then sorts them into ascending order using a Shell sort algorithm. It acquires timings for sorting vectors of sizes 100, 1000, and 10000. The Shell sort is interesting in its own right and requires some explanation.

To see how a Shell sort works, one should first understand how a simple insertion sort works. Consider the vector (2,-1,1,6,10,-8,18,0). To sort this vector into ascending order, one could proceed from left to right starting with the second element and inserting each element into the sorted list to its left. Thus, -1 would be examined first and inserted into the list to its left (which contains only the value 2); the result would be (-1,2,1,6,10,-8,18,0). Then the third element would be examined and inserted into the sorted list to its left, producing (-1,1,2,6,10,-8,18,0). The fourth element would be left unchanged, as would the fifth; they are already in correct order. Processing the sixth element results in (-8,-1,1,2,6,10,18,0). The seventh element would be left unchanged. Finally, processing the last element would give (-8,-1,0,1,2,6,10,18). This process of inserting each new element into the sorted list to its left is the essential idea behind insertion sorting.

The problem with simple insertion sorting is that a large number of comparisons may be required to move a small number that occurs late in the list into its correct location. The Shell sort corrects this with a rather ingenious idea. Again, consider the vector (2,-1,1,6,10,-8,18,0). Now suppose that the sort were to take place in two stages. In the first stage, the original list of 8 elements is viewed as four interleaved lists. The first list is composed of the first element and the fifth (i.e., 2 and 10); the second list is (-1,-8); the third is (1,18); and the fourth is (6,0). During the first stage, each of these lists is ordered using a simple insertion sort. giving (2,-8,1,0,10,-1,18,6). Clearly, fairly long moves can occur during the first stage. Then the resulting list can be sorted with a simple insertion sort.

This notion becomes quite significant when the original vector is long. Of course, we can carry the idea further and use more stages with gradually diminishing numbers of lists, as long as the last stage treats the whole vector as a single list.

This basic notion led to the following algorithm for sorting a vector V containing N elements:

```
procedure shellsort(V,N)

    compute h(1), h(2),...h(i+2) such that h(1)=1,
```

```
                h(k) = (3*h(k-1)) + 1, h(i+1) < N, and h(i+2) > N.

        set gap = h(i)

        while (gap > 0) do

            set nextel = gap + 1

            while (nextel <= N) do

                sortel = nextel - gap

                while (sortel > 0) and (V(sortel) > V(sortel+gap)do

                    exchange V(sortel) and V(sortel+gap)

                    set sortel = sortel - gap

                enddo

                set nextel = nextel + 1

            enddo

            set gap = (gap-1)/3

        enddo

    endproc
```

The sort algorithm is somewhat complex, but it does represent a fairly good sort algorithm that is easily implemented.

The above algorithm can clearly take advantage of multiprocessing on all but the last pass (i.e., on all executions of the main loop with a "gap" size greater than 1). This is achieved by allowing separate processes to sort the interleaved lists. The program that achieves this result using self-scheduling DO-loops and barrier synchronization is as follows:

```
1          define(mode,REAL)
2    **********************************************************************
3    *
4    * THIS PROGRAM DEMONSTRATES THE "BARRIER" AND "SELF-SCHEDULING DO-LOOP"
5    * SYNCHRONIZATION PRIMITIVES.  IT FILLS IN A VECTOR (A) WITH VALUES IN
6    * DESCENDING ORDER.  THEN IT USES A SHELL SORT (SEE KNUTH'S 3RD VOLUME
7    * ON SORTING AND SEARCHING ALGORITHMS) TO SORT THE VALUES INTO
8    * ASCENDING ORDER.  TIMES ARE ACQUIRED FOR TABLE SIZES OF 100, 1000, AND
9    * 10000.
10   *
11   **********************************************************************
12
13          PROGRAM SRTPGM
14   *
15   * COMMON AREA VARIABLES
16   *
17          mode A(10000)
18          INTEGER NPROCS, N, GAP
19          LOGICAL PGDONE
20          COMMON /MAINC/ GAP, A, PGDONE, N, NPROCS
21   *
22          gsdec(GS)
23          bardec(B1)
24   *
25          INTEGER I,J
26   *
27          initenv
28   *
29   **********************************************************************
30   *
31   *   INITIALIZE THE BARRIER AND SELF-SCHEDULING DO-LOOP MONITORS
32   *
33   **********************************************************************
34   *
35          gsinit(GS)
36          barinit(B1)
37   *
38          PGDONE = .FALSE.
39   *
40          READ (5,10) NPROCS
```

```
41    10    FORMAT(I4)
42          WRITE(6,20) NPROCS
43    20    FORMAT(' NPROCS = ',I4)
44    *
45          DO 30 I=1,NPROCS-1
46                create(SLAVE)
47    30    CONTINUE
48    *
49    ***************************************************************
50    *
51    *     THE MAIN LOGIC JUST FILLS IN THE TABLE AND SORTS IT.
52    *     TIMINGS ARE TAKEN FOR TABLES OF 100, 1000, AND 10000.
53    *
54    ***************************************************************
55    *
56          N = 10
57          DO 50 I=1,3
58                N = 10 * N
59                CALL FILL
60    *
61                clock(J)
62                T1 = J
63    *
64                CALL SORT
65    *
66                clock(J)
67                T2 = J - T1
68    *
69                WRITE(6,40) N, T2
70    40          FORMAT(' SIZE = ',I5,'  TOTAL TIME = ',E12.5)
71    *
72    50    CONTINUE
73    *
74    ***************************************************************
75    *
76    *     ONE LAST CALL TO LOOP IS REQUIRED TO FREE THE OTHER PROCESSES
77    *     FROM THE BARRIER (SO THEY CAN EXIT).
78    *
79    ***************************************************************
80    *
81          PGDONE = .TRUE.
82          CALL LOOP(0)
83          STOP
```

```
84          END
85    *
86    ********************************************************************
87    *
88    *    THE FOLLOWING LITTLE ROUTINE JUST FILLS THE VECTOR WITH VALUES
89    *    IN DESCENDING ORDER.
90    *
91    ********************************************************************
92    *
93          SUBROUTINE FILL
94    *
95          mode A(10000)
96          INTEGER NPROCS, N, GAP
97          LOGICAL PGDONE
98          COMMON /MAINC/ GAP, A, PGDONE, N, NPROCS
99    *
100         INTEGER I
101   *
102         DO 10 I=1,N
103             A(I) = (N - I) + 1.0
104   10    CONTINUE
105         RETURN
106         END
107   *
108   ********************************************************************
109   *
110   *    THE SLAVE PROCESSES JUST HANG ON THE BARRIER IN THE "LOOP"
111   *    AND HELP WHEN A TABLE IS TO BE SORTED.
112   *
113   ********************************************************************
114   *
115         SUBROUTINE SLAVE
116   *
117         CALL LOOP(1)
118         RETURN
119         END
120   *
121   ********************************************************************
122   *
123   *    THE SORT ROUTINE IS EXECUTED BY THE MASTER PROCESS.  IT JUST
124   *    CALCULATES THE RADIX FOR EACH PASS OF THE SHELL SORT, AND JOINS
125   *    THE SLAVE PROCESSES WHEN WORKING ON EACH PASS.
126   *    THE RADIX VALUES ARE HT, ... H2, H1: H1 IS 1; HI IS (3*H(I-1) + 1);
```

```
127    *    H(T+2) >= N.  SEE KNUTH FOR ARGUMENTS IN FAVOR OF THESE VALUES.
128    *
129    ***********************************************************************
130    *
131         SUBROUTINE SORT
132    *
133         mode A(10000)
134         INTEGER NPROCS, N, GAP
135         LOGICAL PGDONE
136         COMMON /MAINC/ GAP, A, PGDONE, N, NPROCS
137    *
138         INTEGER I1,I2,I3
139    *
140         I1 = 1
141         I2 = (I1 * 3) + 1
142         I3 = (I2 * 3) + 1
143    10   CONTINUE
144         IF (I3 .GE. N) GO TO 20
145              I1 = I2
146              I2 = I3
147              I3 = (I2 * 3) + 1
148              GO TO 10
149    20   CONTINUE
150    *
151         GAP = I1
152    30   CONTINUE
153         IF (GAP .LE. 0) GO TO 40
154    *
155              CALL LOOP(0)
156              GAP = (GAP - 1) / 3
157              GO TO 30
158    40   CONTINUE
159         RETURN
160         END
161    *
162    ***********************************************************************
163    *
164    *    THE LOOP ROUTINE IS THE CODE REQUIRED TO COORDINATE THE NPROCS
165    *    PROCESSES AS THEY EXECUTE ONE PASS OF A SHELL SORT.  NOTE THE
166    *    BARRIER AT THE TOP, WHICH IS USED TO CAUSE THE PROCESSES TO
167    *    WAIT FOR THE VECTOR TO BE SET UP AND THE INCREMENT CHOSEN.
168    *    THEN A SELF-SCHEDULING DO-LOOP IS USED TO ALLOCATE SUBSCRIPTS.
169    *    NOTE THAT THE MASTER PARTICIPATES IN THIS LOGIC, SO THE PROGRAM
```

```
170   *   CAN BE RUN WITH NPROCS SET TO 1.
171   *
172   ***************************************************************************
173   *
174       SUBROUTINE LOOP(WHO)
175       INTEGER WHO
176   *
177       mode A(10000)
178       INTEGER NPROCS, N, GAP
179       LOGICAL PGDONE
180       COMMON /MAINC/ GAP, A, PGDONE, N, NPROCS
181   *
182       LOGICAL DONE
183       mode T
184   *
185       bardec(B1)
186       gsdec(GS)
187   *
188   10  CONTINUE
189       barrier(B1,NPROCS)
190       IF (PGDONE) GO TO 80
191   *
192   20  CONTINUE
193       getsub(GS,J,GAP,NPROCS)
194       IF (J .EQ. 0) GO TO 70
195   *
196           K = J + GAP
197   30      CONTINUE
198           IF (K .GT. N) GO TO 60
199               K1 = K - GAP
200               DONE = .FALSE.
201   40          CONTINUE
202               IF (DONE .OR. (K1 .LT. 1)) GO TO 50
203                   IF (A(K1) .LE. A(K1+GAP)) THEN
204                       DONE = .TRUE.
205                   ELSE
206                       T = A(K1)
207                       A(K1) = A(K1+GAP)
208                       A(K1+GAP) = T
209                       K1 = K1 - GAP
210                   ENDIF
211                   GO TO 40
212   50          CONTINUE
```

```
213                    K = K + GAP
214                    GO TO 30
215      60      CONTINUE
216                    GO TO 20
217      70      CONTINUE
218              IF (WHO .EQ. 1) GO TO 10
219      80      CONTINUE
220              RETURN
221              END
222      *
223              env
```

Again, several features of this program merit discussion:

1. First, line 1 is an example of a very simple macro. It states that every occurrence of the word "mode" will be replaced by the word "REAL". This macro allows a programmer to easily alter features of a program. We use the UNIX macro processor *m4*. Any macro processor will work equally well, but *m4* is a standard UNIX utility and will become commonly available. Because our approach to coding requires you to code simple macros, we encourage you to gain familiarity with its use. We hope that all of the required details will be adequately covered in this document, but for more details you should consult the UNIX documentation.

2. The variable PGDONE is set to TRUE when there are no more vectors to sort. It is referenced by the slave processes when they fall through the barrier in LOOP. It is used as a signal to the slaves to destroy themselves.

3. The main routine just constructs vectors to sort (by calling FILL) and accumulates the time required to sort each table. Note the use of the *clock* macro to read the system clock (lines 61 and 66). In environments that do not support a system clock, the macro generates code to return a meaningless value (as is done, for example, with the macros designed for use on UNIX in a uniprocessing environment).

4. In this code the routine LOOP is multiprocessed logic. Since the master process prepares computational tasks (i.e., sets up vectors to sort, and creates the parameters for each stage of a sort), it will exit LOOP after each stage of a sort. The slaves, on the other hand, always wait in LOOP for the next stage of a sort (they hang on the barrier in LOOP, waiting for the master to set up the problem and join them at the barrier). This type of logic requires that each process know whether it is a slave or the master. This is achieved by passing a parameter (0 for the master; 1 for a slave) whenever the LOOP subroutine is called (lines 82, 117, and 155).

5. The slaves are created and wait in LOOP for the master to join them. Before joining them, the master process (in the routine SORT) calculates the "gap" required on the next stage of a sort. The master calls LOOP with decreasing "gap" lengths until the a vector is completely sorted (i.e., until after calling LOOP with GAP set to 1).

6. The logic of LOOP is based on the idea that each process selects one of the "interleaved lists" and sorts it into order. For each stage of a sort, there will be GAP lists to sort.

This sort certainly does not fully utilize all available parallelism. In fact, the last stage of each sort (with GAP=1) is handled by a single process. However, on large vectors it does give a speedup roughly equal to half the number of available processors. It is, perhaps, worth noting that with somewhat more thought one can create good sort algorithms that do come much closer to fully utilizing the available processing components.

5. The Concept of Monitors

We have deferred discussion of exactly what we mean by a monitor to allow you to become familiar with a number of the details involved in our basic approach to implementing multiprocessing algorithms. It is now time to analyze the concept of monitors in some detail.

In our examples of self-scheduling DO-loops and barriers, it was very important that each process be able to view execution of *getsub* and *barrier* commands as indivisible operations. The implementation of these commands involves data structures (generated by *gsdec* and *bardec* macros) that are shared among a number of processes. The essential problem here is to make sure that access and updates are carefully synchronized to prevent destructive interference among the processes. Sections of code that can safely be executed by only a single process at a time are called *critical sections*.

For each set of shared data structures, there is a set of operations that represent critical sections. In the case of a self-scheduling DO-loop, there is a single critical section (claiming the next subscript) associated with the data structures. In more complex cases, there may be a number of critical sections.

A *monitor* is a conceptual abstraction composed of three distinct parts:

1. The data that are shared,

2. The operations that represent critical sections associated with the shared data, and

3. The code required to initialize the shared structures.

Thus, when we speak of using a monitor to coordinate activity based on some shared data, we mean that the programmer carefully defines the shared data, the operations on the shared data, and the operations required to initialize the data. The details of how monitor operations are implemented to prevent destructive interfence represent the central difficulty. When a process has begun to execute a critical section (i.e., when it enters a monitor operation), we refer to this as "having entered the monitor". Only one process may be "in a monitor" at any given point. This is achieved conceptually by setting a lock at the point where the operation is entered and releasing the lock at the point where the operation is exited. Thus, in a self-scheduling DO-loop, the operation *getsub* is basically

set a lock
claim the next subscript (which is a shared variable)
release the lock.

In the case of the self-scheduling DO-loop, the *gsdec (GS)* defines the shared data in a COMMON block; The *gsinit(GS)* initializes the lock to "not set" and the subscript to 1. However, in the case in which there are no more available subscripts, we decided to cause the process issuing the *getsub* to "hang" until all of the remaining processes were also requesting a subscript. Only then will the **getsub** release them all (with a value of 0 to indicate that they were not successful in claiming a subscript). Conceptually, we "hang" a process as follows.

When a process is in a monitor and cannot complete the operation until a later point, it is *delayed*. This means that the process relinquishes the monitor and is placed in a queue. A delay queue can contain any number of "hung" processes, in arbitrary order. Each delayed process can be reactivated only by another process issuing a *continue*. It is important that only one process ever be "in a monitor". Thus, the process that issues the *continue* (which can be done only when it is in the monitor) exits from the monitor at the same instant that the (arbitrarily chosen) delayed process is reactivated (and regains control of the monitor).

Summarizing, we have identified four basic monitor operations:

menter(<monitor-name>): this operation is the first instruction in a monitor operation. It sets a lock, which ensures that the process can enter the monitor operation only in the case in which no other process is active in any operation associated with <monitor-name>.

mexit(<monitor-name>): this operation is the last instruction in a monitor. It releases the lock set by *menter(<monitor-name>)*.

delay(<monitor-name>,<queue-number>): this operation causes the process that is in the monitor to be delayed in the queue designated by <queue-number>. The process loses control of the monitor.

continue(<monitor-name>,<queue-number>): this operation causes the active process to immediately exit from the monitor. If there are any delayed processes in the designated queue, one of them will be activated (thus, inheriting the lock set by the process leaving the monitor). Otherwise, the lock will be released by the exiting process.

With these definitions in hand, we can now give the exact logic of the *get-sub* monitor:

getsub(<monitor-name>,<returned-subscript>,<max-val>,<num-proc>)

    menter(<monitor-name>)

    if (the shared subscript is less than or equal to <max-val>) then

        set <returned-subscript> to the value of the shared subscript

        increment the shared subscript

    else

        set <returned-subscript> to 0

        if (fewer than (<num-proc> - 1) processes are in delay-queue-1)

            delay(<monitor-name>,1)

        endif

        reset the shared subscript to 1

        continue(<monitor-name>,1)

    endif

    mexit(<monitor-name>)

Once this logic is understood, the logic for barrier synchronization becomes trivial:

    barrier(<monitor-name>,<num-proc>)

        menter(<monitor-name>)

        if (fewer than (<num-proc> - 1) processes are in
            delay-queue-1)

            delay(<monitor-name>,1)

        endif

        continue(<monitor-name>,1)

        mexit(<monitor-name>)

We do not intend to introduce you to all of the features available in *m4* for implementing such monitors as macro invocations. However, you will need to understand the essential features of *m4* in order to work with our more complex monitors (and to code your own monitor operations, when necessary). Therefore, let us introduce you to *m4* by presenting a macro definition of the **barrier** operation:

```
define(barrier,
        [menter($1)
        IF ($1C1 .LT. ($2 - 1)) THEN
            delay($1,1)
        ENDIF
        continue($1,1)
        mexit($1)]
    )
```

The *define* command is used to create new macros. It contains two arguments -- the name of the macro and what should be generated by the macro. In this simple example, "barrier" is the name, and the text surrounded by the square brackets is the replacement text. *m4* can be used to search for strings of the form "barrier(a1,a2)", which represent invocations of the macro. Whenever such a string is found, the replacement text will replace it. The only complexity involves the arguments of the invocation: wherever $1 occurs in the replacement text, the first argument of the macro invocation will be used, and similarly for any number of arguments. Thus,

> barrier(BA,NPROCS)

would generate

```
menter(BA)
IF (BAC1 .LT. (NPROCS - 1)) THEN
    delay(BA,1)
ENDIF
continue(BA,1)
mexit(BA)
```

This code would then be expanded to actual FORTRAN using definitions of the basic monitor operations that we supply for different machines.

Before leaving this example, one more comment is required. The variable $1C1 occurs in the macro definition (and gets expanded in our example to BAC1). This variable, by definition, contains the number of processes delayed in the first delay queue for the monitor.

6. An Introduction to the Askfor Monitor

In our studies of implementing algorithms for multiprocessors, we have become increasingly aware of the significance of a single synchronization pattern. It appears with surprising frequency in both numeric and non-numeric applications. The pattern involves the concept of "a pool of tasks", where processes "ask for a task to work on" and "add tasks to the pool". In some sense, this is exactly what a self-scheduling DO-loop does, except that for the DO-loop processes never add new tasks to the pool. In the case of the DO-loop, the pool of problems is represented by a subscript; if the shared subscript is I and the maximum value is N, then the pool of remaining tasks to be parcelled out is the subscript values from the current value of I to the maximum value N. This fairly simple special case, however, is not sufficient for many applications. Frequently, the pool of remaining problems cannot be represented by a single subscript; in fact, the structure required to represent the pool is often quite complex.

Let us first give a more precise description of the general pattern:

1) A sequence of computational tasks (i.e., problems) must be solved. We shall refer to these as the "major" tasks T_1, T_2, ...

2) Each major task T_i may be decomposed into one or more minor tasks t_{i1}, t_{i2}, ...

3) A minor task may itself be decomposed.

4) At any point in the computation, the solution of a minor task may result in a solution for the current major task. Thus, the current major task is thought of as "unsolved" until either a sub-computation produces a solution or until all subcomputations are completed. We refer to this latter situation as a solution by *exhaustion*.

Let us illustrate one instance of this pattern that we found in writing a routine to perform QR-factorization of a sequence of matrices. In this case, each major task amounts to computing the desired factorization. We use Householder's algorithm for performing the factorization. It is not important that you understand what this algorithm does; it is necessary only to understand the following synchronization requirements:

1. The first step in factoring a matrix is to create the reflection for column 1. This reflection can then be applied to all remaining columns. In general, you create the reflection for column k after the previous k-1 columns have all had their reflections created and applied to column k.

2. A reflection for a column k can be applied to all columns to the right of k. However, the reflections must be applied in order. That is, the reflection created from column 1 must be applied to column 3 before the reflection created from column 2 is applied to column 3.

In this case, the pool of remaining tasks includes two types of minor tasks: create a reflection for column i and apply the reflection for column i to column j. Initially, the pool will contain only the minor task "create the reflection for column 1". The solution of the first minor task will cause a number of new minor tasks (to apply the reflection to each of the remaining columns) to be added to the pool. Processes claim minor tasks and add them to the pool until the pool is exhausted, representing completion of the major task. In this particular case, all major tasks are solved by exhaustion (and are solved "successfully"). This is frequently not the case. The challenge involved in setting up the problem is how to represent the "pool of problems" in a reasonably efficient manner. This is a problem-dependent aspect of the synchronization: different problems utilize widely different representations of the problem pool. Thus, special-purpose logic will be needed to "claim a problem from the pool" or to "insert a problem into the pool".

We have found this pattern of synchronization, which we will call the *askfor* monitor (since processes "ask for" the next available task to perform), to be quite difficult to implement properly. The fact that problem-dependent code is required to manage the pool of outstanding tasks makes the use of our *askfor* monitor more complex than using the *barrier* or *getsub* monitors. We begin, therefore, with the simplest of settings -- our first example that adds two vectors to produce a third. In this case, since it is a self-scheduling DO-loop, the pool of problems can be managed by a single shared subscript. The code is as follows:

```
1       define(getprob,
2               [IF (SUB .LE. $2) THEN
3                       $1 = SUB
4                       SUB = SUB + 1
5                       $3 = 0
6               ENDIF]
7           )
8       *******************************************************************
9       *
10      * THIS PROGRAM DEMONSTRATES THE "ASKFOR" SYNCHRONIZATION PRIMITIVE.
11      * IT READS IN TWO VECTORS, ADDS THEM, AND PRINTS THE RESULT.
12      *
13      *******************************************************************
14      *
15              PROGRAM ADDTWO
16      *
17      * COMMON AREA VARIABLES
18      *
19              INTEGER A(1000), B(1000), C(1000)
```

```
20          INTEGER NPROCS, N
21          COMMON /MAINC/ A, B, C, N, NPROCS
22     *
23     *******************************************************************
24     *
25     *   DECLARE THE VARIABLES AND COMMON TO SUPPORT THE MONITOR
26     *
27     *******************************************************************
28     *
29          adec(MO)
30     *
31          INTEGER SUB
32          COMMON /POOL/ SUB
33     *
34          INTEGER I
35     *
36     *******************************************************************
37     *
38     *   INITIALIZE THE ENVIRONMENT (ON HEP THIS MEANS SET THE TIMEBOMB)
39     *
40     *******************************************************************
41     *
42          initenv
43     *
44     *******************************************************************
45     *
46     *   INITIALIZE ASKFOR MONITOR
47     *
48     *******************************************************************
49     *
50          ainit(MO)
51          SUB = 1
52     *
53     *******************************************************************
54     *
55     *   READ IN THE NUMBER OF PROCESSES TO RUN IN PARALLEL
56     *
57     *******************************************************************
58     *
59          READ (5,10) NPROCS
60     10   FORMAT(I4)
61          WRITE(6,20) NPROCS
62     20   FORMAT(' NPROCS = ',I4)
```

```
63    *
64    ***********************************************************************
65    *
66    *    READ IN THE TWO INPUT VECTORS
67    *
68    ***********************************************************************
69    *
70         READ (5,10) N
71         READ (5,10) (A(I), I = 1,N)
72         READ (5,10) (B(I), I = 1,N)
73    *
74    ***********************************************************************
75    *
76    *    CREATE THE SLAVE PROCESSES
77    *
78    ***********************************************************************
79    *
80         DO 30 I=1,NPROCS-1
81              create(SLAVE)
82    30    CONTINUE
83    *
84         CALL WORK
85    *
86         WRITE (6,10) (C(I), I = 1,N)
87         STOP
88         END
89    *
90    ***********************************************************************
91    *
92    *    THE SLAVE PROCESSES JUST CALL THE WORK SUBROUTINE TO ADD UP
93    *    ELEMENTS UNTIL THE END OF THE VECTOR IS REACHED.  THE PROCESSES
94    *    THEN EXIT (WHICH IS ASSUMED TO DESTROY THEM).
95    *
96    ***********************************************************************
97    *
98         SUBROUTINE SLAVE
99    *
100        CALL WORK
101        RETURN
102        END
103   *
104   ***********************************************************************
105   *
```

```
106     * THE WORK SUBROUTINE JUST CAUSES A PROCESS TO GRAB AVAILABLE
107     * SUBSCRIPTS UNTIL ALL OF THE WORK AS BEEN COMPLETED.  AT THAT
108     * POINT THE SUBROUTINE EXITS.  NOTE THAT IF THERE IS A SINGLE
109     * PROCESS (I.E., NO SLAVES), THE ALGORITHM STILL WORKS JUST
110     * FINE.
111     *
112     ***************************************************************
113     *
114           SUBROUTINE WORK
115     *
116     * COMMON AREA VARIABLES
117     *
118           INTEGER A(1000), B(1000), C(1000)
119           INTEGER NPROCS, N
120           COMMON /MAINC/ A, B, C, N, NPROCS
121     *
122           adec(MO)
123     *
124           INTEGER SUB
125           COMMON /POOL/ SUB
126     *
127           INTEGER I,RC
128     *
129     10    CONTINUE
130     *
131     ***************************************************************
132     *
133     *     CLAIM THE NEXT AVAILABLE SUBSCRIPT (RETURNED IN I)
134     *
135     ***************************************************************
136           askfor(MO,RC,NPROCS,getprob(I,N,RC),)
137     *
138           IF (RC .NE. 0) GO TO 20
139     *
140           C(I) = A(I) + B(I)
141           GO TO 10
142     *
143     20    CONTINUE
144           RETURN
145           END
146     *
147           env
```

To understand this program, the reader should compare it to the version using self-scheduling DO-loops. Several points are worth mentioning:

1. First, note that the programmer explicitly gives the shared COMMON used to manage the pool of processes (lines 31-32). He must also initialize his representation of the pool (line 51).

2. The *getsub* operation has been replaced with an invocation of the *askfor* monitor operation (line 136):

     136   askfor(MO,RC,NPROCS,getprob(I,N,RC),)

     Here, the first argument (MO) is the name of the monitor. The second argument (RC) is a variable set by the monitor operation to indicate whether a problem could be taken from the pool (set to 0 on successful acquisition of a problem; otherwise it will get set to 1). The third argument (NPROCS) gives the number of processes sharing the pool. The fifth argument gives a macro invocation that can be used to generate the problem-dependent logic required to try to claim a problem from the pool. There is a missing sixth argument which is used to generate the code required to reinitialize the pool; since we are only adding one pair of vectors, there is no need to reinitialize the pool.

The intrinsic complexity involved in the *askfor* monitor is based on the fact that the user has to provide a macro to generate the logic to claim tasks (and the logic to reinitialize the pool, if a sequence of major tasks are to be processed). The logic to claim a problem is generated by the macro *getprob*, which is defined in lines 1-7 of the program. Note that *getprob* does not generate a monitor operation; rather, it generates a block of code in the middle of the *askfor* monitor operation. This is why it does not begin with an *menter* nor end with a *mexit*.

7. A More Complex Example of the Askfor Monitor

Many applications of the *askfor* monitor are substantially more complex than our last example. Frequently, the complexity originates in the representation of the pool of problems. However, there can be other sources of complexity:

1. Some problems can be "solved" by any arbitrary process working on a minor task. All processes must (on their next request for a task) be notified of "problem end" by a positive value in the return code. For example, suppose that the object of our previous problem were to determine whether the sum of any two corresponding elements in A and B exceeded 100. In this case, a solution by exhaustion (return code of 1) would indicate that no values did exceed 100. On the other hand, any process that found a sum that exceeded 100 could "post" end-of-problem, using the actual sum as the return code (actually any value greater than 1 would be adequate). Posting an end-of-problem condition is accomplished with the *probend* macro.

2. Some programs must compute solutions to a sequence of major tasks. This requires the inclusion of an extra parameter on the *askfor* invocation giving a macro that can be used to reinitialize the monitor. Furthermore, each process should receive the end-of-problem return code exactly. Once a process has received such a return code, it can ask for another task (which is what slave processes normally do) or itself go and acquire another major task to solve (which is what the master process would normally do).

3. In the cases where a sequence of major tasks are to be solved, some means must exist for signalling "end of program" to processes. This is done by invoking the *progend* macro. In this case, every process that has been delayed or requests another task will receive a return code value of -1.

To see exactly how these concepts come into play, let us consider a modified version of our earlier example. In this example, a sequence of pairs of input vectors are processed. For each pair, the question

"Does the sum of any corresponding elements exceed 100?"

is answered. Between problems, the reset logic just resets the shared subscript to 0. The subscript is set to 1 when a new pair of vectors are ready to be processed.

```
1     define(getprob,
2            [IF (SUB .GT. 0) THEN
```

```
3                      IF (SUB .LE. $2) THEN
4                           $1 = SUB
5                           SUB = SUB + 1
6                           $3 = 0
7                      ENDIF
8                 ENDIF]
9             )
10     define(reset,
11           [SUB = 0]
12           )
13     define(probstart,
14           [menter(MO)
15            SUB = 1
16            continue(MO,1)
17            mexit(MO)]
18           )
19     ***********************************************************************
20     *
21     * THIS PROGRAM DEMONSTRATES THE "ASKFOR" SYNCHRONIZATION PRIMITIVE.
22     * IT READS IN PAIRS OF VECTORS.  FOR EACH PAIR, IT DETERMINES
23     * WHETHER OR NOT THE SUM OF ANY TWO CORRESPONDING ELEMENTS
24     * EXCEEDS 100.
25     *
26     ***********************************************************************
27     *
28           PROGRAM CHKTWO
29     *
30     * COMMON AREA VARIABLES
31     *
32           INTEGER A(1000), B(1000)
33           INTEGER NPROCS, N
34           COMMON /MAINC/ A, B, N, NPROCS
35     *
36     ***********************************************************************
37     *
38     *   DECLARE THE VARIABLES AND COMMON TO SUPPORT THE MONITOR
39     *
40     ***********************************************************************
41     *
42           adec(MO)
43     *
44           INTEGER SUB
45           COMMON /POOL/ SUB
```

```
46    *
47          INTEGER I, J, NPROBS
48    *
49    ***************************************************************
50    *
51    *   INITIALIZE THE ENVIRONMENT (ON HEP THIS MEANS SET THE TIMEBOMB)
52    *
53    ***************************************************************
54    *
55          initenv
56    *
57    ***************************************************************
58    *
59    *   INITIALIZE ASKFOR MONITOR
60    *
61    ***************************************************************
62    *
63          ainit(MO)
64          SUB = 0
65    *
66    ***************************************************************
67    *
68    *   READ IN THE NUMBER OF PROCESSES TO RUN IN PARALLEL
69    *
70    ***************************************************************
71    *
72          READ (5,10) NPROCS
73    10    FORMAT(I4)
74          WRITE(6,20) NPROCS
75    20    FORMAT(' NPROCS = ',I4)
76    *
77    ***************************************************************
78    *
79    *   CREATE THE SLAVE PROCESSES
80    *
81    ***************************************************************
82    *
83          DO 30 I=1,NPROCS-1
84              create(SLAVE)
85    30    CONTINUE
86    *
87    ***************************************************************
88    *
```

```
89    *    READ IN THE NUMBER OF PAIRS TO PROCESS
90    *
91    *****************************************************************
92    *
93
94          READ (5,10) NPROBS
95          DO 40 J = 1,NPROBS
96    *
97    *****************************************************************
98    *
99    *    READ IN THE TWO INPUT VECTORS
100   *
101   *****************************************************************
102   *
103          READ (5,10) N
104          READ (5,10) (A(I), I = 1,N)
105          READ (5,10) (B(I), I = 1,N)
106   *
107          probstart
108          CALL WORK(0)
109   40     CONTINUE
110          progend(MO)
111   *
112          STOP
113          END
114   *
115   *****************************************************************
116   *
117   *              S L A V E   P R O C E S S E S
118   *
119   *****************************************************************
120   *
121          SUBROUTINE SLAVE
122   *
123          CALL WORK(1)
124          RETURN
125          END
126   *
127   *****************************************************************
128   *
129   *              W O R K   S U B R O U T I N E
130   *
131   *****************************************************************
```

```
132    *
133            SUBROUTINE WORK(WHO)
134            INTEGER WHO
135    *
136    * COMMON AREA VARIABLES
137    *
138            INTEGER A(1000), B(1000)
139            INTEGER NPROCS, N
140            COMMON /MAINC/ A, B, N, NPROCS
141    *
142            adec(MO)
143    *
144            INTEGER SUB
145            COMMON /POOL/ SUB
146    *
147            INTEGER I, RC, SUM
148    *
149    10      CONTINUE
150    *
151    *************************************************************************
152    *
153    *       CLAIM THE NEXT AVAILABLE SUBSCRIPT (RETURNED IN I)
154    *
155    *************************************************************************
156            askfor(MO,RC,NPROCS,getprob(I,N,RC),reset)
157    *
158            IF (RC .NE. 0) GO TO 20
159    *
160            SUM = A(I) + B(I)
161            IF (SUM .GT. 100) THEN
162                probend(MO,2)
163            ENDIF
164    *
165            GO TO 10
166    *
167    20      CONTINUE
168            IF ((RC .NE. -1) .AND. (WHO .EQ. 1)) GO TO 10
169            IF (WHO .EQ. 0) THEN
170                WRITE(6,30) RC
171    30          FORMAT(' THE RETURN CODE = ',I4)
172            ENDIF
173            RETURN
174            END
```

Note the following points:

1. The *getprob* logic must now check to make sure that there is an active problem. If the logic does not alter RC, then the requesting process will be delayed until *probstart* is executed. Here *probstart* is an actual monitor operation. It issues a *continue* to activate any processes that might be waiting for work to arrive.

2. If a process recognizes an end-of-problem condition, it still must go through the *askfor* requesting a task. Our logic insists on returning the end-of-job return code to each of the cooperating processes (and waits for them all to be delayed, so that it can release them all with the appropriate return code).

3. The WHO variable is used in the WORK routine to distinguish the master process, which prints the return code and goes to get the next problem.

4. The second operand on the *probend* monitor operation is the return code to be passed back to each process. It should always be greater than 1.

The reader should note that the logic to support the full *askfor* monitor is somewhat complex. For a detailed description, you should consult[8]. However, we do include a summary of the logic here for the interested reader:

```
askfor: procedure(<returned-task>,<return-code>)
        if ((not program done) and (problem done)) then
            if (other nondelayed processes) then
                delay
            endif
        else
            <return-code> <- "undetermined"
            while ((not program done) and (not problem done)) do
                try to claim a problem
                if (success) then
                    continue
                else
                    if (last active process)
                        set problem done (set code to "exhausted")
                    else
                        delay
                    endif
                endif
            enddo
        endif
        if (program done) then
            <return-code> <- "program done"
            continue
        else
            <return-code> <- "problem done (set code)"
            if (no more delayed processes) then
                reset variables (for next problem)
            endif
            continue
        endif
        end procedure
```

We have obviously left out the details introduced by the user having to
pass the logic to "try to claim a problem" or to "reset variables", but the
logic does accurately represent our macro implementation.

8. Locks

Before ending this discussion of basic synchronization primitives, some discussion of "locks" should be included. Consider the problem of computing a dot product of two vectors A and B, storing the result in the integer I. If a self-cheduling DO-loop is used, processes are allocated distinct subscripts. However, the problem remains of exactly how to synchonize the addition of values into the integer I. The basic idea behind the use of monitors would suggest that a monitor be established for the variable I, with the single operation of adding a value to the variable. This is a perfectly reasonable way to handle the problem.

However, in some problems it becomes necessary to selectively gain access to a variety of data items and then to update them in fairly complex patterns. This can be done most easily using "locks". A lock amounts to a "monitor enter" operation, while an "unlock" is the corresponding "monitor exit" operation. When utilizing locks, there is no notion of delaying the process. The process simply gains control of the lock, performs the critical section, and releases the lock.

To allow this style of programming, we have include for macros in our standard package:

> *lockdec(N)* declares the variables required to support N locks. These locks are based on an array (named LO) of monitors.

> *lockinit(N)* initializes the N locks.

> *lock(J)* acquires the Jth lock. This amounts to an *menter(LO,J)* operation, which acquires entry to the Jth monitor of the array named LO.

> *unlock(J)* releases the Jth lock.

To update the shared variable I, one would then use

```
lock(1)
I = I + some value
unlock(1)
```

where the single lock would be decared with

```
lockdef(1)
```

and initialization would be accomplished with

```
lockinit(1)
```

In those cases where a number of locks must he held before updating a set of values, the programmer should always acquire the locks in some fixed order (e.g., increasing order of lock number). This technique is called a *standard allocation pattern* and will guarantee that a deadlock will not occur between two processes attempting to claim overlapping sets of locks. Thus, if process 1 requires locks 1 and 2, while process 2 requires locks 2, 3, and 1, a deadlock could occur unless the fixed order of locking is observed (forcing process 2 to claim lock 1 before lock 2, and lock 2 before lock 3).

9. The Fetch-and-Add

There has been a great deal of interest in the use of the fetch-and-add as a primitive operation in a multiprocessing environment[2]. For many applications, it can be used to eliminate critical sections. It seems quite likely that, as people contemplate the potential advantages of machines with thousands of processors, the significance of the fetch-and-add operation will turn out to be substantial.

To allow researchers to develop codes for machines that support fetch-and-add on multiprocessors that do not (or to allow portability from systems that do to those that do not), we have written a set of macros that allow one to code using the fetch-and-add. On systems that do not support the operation as a primitive, the macros generate the code to support it as a monitor operation (with the implied overhead associated with the critical section).

The macros to support fetch-and-add are as follows:

fadec(<monitor-name>,<type>) is used to generate the variables and COMMON area required to support the monitor. Here <type> should be INTEGER or REAL, giving the type associated with the value maintained by the monitor.

fainit(<monitor-name>)) initializes the monitor, setting the associated value to 0.

fadd(<monitor-name>,<old>,<new>,<incr>) returns the "old" value in <old>, increments it with <incr>, and returns the "new" value in <new>. The value associated with the monitor takes on the "new" value.

Thus, the macros might be used as follows:

```
fadec(F1,INTEGER)
fainint(F1)
       .
       .
       .

fadd(F1,OLDI,NEWI,J)
       .
       .
       .
```

Here the integer value associated with F1 is incremented by the fetch-and-add. The original value is returned in OLDI, and the new value in NEWI.

This method really does not convey the full power of fetch-and-add, since the operation is designed to be applicable on any word in memory. If you think of its use in manipulating linked lists, then the above version of the macros is really quite inadequate. To somewhat improve the situation, we allow you to declare and manipulate an array of monitors, rather than a single monitor. When this is done, the subscript of the desired monitor (which can be thought of as a "cell" address) is used as the last argument. For example,

```
fadec(F1,INTEGER,100)
fainint(F1,100)
```

.
.
.

```
fadd(F1,OLDI,NEWI,J,CELL)
```

.
.
.

declares and utilizes 100 monitors. Here the *fadd* includes an extra argument, which is the subscript of the monitor for which the operation applies.

10. Running the Package

To prepare a program for execution on some particular machine, you must expand the macro definitions into versions for the desired machine. Typically, you would keep one file of macro definitions for all monitors. This file would not include the basic macro package (which includes *menter* and *mexit*). The basic macro package is machine-specific. User-defined macros specific to a given program are normally included at the front of the program. Following these conventions,

```
m4 <basic-macro-library> <standard-monitors> <user-source> >! <dest>
```

can be used to create the desired source in <dest>. We can supply versions of the <basic-macro-library> for both UNIX uniprocessors (for debugging on a uniprocessor system) and HEP FORTRAN. The <standard-monitors> code at this point includes the monitors that we have discussed in this document, as well as a number of other standard monitors (which we hope to discuss in future reports).

11. Conclusion

This tutorial focuses on the use of three of our macro packages -- those for the self-scheduling DO-loop, barrier, and askfor monitors. We have not discussed all features of these macros, but we have covered their most common uses. We believe, however, that the monitors have wide applicability in more demanding contexts.

References

1. M. Ben-Ari, *Principles of Concurrent Programming*, Prentice-Hall, Inc., Englewood Cliffs, New Jersey (1982).

2. Allan Gottlieb and J. T. Schwartz, "Networks and algorithms for very-large-scale parallel computation," *Computer Magazine*, pp. 27-36 (January 1982).

3. Per Brinch Hansen, "The programming language Concurrent Pascal," *IEEE Transactions on Software Engineering SE-1* **2** pp. 199-207 (June 1975).

4. Per Brinch Hansen, *The Architecture of Concurrent Programs*, Prentice-Hall, Inc., Englewood Cliffs, New Jersey (1977).

5. C. A. R. Hoare, "Monitors: an operating system structuring concept," *Communications of the ACM*, pp. 549-557 (October 1974).

6. R. C. Holt, G. S. Graham, E. D. Lazowska, and M. A. Scott, *Structured Concurrent Programming with Operating Systems Applications*, Addison-Wesley Publishing Co., Menlo Park, California (1978).

7. Ewing L. Lusk and Ross A. Overbeek, "An Approach to Programming Multiprocessing Algorithms on the Denelcor HEP," Technical Report ANL-83-96, Argonne National Laboratory, Argonne, Illinois (December 1983).

8. Ewing L. Lusk and Ross A. Overbeek, "Implementation of Monitors with Macros: A Programming Aid for the HEP and Other Parallel Processors," Technical Report ANL-83-97, Argonne National Laboratory, Argonne, Illinois (December 1983).

9. N. Wirth, "MODULA: a language for modular programming," *Software Practice and Experience* **7** pp. 3-35 (January-February 1977).